IMAGES
of America

WALDWICK

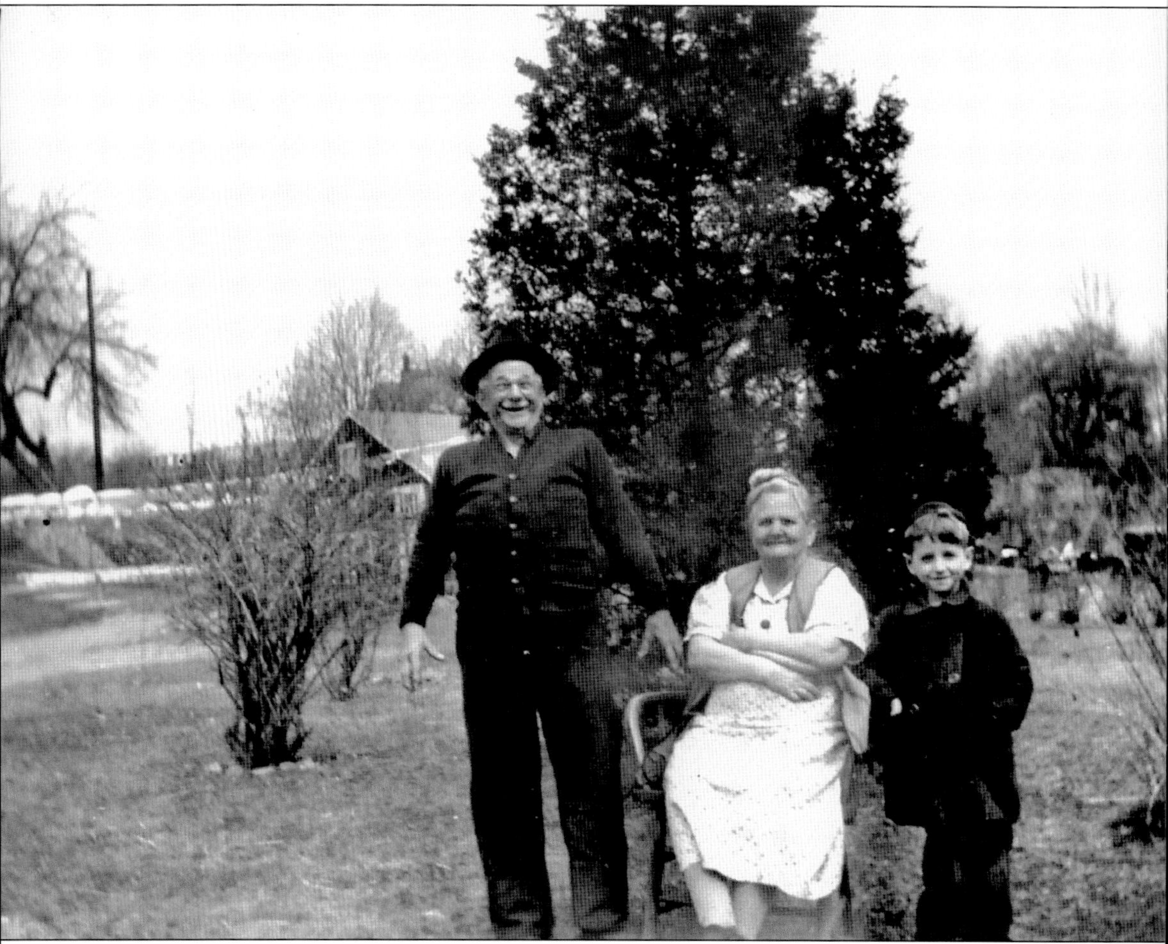

In a 1940s view of a lighthearted moment in "the hollow" along the Ho-Ho-Kus Brook, George and Mary Morgan, with grandson Howie Van Dyke, welcome readers to this pictorial history of Waldwick.

IMAGES
of America

WALDWICK

Michael Brunkhorst and Glenn P. Corbett

ARCADIA
PUBLISHING

ISBN 978-0-7385-1307-2

Published by Arcadia Publishing
Charleston, South Carolina

Printed in the United States of America

Library of Congress Catalog Card Number: 2003107453

For all general information contact Arcadia Publishing at:
Telephone 843-853-2070
Fax 843-853-0044
E-mail sales@arcadiapublishing.com
For customer service and orders:
Toll-Free 1-888-313-2665

Visit us on the Internet at www.arcadiapublishing.com

This book is lovingly dedicated to our spouses—Christl Brunkhorst and Sharon Corbett—whose tolerance for losing us to this volume on Waldwick's past is equaled only by their resolve not to let us do this again.

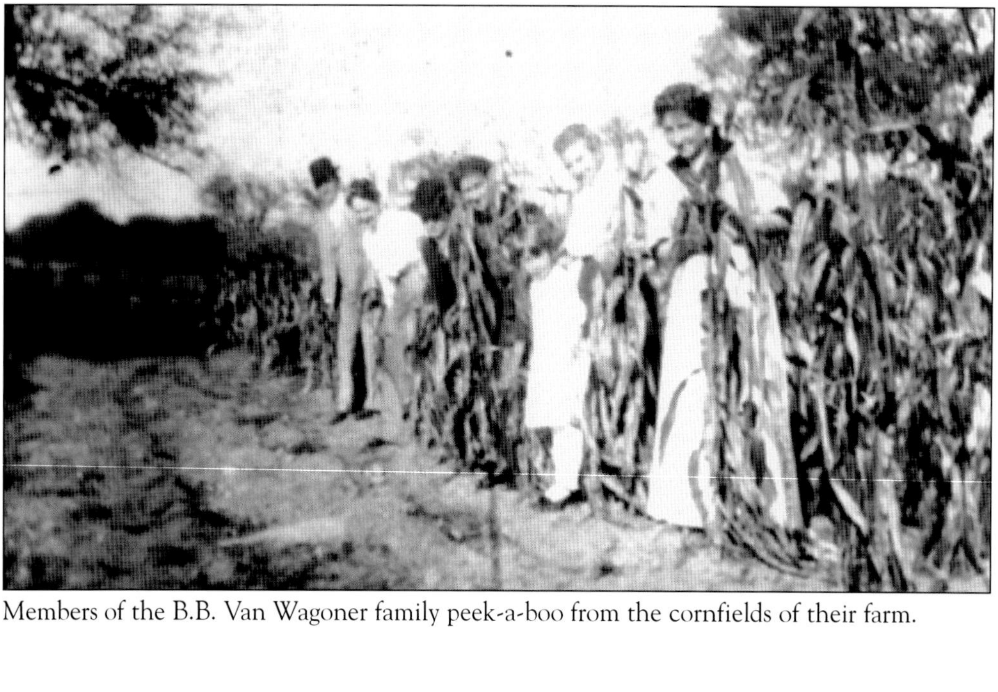

Members of the B.B. Van Wagoner family peek-a-boo from the cornfields of their farm.

Contents

ACKNOWLEDGMENTS

Although this book has two authors, many people and organizations assisted in a myriad of different ways. They include, in no particular order, Ralph Scrofani, Curtis Springstead, Andrea Mistretta, Perry Quaranta, Paula Jaegge, Barbara Flurchick, Dot Pangburn, Robert Griffin, Nancy and Ben Groo, Frank Holley, John Becica, Butch Wagner, Harold Anthony, Kevin Smith, Janet Kelso, Isabel Tringone, Anne Pope, Marcy Peterman, Dave Anderson, Giacomo DeStefano, Joseph Costa, Edna Bainbridge, Edith Whilden, Edna Corbett, Sarit Hand, Pamela Smith, George Zumbano, Todd Schust, Carmelita Garofalini, Sean O'Leary, Janet Strom, and Elio from the Village Restaurant.

Those who provided images and, in some cases, information for this book are listed below according to the page on which their contributions appear. Abbreviations are used after the page numbers to indicate the top, bottom, left, and right of the page.

George Fredricks (cover, 32t, 37b, 46b, 48b, 63b, 64b, 65b, 68t, 69b, 71t, 72t, 78t, 87b, 92t, 119t), Keith Morgan (2, 38b, 44t, 105t), Joanne Thompson (105b), Lillian Lockwood (106t), Keith Giovanolli (4, 24b, 29b, 51b, 60b, 76, 77t, 85b, 86), the Riccardi family (8, 101t, 109, 113), Neil Borrelli (114b), Ed Moderacki (115t), North Jersey Media Group (12b, 121b), Jean Willson (14, 16, 36, 54b, 62, 63t, 82, 96b, 125t), the Ridgewood Historical Society (15t, 19t, 20, 26b, 27, 41, 58t), Kevin Smith (88t, 94t, 116b), Jim Zumbano (110t, 116t, 123t), Mr. Adamo (110b), Elizabeth VanderEls (88b, 89t, 91b, 118b), Deedee Burnside (89b), Joe Evans (17t, 112t), Ruth Amster (92b), Dave and Sue Cubby (93t), the U.S. Library of Congress (18, 30, 42t), Madeline Anthony (21t, 60t, 74t, 84b, 98t, 99b), Judy Shields (83t), Rose Mistretta (84b, 102t, 103b, 122t), the Paterson Museum (85t), the Collection of the Hermitage, New Jersey Division of Parks and Forestry (21b, 28t, 33t, 38, 39, 42b, 45b, 48, 49, 50b, 58b, 68b), the Bergen County Office of Cultural Affairs (25t, 33b, 34t, 40b, 47t), Nancy Groo (34b), Ralph Ten Eyck (78b), the Smithsonian Institution (79), Uncle Richard Brunkhorst (35t), John and Ruth Livesy (43, 54t, 52, 53), Dorothy Becica (45t, 57t, 104t), Town Clerk Paula Jaegge (57b), the Registry Division of the Bergen County Clerk (46t), the Waldwick Historical Society (50t, 59tr, 64t, 70b, 80t, 83b, 94b, 96t, 104b, 106b), Drew Churchson (107t, 117b), Ralph Ten Eyck Sr. (95t, 98t, 111t), Maurice Farissier (95b), James Wrocklage (80b), Dominic LaPorta (81t, 87t, 101b), Bill Blom (60), Chuck and Jack Wanamaker (77b), Sue Cutler (73), the Waldwick Fire Department (70t), Doris Wagner (71b, 82, 90, 100t, 102b, 103t, 107b, 128b), Angelo Biele (91t, 93b, 117t), Waldwick Public Library (74t), Alain Koch (75), Jo Wrocklage (100b), Ruth Swallow (née Lumley) and Joan Powers (née Lumley) (115b), Dan Lupo (120t), Edna Mills (120b), Crescent School librarian Nancy Strife (122b), Sherri Gusta of the Waldwick Ambulance Corps (123b), Ralph Olivieri (125bl), and William Branagh (126).

Special credit must be given to four people—Beatrice Cannon, Kay Williams, John Huska, and town historian George Fredricks, all of whom have conducted significant research into Waldwick's history. We are greatly indebted to them; their dedication to accurately preserving Waldwick's history forms the foundation on which much of this history is based.

Deedee Burnside, a nationally known calligrapher from Waldwick, volunteered her time to prepare the wonderful map found at the beginning of chapter 1.

The Brunkhorst children all deserve special thanks for their contributions. Jonathon performed all of the digital work in preparing the images. Michelle and Clara both used their professional typing skills, and David helped gather historical interviews.

INTRODUCTION

When the Waldwick railroad station opened in 1886, the town changed forever. This critical event unleashed forces that led to rapid development. Yet, history was being made long before this defining moment. This book attempts to take a broad look at Waldwick's past, stopping along the way to take look at the people and events that have shaped the town.

For thousands of years, Native Americans populated much of the eastern seaboard. The Delaware Indians, or Lenne Lenape, made much of New Jersey, including Waldwick, their home. They hunted in the same woods and fished along the same brooks that are still found within our borders.

Other tribes came through this area as well. The Tuscaroura passed through Waldwick on their way to upstate New York c. 1710. At least two of their tribesmen died along the way and were buried near the old Prospect Street School baseball field.

Although the Dutch were the first settlers to the area in the mid- to late 1600s, it was the British Duke of York who took control of the land now called New Jersey. He in turn transferred the land to Sir George Carteret and Lord John Berkley in 1664. The portion of New Jersey including Waldwick was known as East Jersey. Eventually, it was purchased by a group known as the proprietors, who then divided the land into much smaller tracts. It was these small tracts that the early Dutch settlers purchased from the proprietors.

Farming was the major industry in the Waldwick area for nearly 300 years. A variety of crops were grown, including potatoes and corn. Wheat was produced as well, providing the fodder for several gristmills that dotted the landscape around Waldwick.

As the American Revolution approached, residents of Bergen County aligned themselves with either the loyalists or the revolutionaries. At the time, Theodosia Prevost, the owner of the Hermitage in present-day Ho-Ho-Kus, was considered to be a loyalist even as George Washington and his troops camped in the Waldwick area in 1778. No battles were fought in Waldwick, but skirmishes did occur to the south in the present-day Ho-Ho-Kus and Paramus areas.

American independence brought new people to the region. Industry also came to this area in the form of paper and cotton mills. The locale of the present-day Northwest Bergen County Utilities Authority along the Ho-Ho-Kus Brook—known as the hollow—became a thriving place for industry.

The coming of the railroad brought changes to the area. Products—both agricultural and industrial—were now capable of being transported to a much larger area. The railroad also brought additional development and commerce to the region.

The coming of the Waldwick train station in the 1880s brought people, creating the town we know today. Individuals began to populate the area surrounding the train station, putting up new homes along newly created streets. The area around the station remained as the residential and business district for several decades, until the opening of the municipal building in 1927 and the final closure of the railroad crossing in 1935.

The largest and final surge of population growth occurred immediately after World War II.

Most of Waldwick was subdivided throughout the 1950s, creating thousands of new homes and pushing the town's population over 10,000.

Most Waldwick families came to the town in the wave of development following World War II. Some families came during the growth of the railroad. A few families here today have ties to the earliest settlers. What binds them together is a love for Waldwick, many planting deep roots here.

This book opens the window of history, allowing readers to take a brief glance down the path of Waldwick's past. We have attempted to give the reader a taste of our community's history. Hopefully, longtime residents and newcomers will gain a greater understanding of the community in which they live.

The authors encourage the young residents of Waldwick to save their own history, which is happening now, so that others may continue this story.

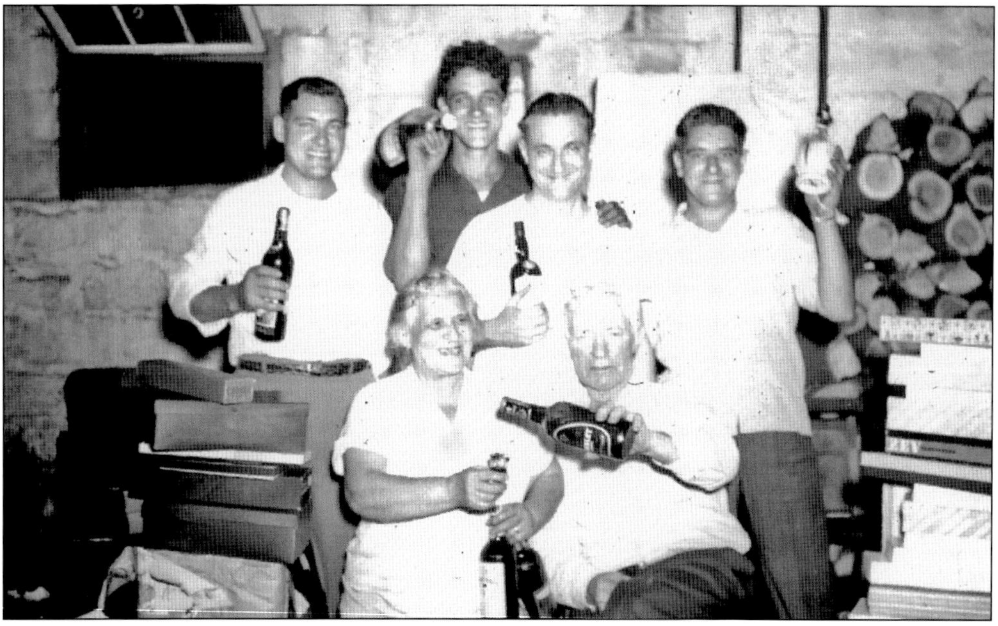

This photograph from the early 1940s shows the Riccardi family in a wine-tasting session in the basement of their home on Zazzetti Street. Winemaking was popular pastime in the Italian neighborhood. From 18 crates of grapes, 55 gallons of wine could be produced. Seen here are, from left to right, the following: (front row) Louise and Louis; (back row) Carmen, Nicholas, Anthony, and John.

One

Natives and First Settlers

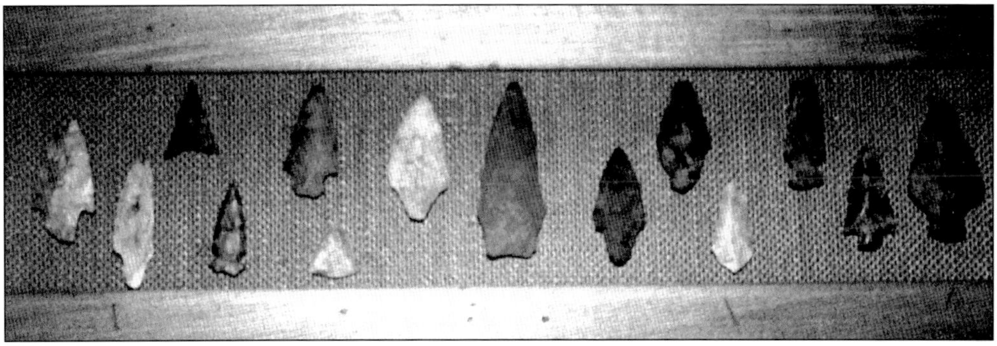

These arrowheads are evidence of a large population of Native Americans who inhabited the Waldwick area for thousands of years. These and many others were collected by numerous generations of the Ackerman family who farmed the area between the Saddle River and Franklin Turnpike. Other locations where arrowheads were found include the rear of the high school and Smoches Vol Creek. Trading between European settlers and Native Americans necessitated the use of wampum, a form of money. It is believed that a wampum factory was located in the northwest corner of Waldwick, along the Allendale border, in the early 1700s.

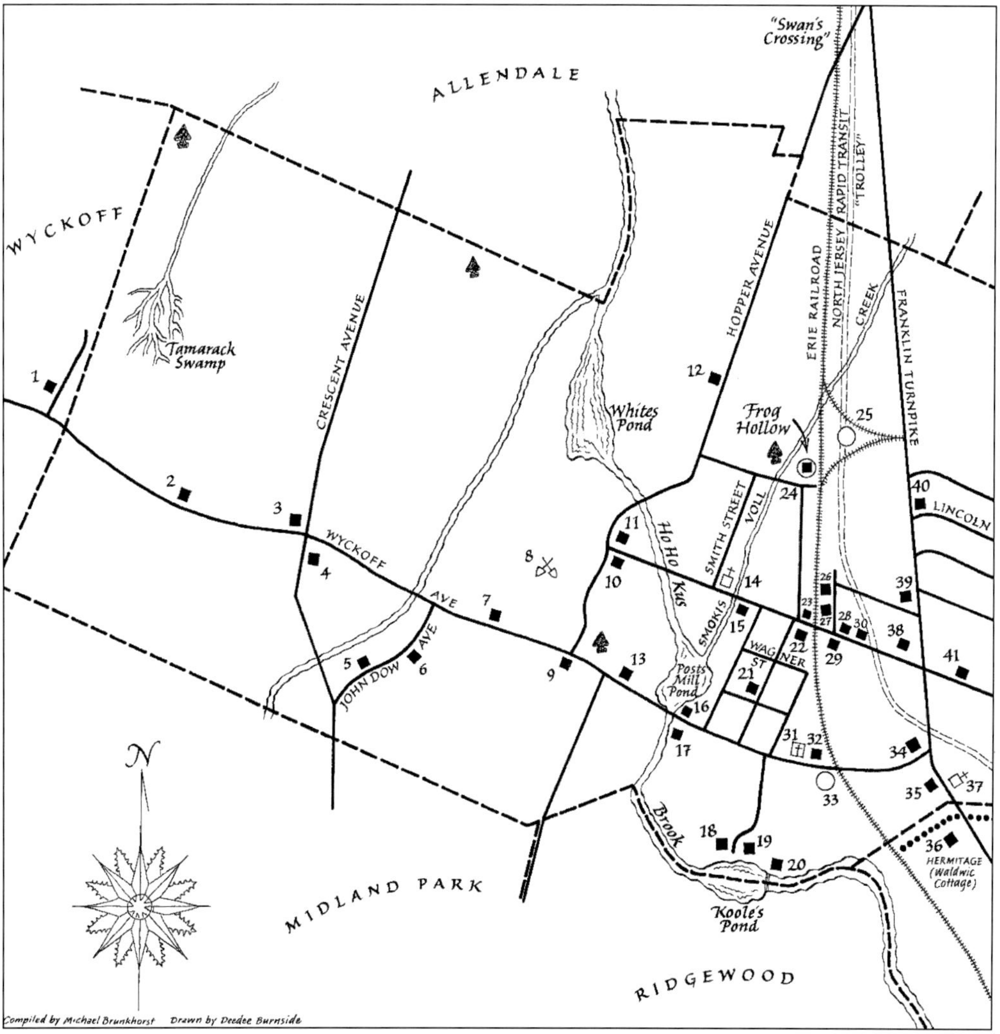

1. Union Hill School (p. 32)
2. Abe Smith house (p. 22)
3. Miller-Green-Ritter-Henderson house (p. 83)
4. Captain Frost estate (p. 40)
5. Koopman-VanderEl house (p. 89)
6. Van Hull house (p. 98)
7. Cornelius Smith house (p. 24)
8. Camp Smith (p. 13)
9. White-Higham house (p. 40)
10. Prospect Street School (p. 104)
11. White paper twine company (p. 32)
12. Henry L. Hopper house (p. 40)
13. Potter-Bender-Van Wagoner house (p. 51)
14. Baptist-Reformed church (p. 61)
15. Site of the "Hankey" Hopper gristmill and Post Silk Mill (p. 47)
16. Ramapo Bleachery-Margroff Mill (p. 74)
17. Blacksmith shop, Garretson house (p. 33)
18. White-Babcock house (p. 34)
19. White tenant house (p. 28)
20. Site of the paper mill, sawmill (p. 39)
21. Redmen's Hall (p. 59)
22. Frank Wagner's Waldwick Hotel (p. 46)
23. Waldwick Coal and Lumber Company (p. 44)
24. Waldwick switching tower "WC" (p. 44)
25. The wye turnaround for train engines (p. 6)

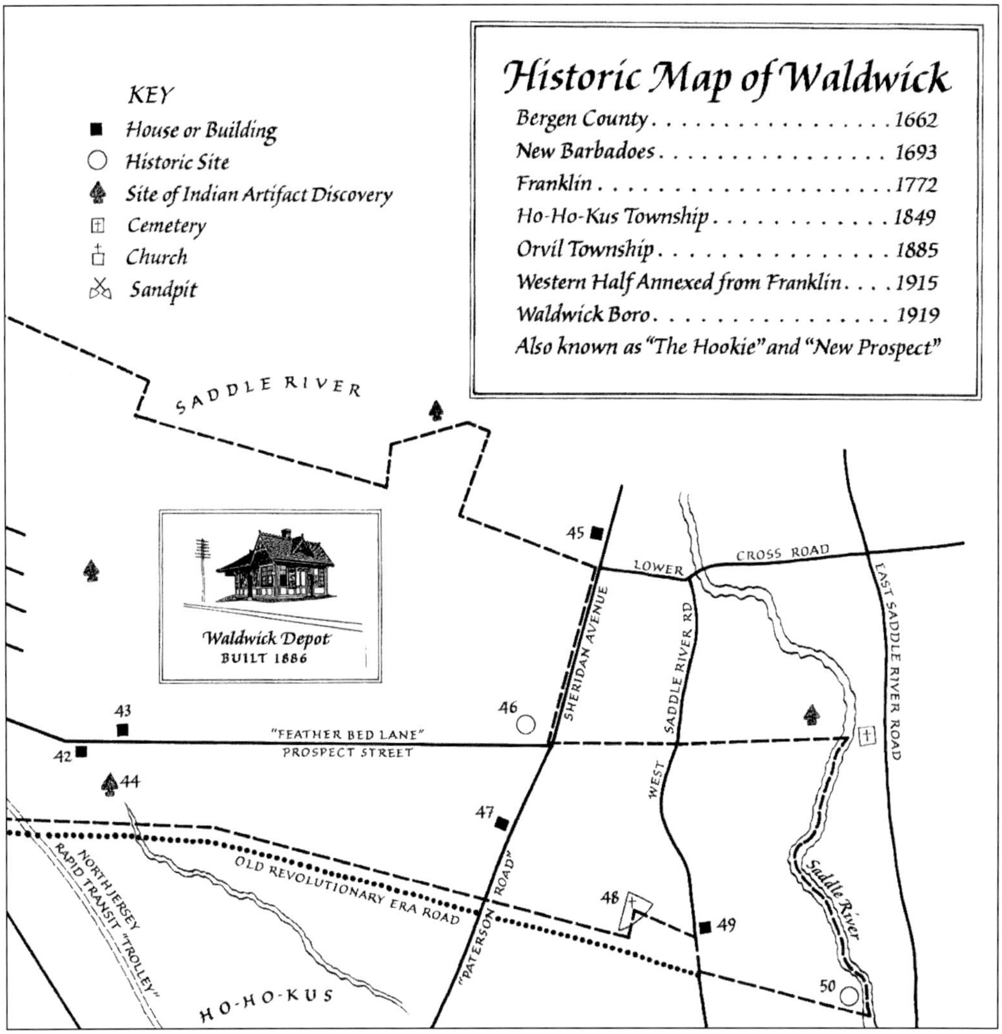

26. Freight depot (p. 55)
27. Waldwick train station, 1886 (p. 43)
28. Orvil House (p. 53)
29. Oughton's-Peterson's grocery store (p. 50, 68)
30. Dieckmann brothers confectionery (p. 63)
31. Hopper burial ground (p. 25)
32. Old Dissenter's Church (p. 25)
33. Railroad cut bridge (p. 64)
34. Larue-Bamper Hotel (p. 21)
35. Stout house (p. 20)
36. "Waldwic Cottage," the Hermitage (p. 31)
37. Methodist church (p. 37)
38. Old School No. 2 and the Cordes cannon (p. 72, 79)
39. John W. Quackenbush house (p. 57)
40. Harvey Springstead house (p. 79)
41. Waldwick Municipal Building (p. 92)
42. Henry G. Ackerman house (p. 62)
43. Abraham H. Hopper house (p. 22)
44. Sites of Native American artifacts (p. 9, 12)
45. Orville Victor residence (p. 41)
46. Revolutionary War encampment, July 1778 (p. 17, 19)
47. H.A. Ackerman house (p. 40)
48. Ackerman family cemetery (p. 17)
49. John T. Ackerman house (p. 36)
50. Site of the 1760s Blue Mill (p. 13)

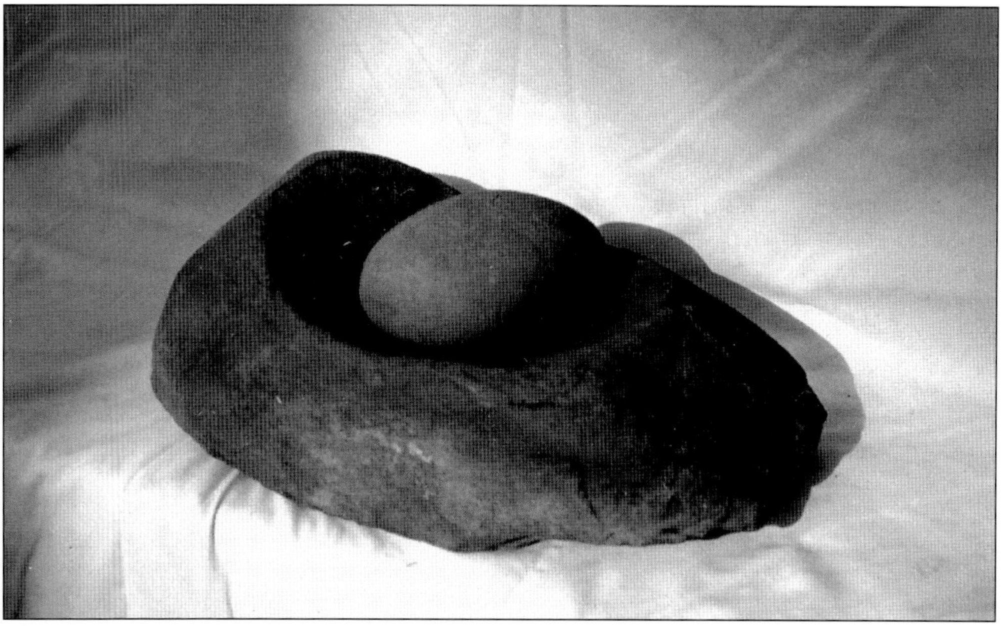

This Native American grinding stone was found in the area of Centre Street, a location believed to have been a Native American campground in the early 1700s. Artifacts have also been found along the Saddle River and in the area of the Traphagen School.

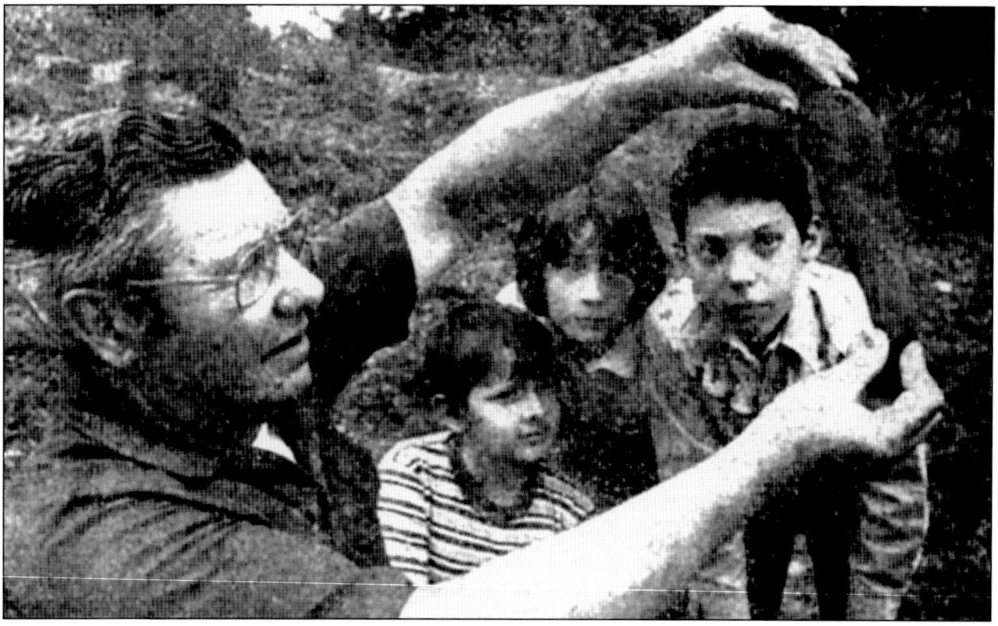

William Mirti is holding a stone pestle used by Native Americans for grinding food. It was found near the Crescent School. Looking on are, from left to right, students Mark Delgaudio, Florence Melville, and Thomas Ott. Other evidence includes the skeletons of two Native Americans unearthed during the excavation of the Prospect Street School baseball field in 1940.

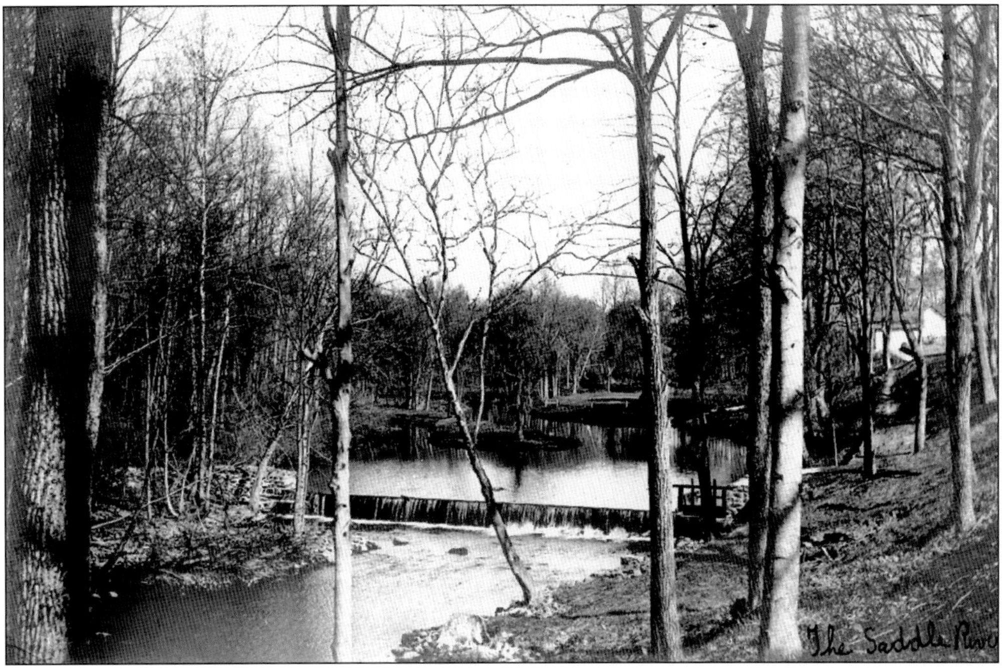

The dam at the location of the Blue Mill is shown in this *c.* 1900 postcard view. The mill was built *c.* 1760 along the west side of the Saddle River, behind Ackerman Avenue.

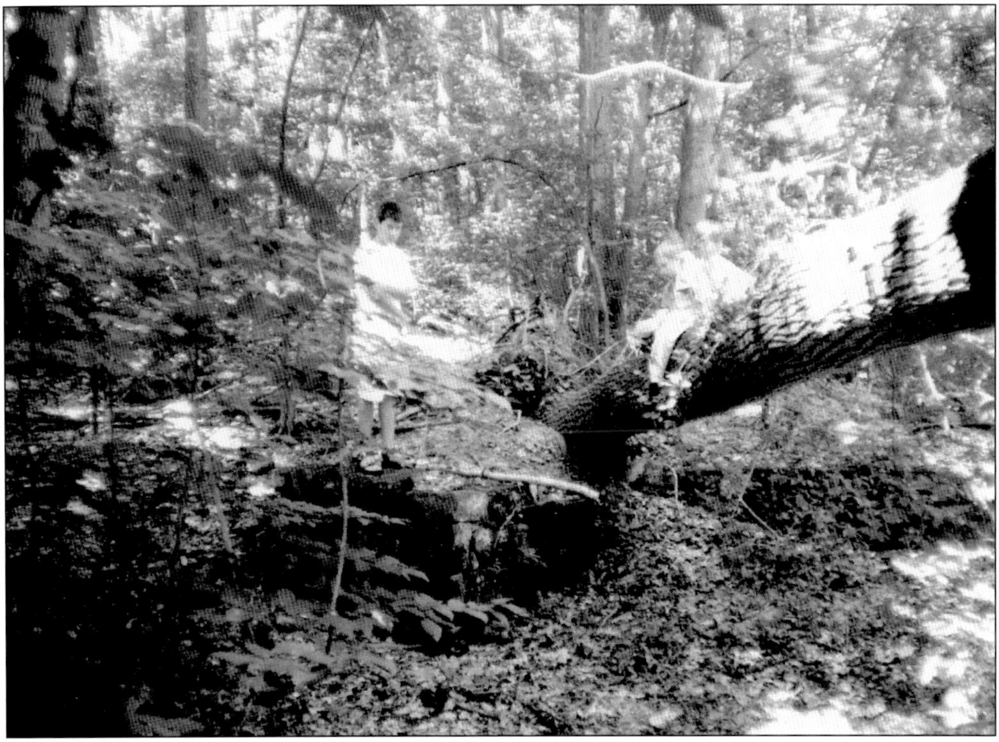
Brunkhorst children stand among the ruins of the Blue Mill. The mill produced cotton and was likely destroyed by fire around the time of the American Revolution.

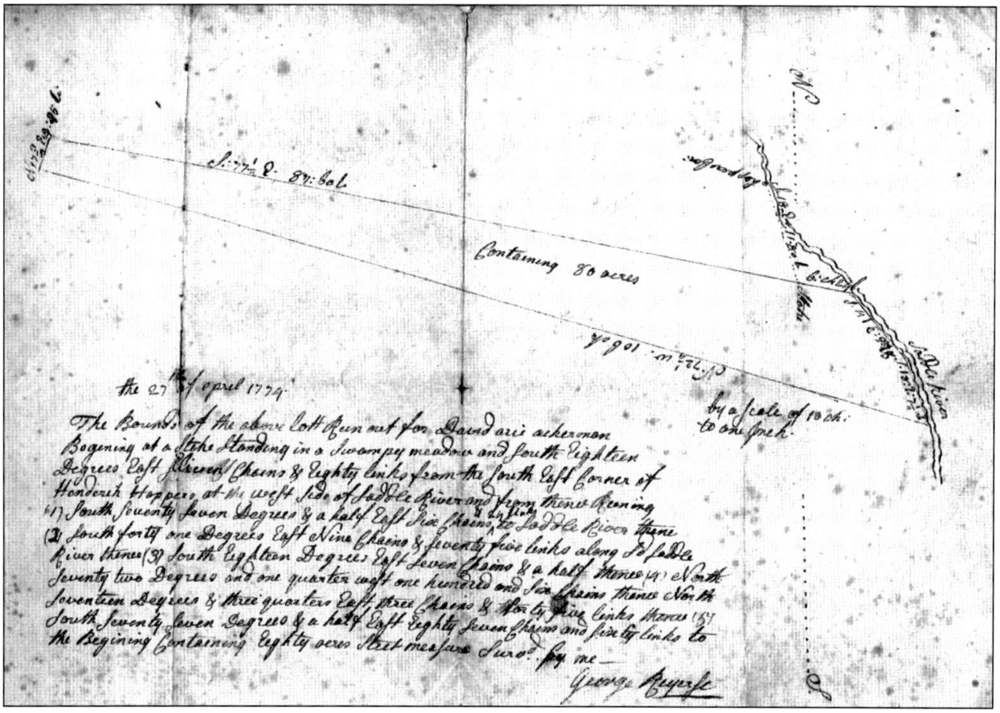

This map depicts an 80-acre parcel that was part of the 323-acre landholdings of Johannes Ackerman. The piece of land extends from the Saddle River to the area of Franklin Turnpike.

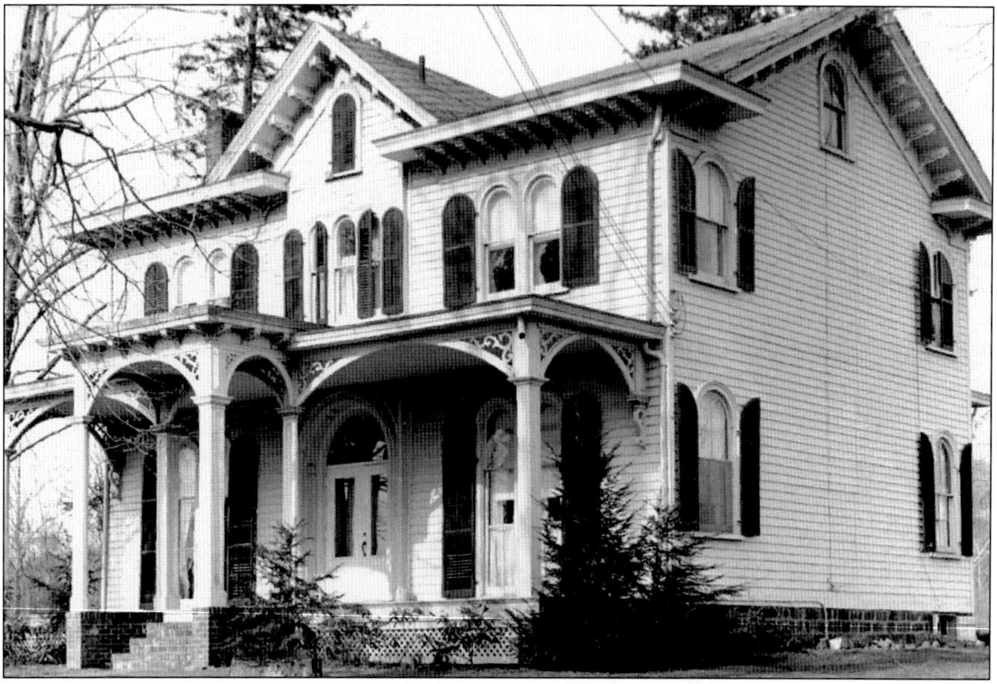

The John Terhune Ackerman house, built in the 1860s, was constructed near the site of the original sandstone Johannes Ackerman house in the 1770s. Legend tells of friendly Native Americans who helped Johannes Ackerman build his first home.

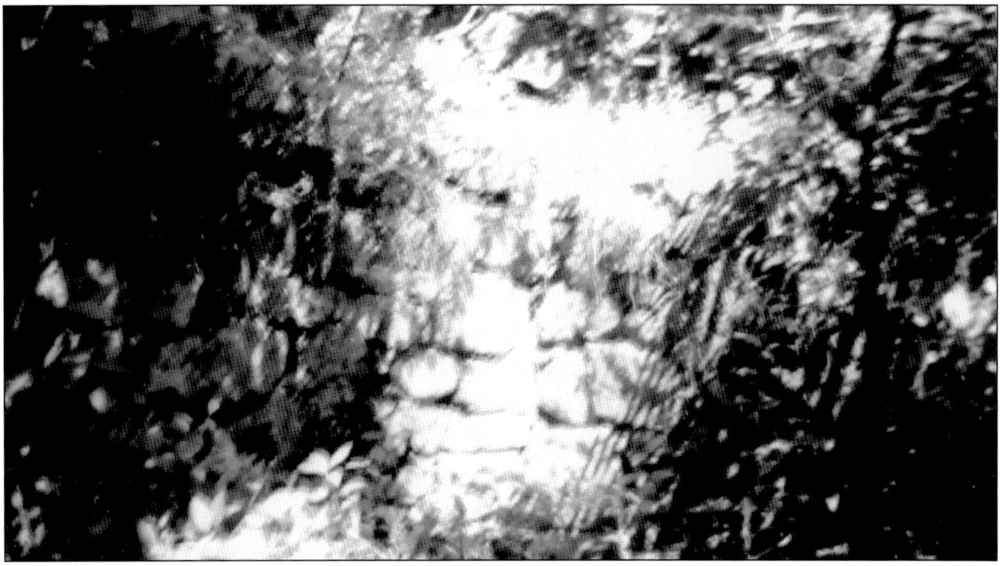

The foundation of an Ackerman slave house is pictured in this 1950s photograph. Slavery was not effectively outlawed in New Jersey until 1804.

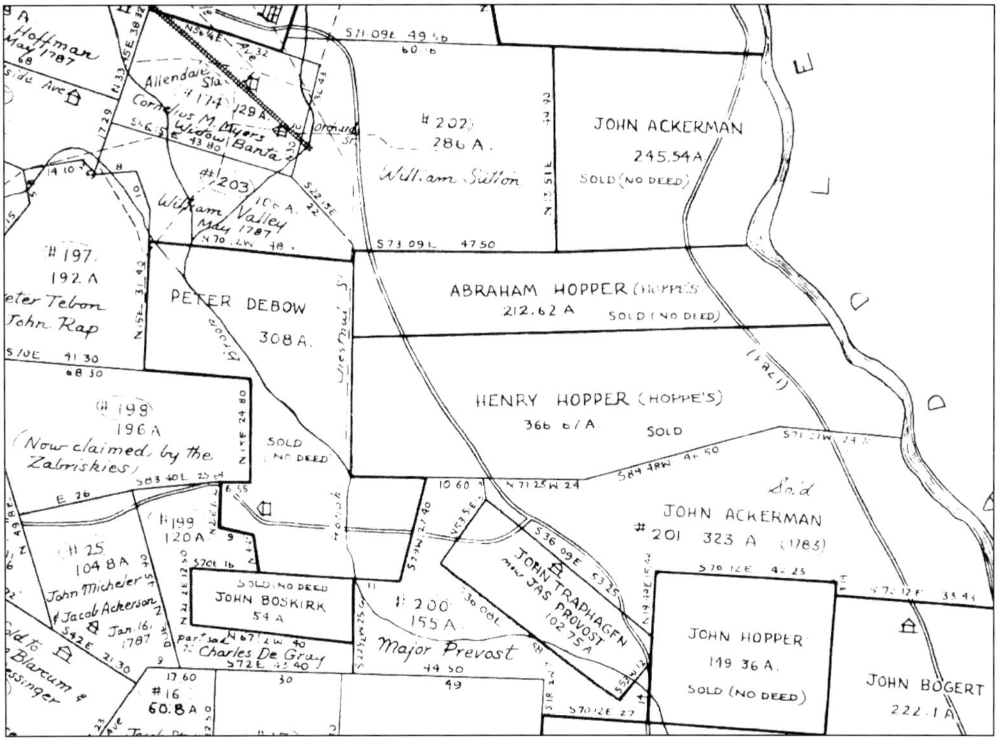

Shown is a modern copy of the Ramapo Tract map, originally created in 1768. The map shows property owners Johannes (John) Ackerman and Henry Hopper in the area that was to become Waldwick.

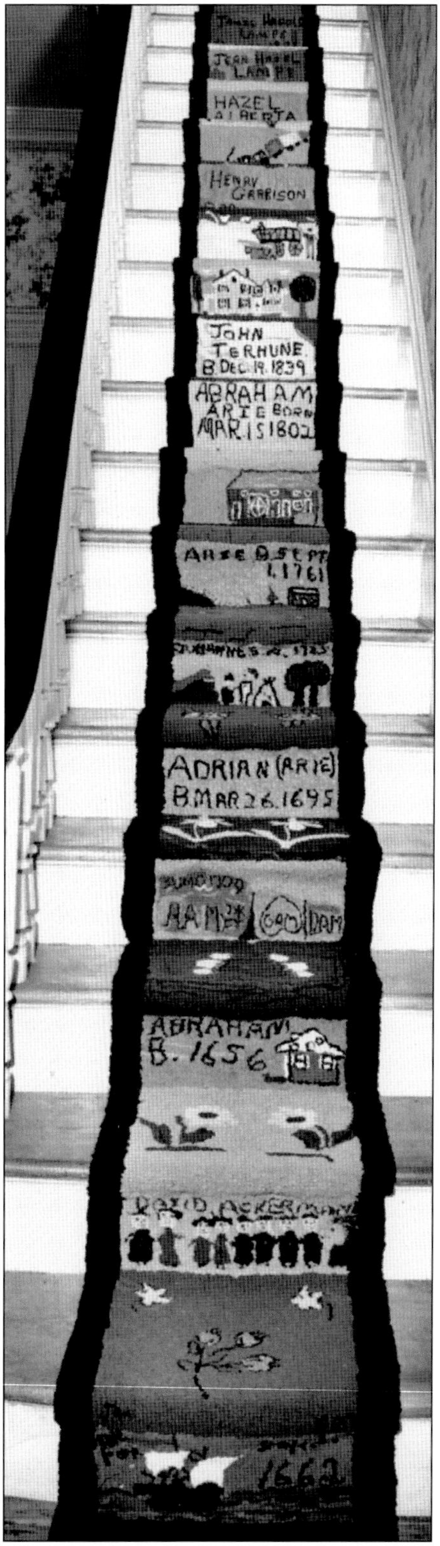

This hook rug stair runner was created by Hazel Lampe (née Ackerman) to depict the many generations of her branch of the Ackerman family. Each riser depicts a name and symbol for each generation. It begins with David Ackerman, who landed in New Amsterdam in 1662.

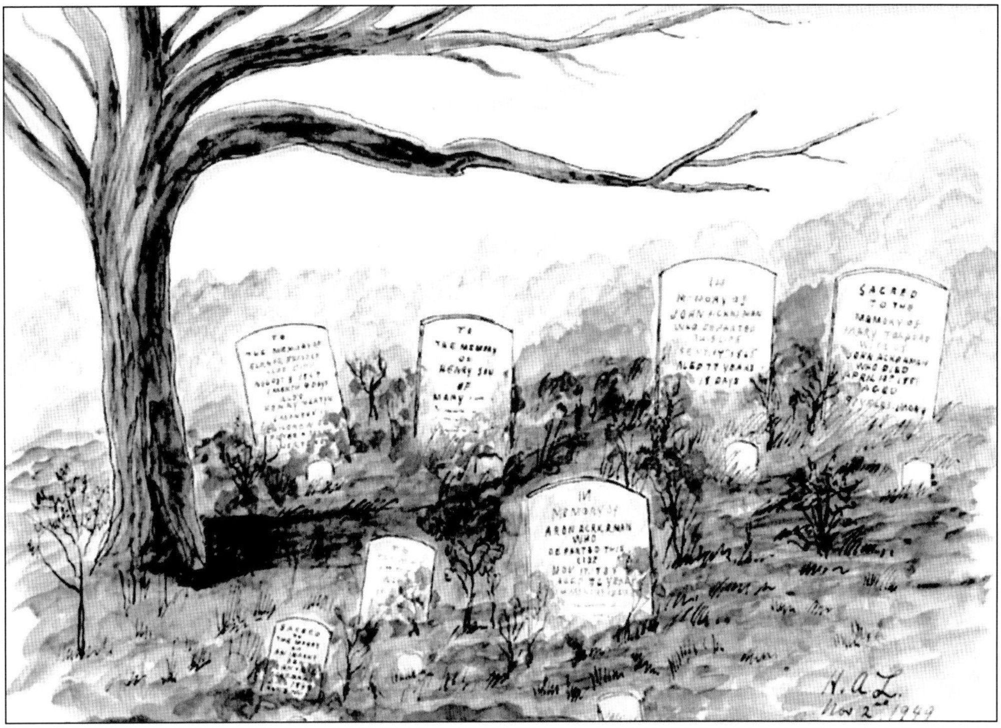

The Ackerman family cemetery, near Saddle River Road and Stuart Street, is depicted in this 1949 watercolor by Harold Lampe. The cemetery was heavily disrupted during construction of a new housing development in Ho-Ho-Kus in the 1980s.

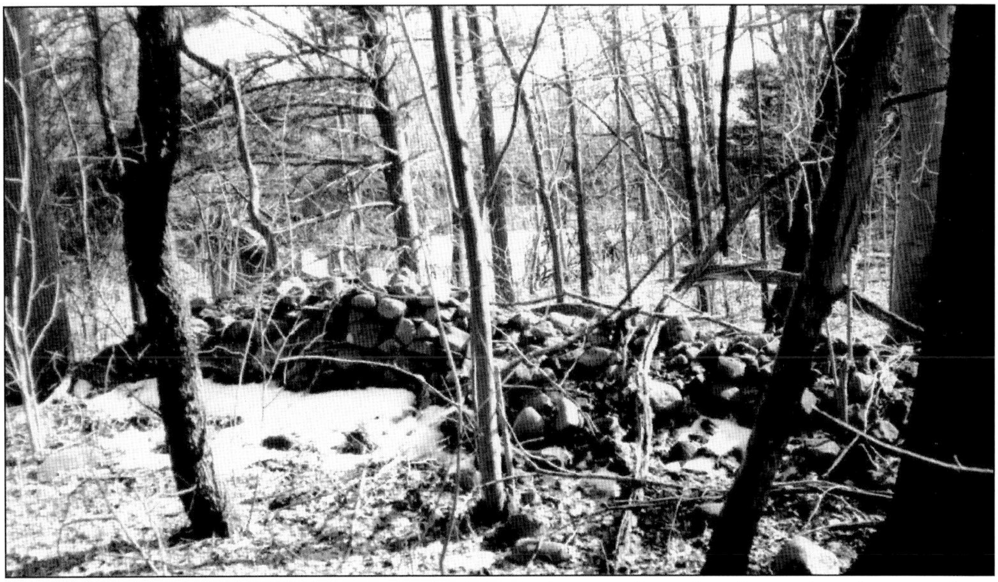

This stone wall is one of the last remnants of the Ackerman farm. It is located in the area along Sheridan Avenue and East Prospect Street where Continental troops were given permission by Johannes Ackerman to clear the land for their encampment in July 1778. The troops had marched to this area (then known broadly as Paramus, which encompassed a large area of northern Bergen County) after the Battle of Monmouth.

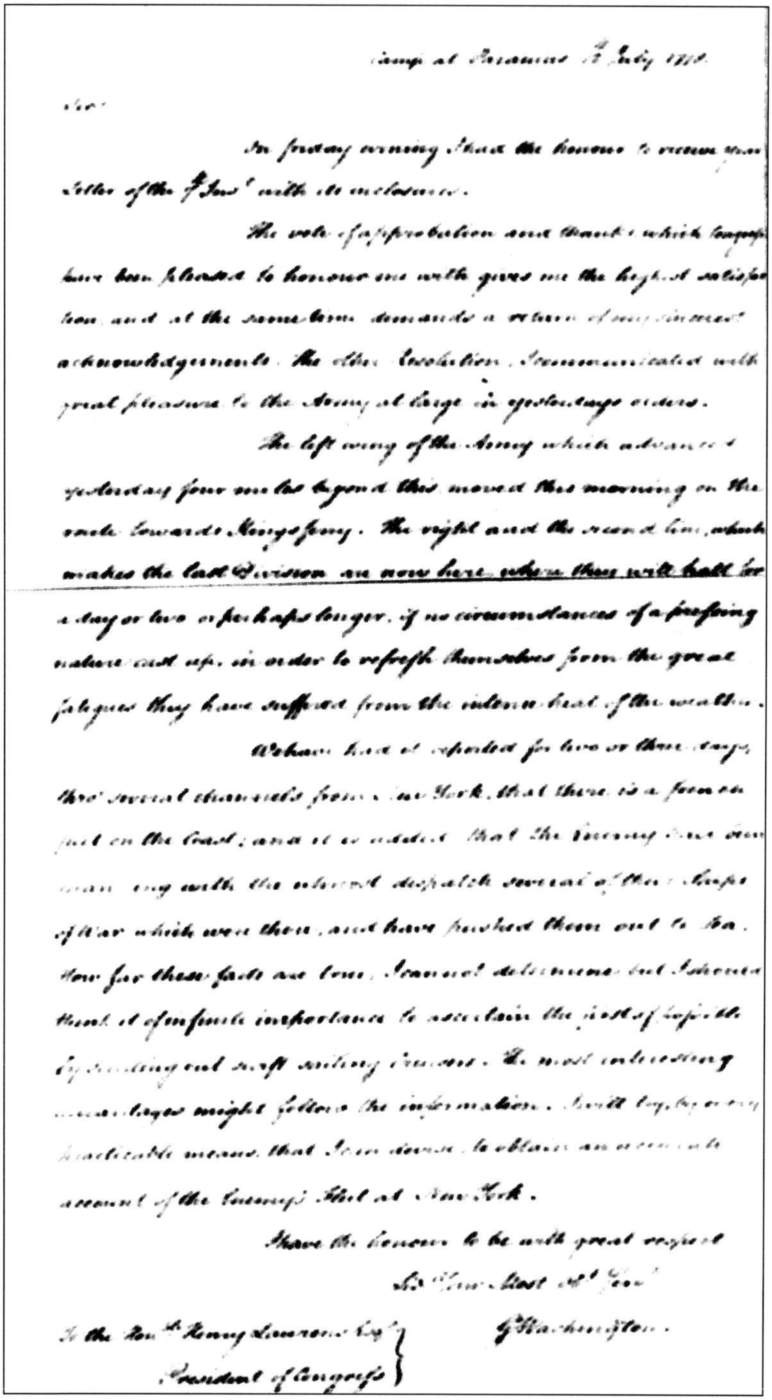
Camp at Paramus 12th July 1778.

Sir

On friday evening I had the honour to receive your Letter of the 9th Inst. with its inclosures.

The vote of approbation and thanks which Congress have been pleased to honour me with gives me the highest satisfaction and at the same time demands a return of my sincerest acknowledgements. The other Resolution I communicated with great pleasure to the Army at large in yesterdays orders.

The left wing of the Army which advanced yesterday four miles beyond this moved this morning on the route towards Kings ferry. The right and the second line, which makes the last Division are now here where they will halt for a day or two or perhaps longer, if no circumstances of a pressing nature cast up, in order to refresh themselves from the great fatigues they have suffered from the intense heat of the weather.

We have had it reported for two or three days, thro' several channels from New York, that there is a French fleet on the Coast; and it is added that the Enemy have been manning with the utmost dispatch several of their Ships of War which were there, and have pushed them out to Sea. How far these facts are true, I cannot determine but I should think it of infinite importance to ascertain the first if possible by sending out swift sailing Vessels. The most interesting advantages might follow the information. I will try, by every practicable means, that I can devise to obtain an accurate account of the Enemy's Fleet at New York.

I have the honour to be with great respect

Sir Your Most obt servt

G Washington.

To the Honble Henry Laurens Esqr
President of Congress

Gen. George Washington wrote this letter from his camp at Paramus on July 12, 1778. He details troop movements, word of the first sighting of the French fleet at the Delaware capes, and the oppressive heat. This is one of at least 19 letters written from Paramus (specifically, from the Old Paramus Church adjacent to present-day Route 17 and from the Hermitage in today's Ho-Ho-Kus).

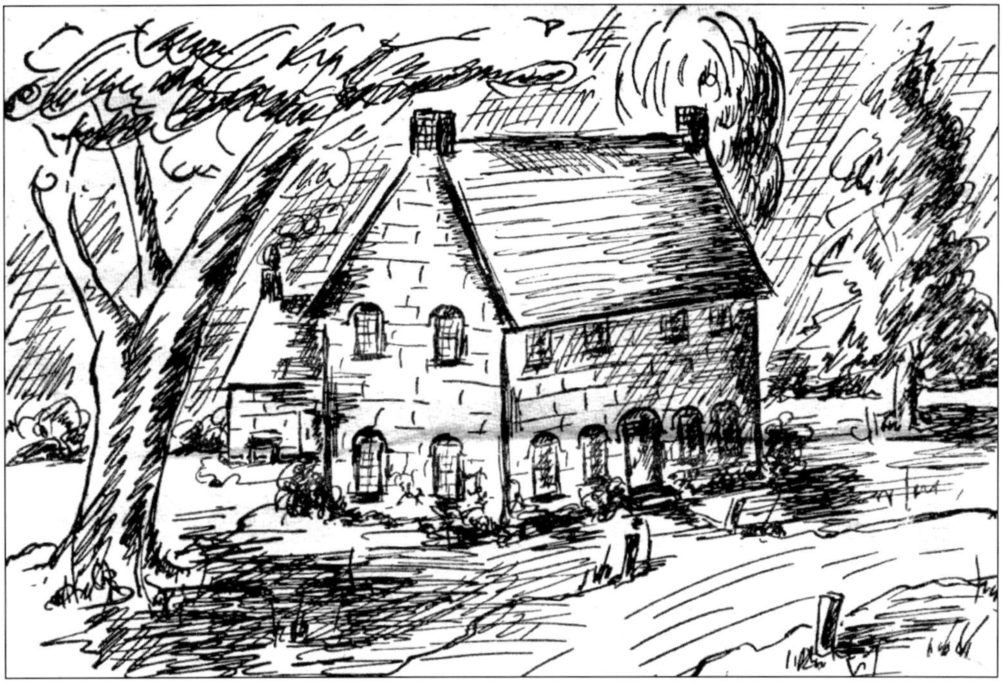

The Hermitage is depicted here as it likely looked during the time of the Revolutionary War. Gen. George Washington stayed at the Hermitage for four days.

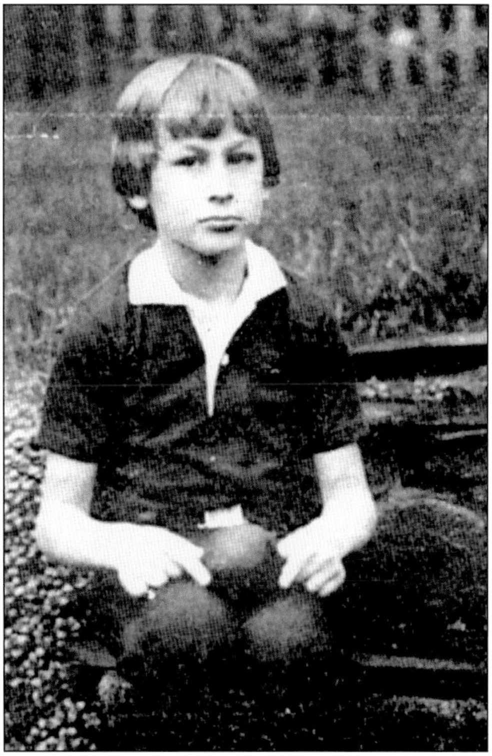

Steven Gross (pictured here) found this cannonball on Hudson Avenue while helping his father repair a stone wall. The cannonball was undoubtedly left behind by Continental troops who were encamped near the present-day Route 17 cloverleaf. Another division of Washington's troops were encamped near the Old Paramus Church.

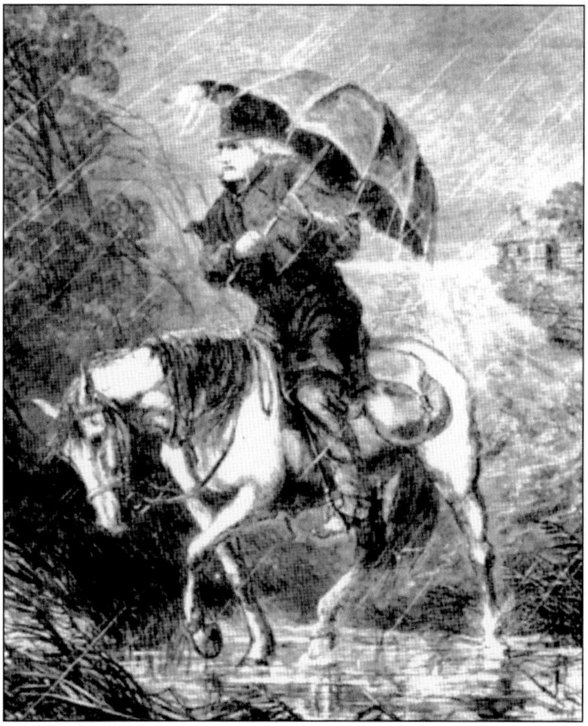

A Methodist circuit rider is seen here. Such clergy were common in rural America, riding a horse from church to church over a large area. As one of the earliest Methodist churches in northern New Jersey, the Paramus Methodist Episcopal Church (located in present-day Waldwick) was officially formed in 1797. The first circuit rider in this area was Richard Watcot. The first church edifice was a vacant building in the hollow behind the Hermitage, near a pond and dam. A door latch from this first church building was found by Elizabeth Rosencrantz, who was one of many Rosencrantz family members who lived in the Hermitage. The church later moved to a new building on Franklin Turnpike, just north of the present-day Golden Block, on December 18, 1819.

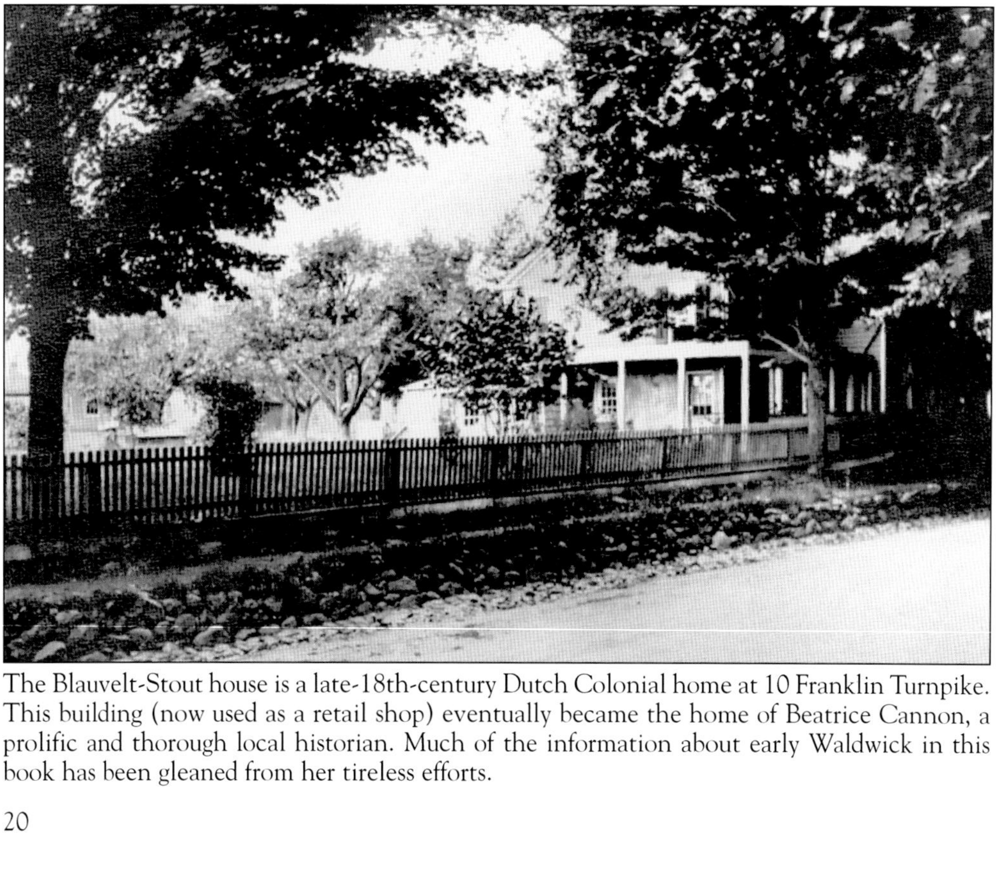

The Blauvelt-Stout house is a late-18th-century Dutch Colonial home at 10 Franklin Turnpike. This building (now used as a retail shop) eventually became the home of Beatrice Cannon, a prolific and thorough local historian. Much of the information about early Waldwick in this book has been gleaned from her tireless efforts.

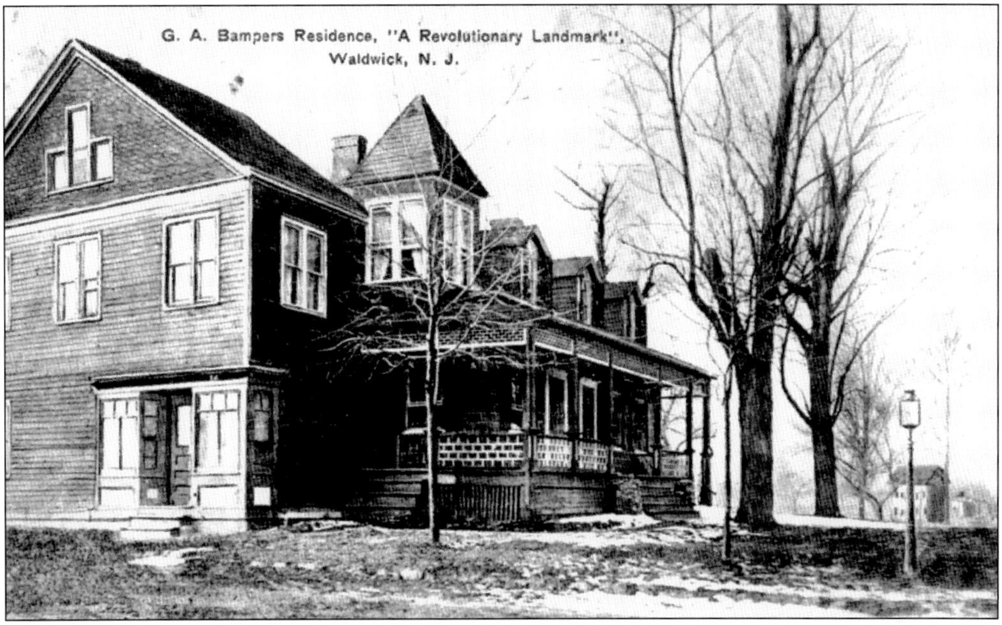

The most famous building in Waldwick was the Berthoff-Larue-Bamper house, which stood on the northwest corner of Wyckoff Avenue and Franklin Turnpike. This pre–Revolutionary War building was used as a tavern, inn, store, court, and even a school over its 200 years of existence. Remnants of a liberty pole were found adjacent to the home.

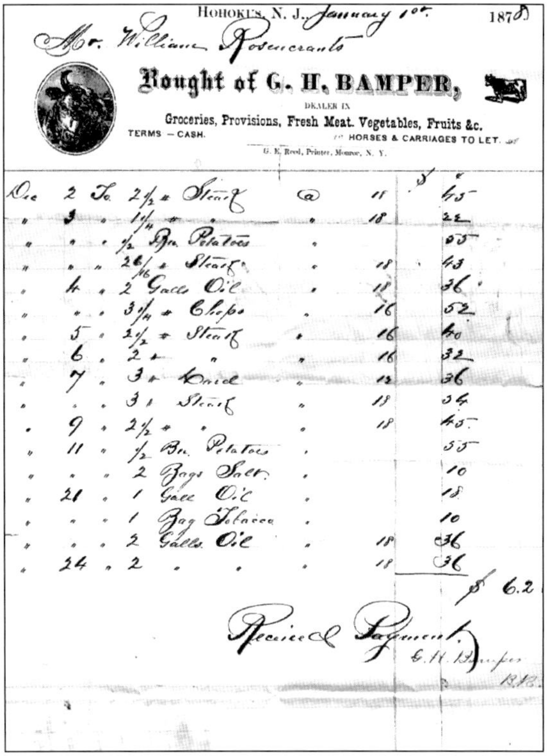

This receipt from Garret H. Bamper for the Rosencrantz of the Hermitage is indicative of the Bamper family's flourishing grocery business in the 1870s. His father (also named Garret) purchased the tavern from James Larue in 1832.

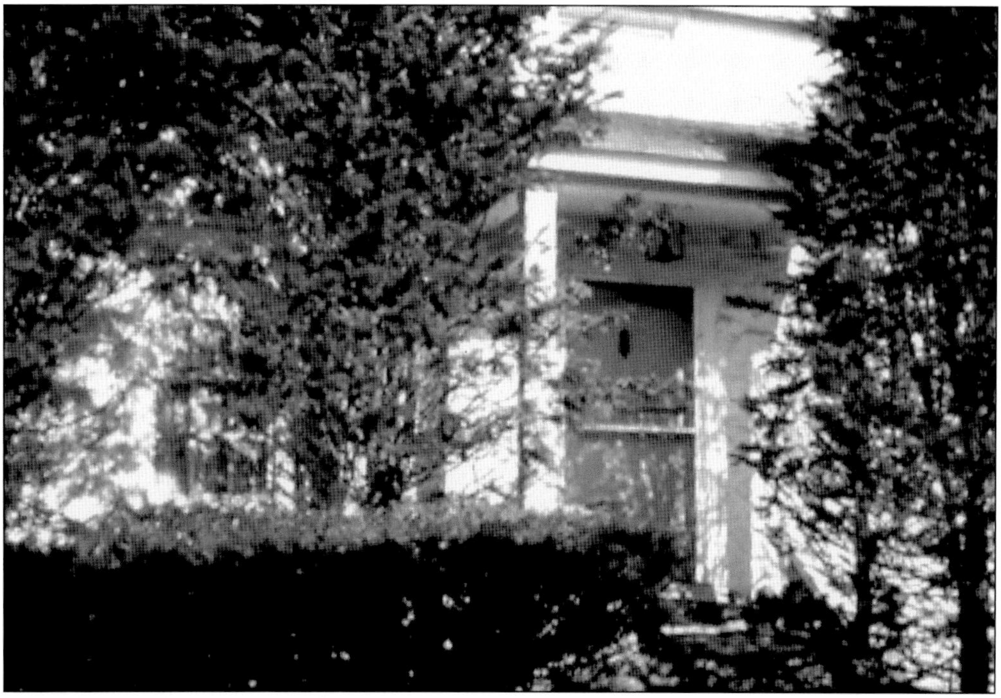

The Abraham Smith house, located on Wyckoff Avenue, is believed to have been built in 1750. The home has been altered over the years but still retains early sandstone walls and hand-hewn timbers in the basement.

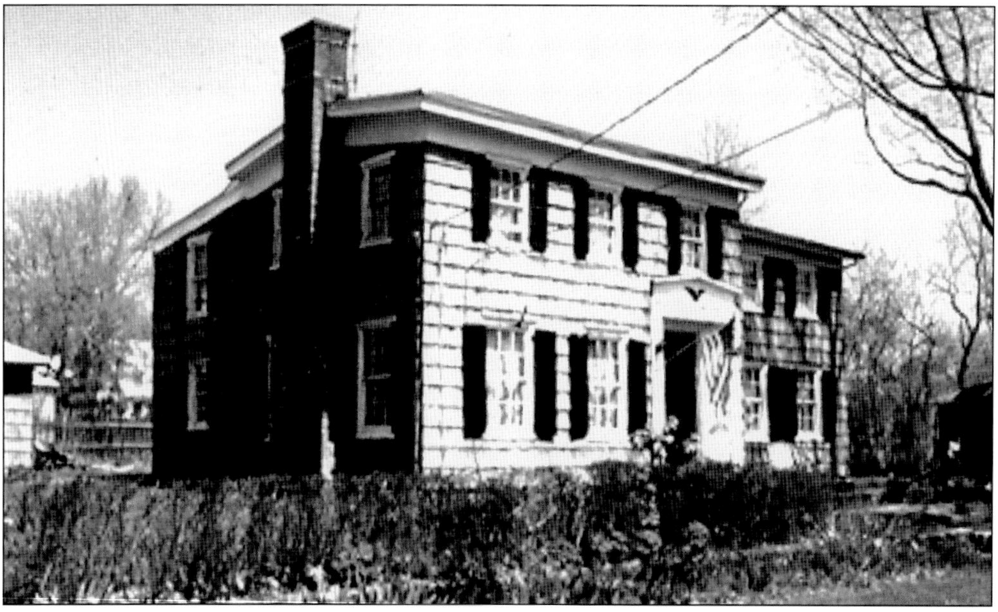

Abraham H. Hopper, father of Henry A. Hopper, built this home in 1794. The house, at the corner of Nordham and Prospect Streets, had several subsequent owners, including A.J. Zabriskie, A.J. Bogert, and George Nordham. Nordham was a noted local architect, designer of the municipal building and the Prospect Street School. The front door of the home was the door from the original Waldwick School on Franklin Turnpike.

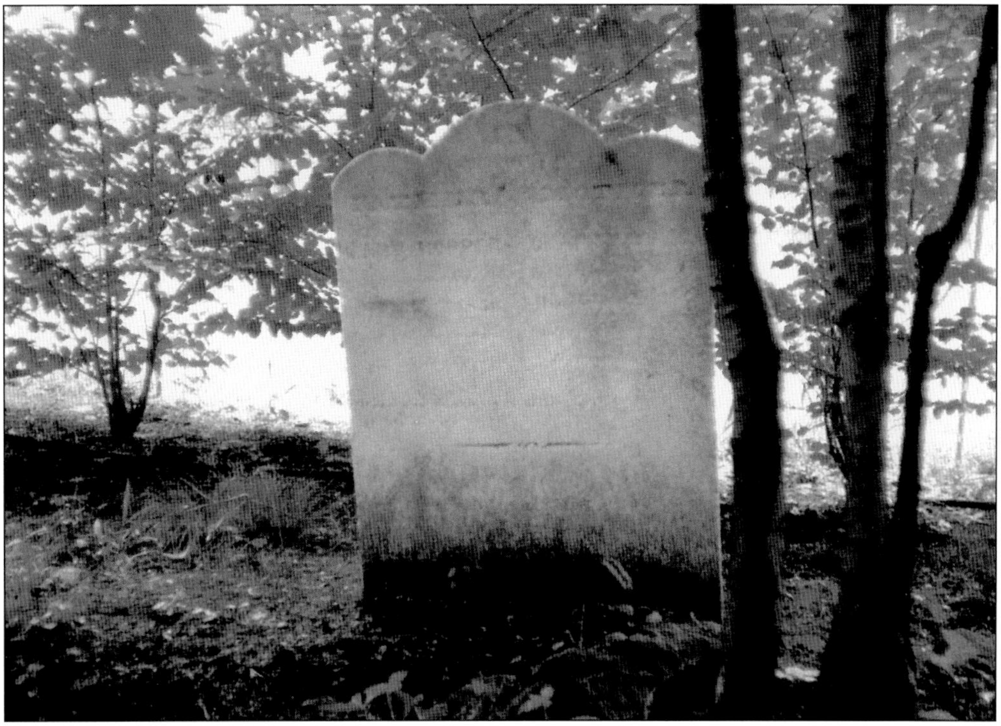

The gravestone of Henry and Charity (née Conklin) Hopper is in the family cemetery near Maple Street and Wyckoff Avenue. Henry Hopper (1770–1856) was a prominent landowner and gristmill operator in Waldwick. He also was the founder of the Dissenter's Church (he was formerly a member of the Paramus Reformed Church), which was located in Waldwick.

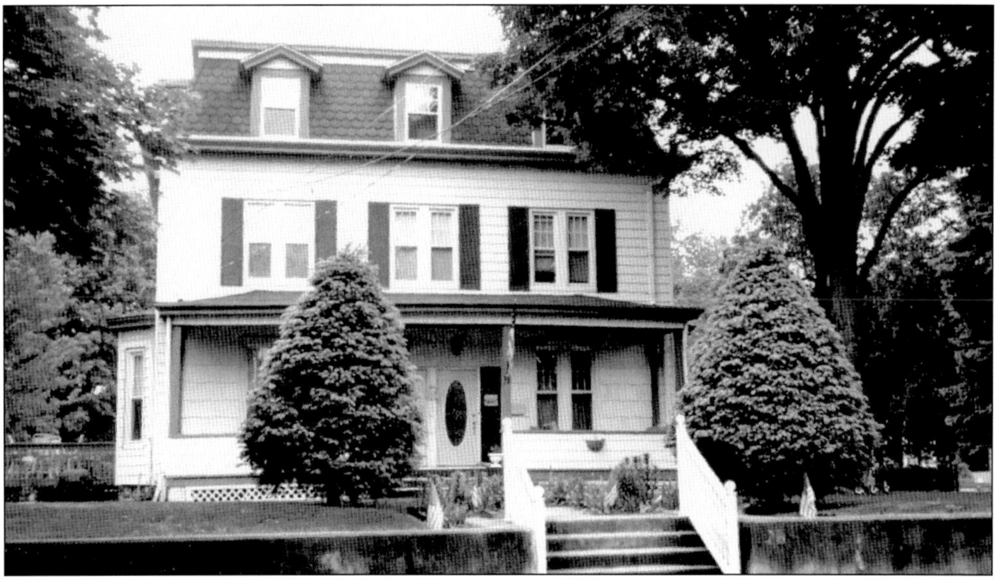

Seen is the home of Lewis Hopper. The son of Henry Hopper, Lewis was also in the milling and farming businesses. He was an owner of slaves, whose stone huts were located near the present-day train station.

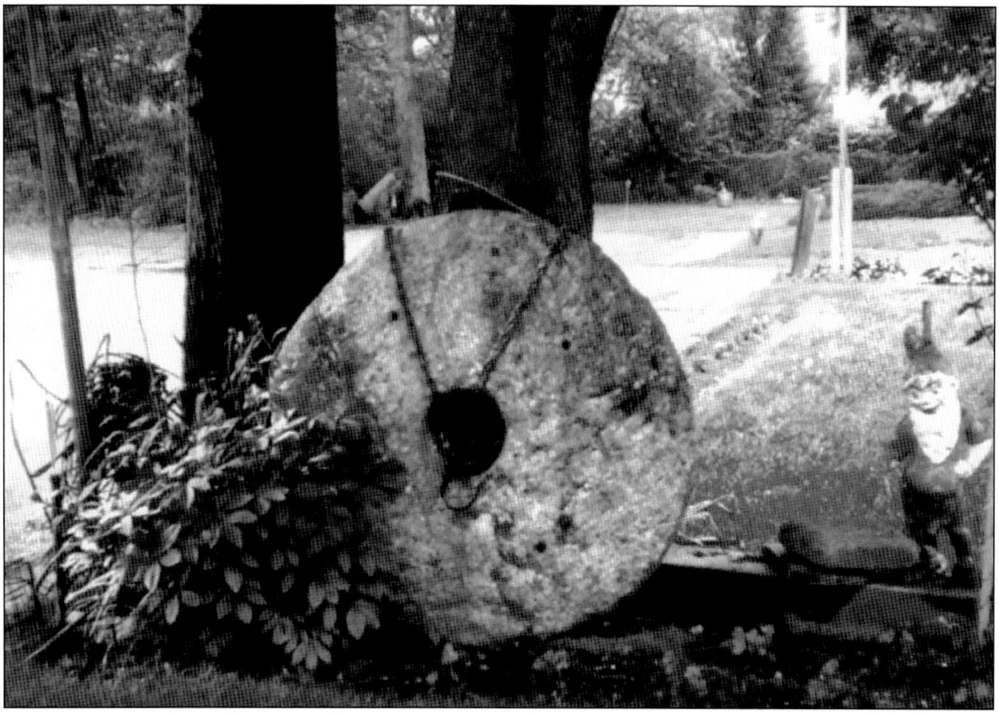

This stone is believed to have been used in the Henry "Hankey" Hopper gristmill. The mill was located along the Ho-Ho-Kus Brook just north of Wyckoff Avenue. A man by the name of Sweeting Miles worked for Hopper and was noted for his high flour yield from grain.

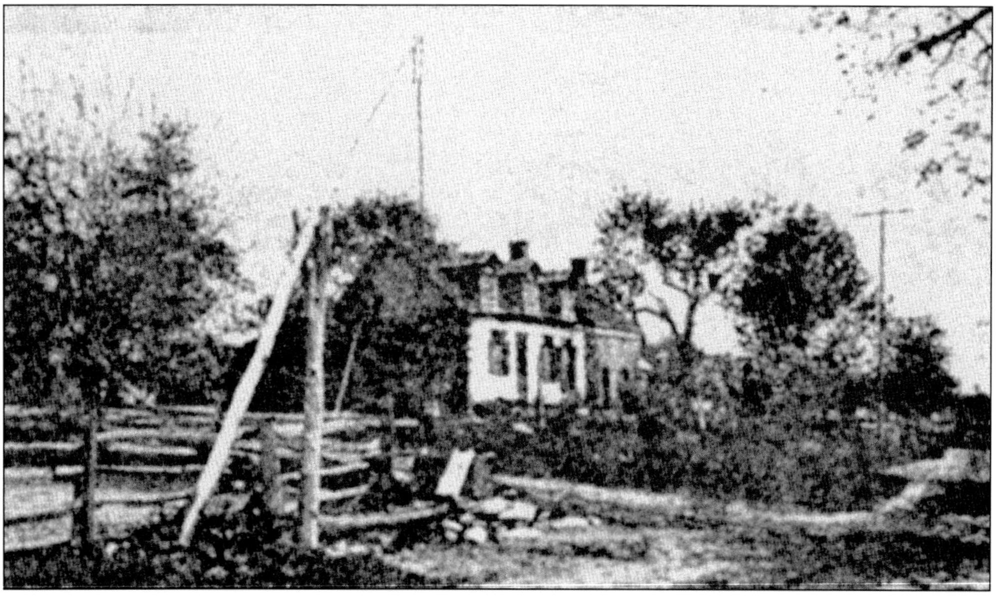

The Cornelius Smith house was located on Wyckoff Avenue near the center of the southern edge of the present-day high school. His first purchase of land was in 1802 from Abraham Hopper. His landholdings eventually encompassed an area of several hundred acres, stretching from Prospect Street south to the Midland Park border, bordered on the east by Hopper Avenue and on the west by Crescent Avenue.

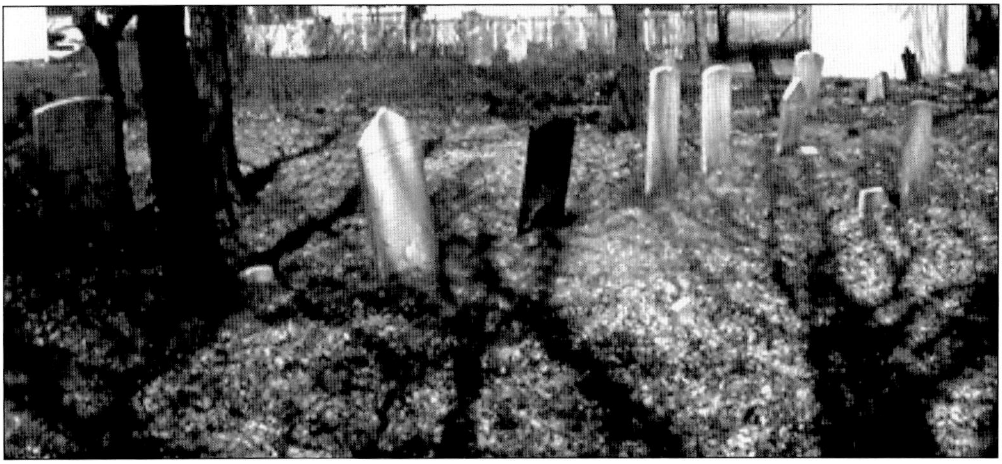

The Hopper family cemetery is adjacent to the former location of the Dissenter's Church. The first interment was in 1814, and the cemetery contains approximately 30 graves.

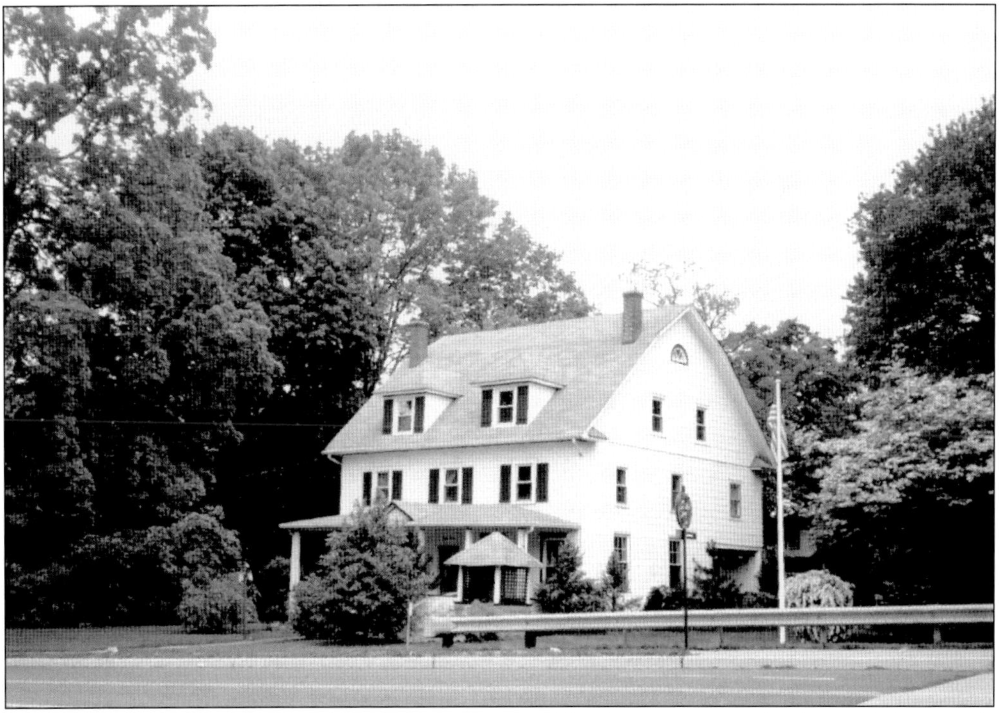

The Monroe house was built in the 1860s on the site of the former Dissenter's Church. This church was started in 1823 and left for Ridgewood in 1858, eventually becoming the First Presbyterian Church. The Monroe house utilized beams and banisters from the old church building.

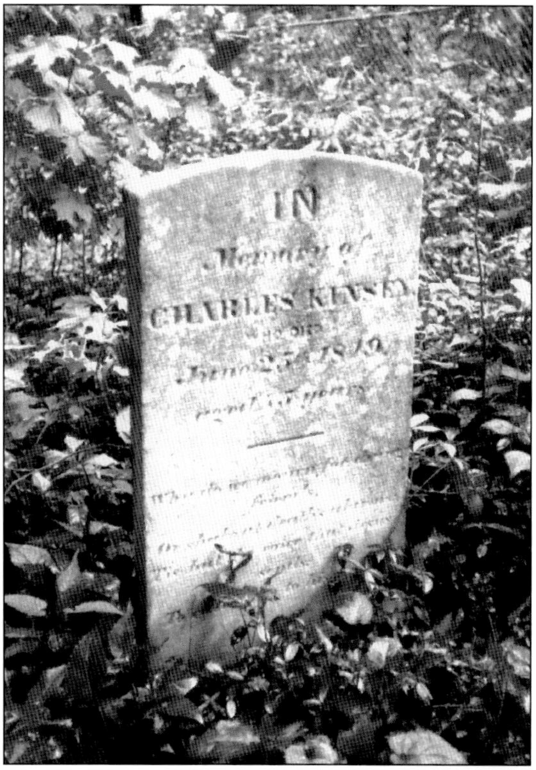

In 1803, paper mill owner Charles Kinsey of Paterson invented and patented a machine that created the first continuous roll of paper. In 1823, he and his family moved to New Prospect (as the Waldwick area was known then), where his son Ingram opened a new paper mill with James Larue. This is Charles Kinsey's gravestone at the Union Hill Cemetery in Wyckoff.

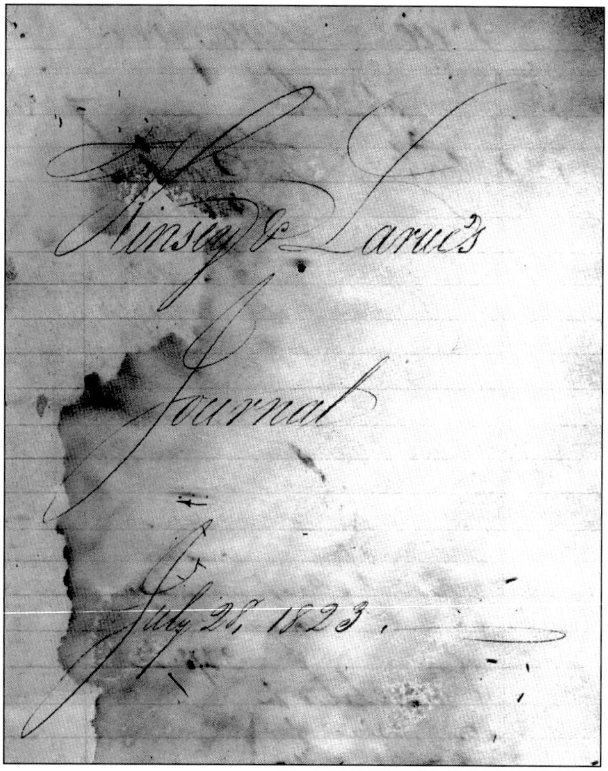

Kinsey & Larue's
Journal
July 28, 1823.

Ingram Kinsey and James Larue operated the paper mill from 1823 to at least 1830. The mill itself was a wood-frame building located along the Ho-Ho-Kus Brook near the present-day sewage-treatment facility. This is the title page from their daybook.

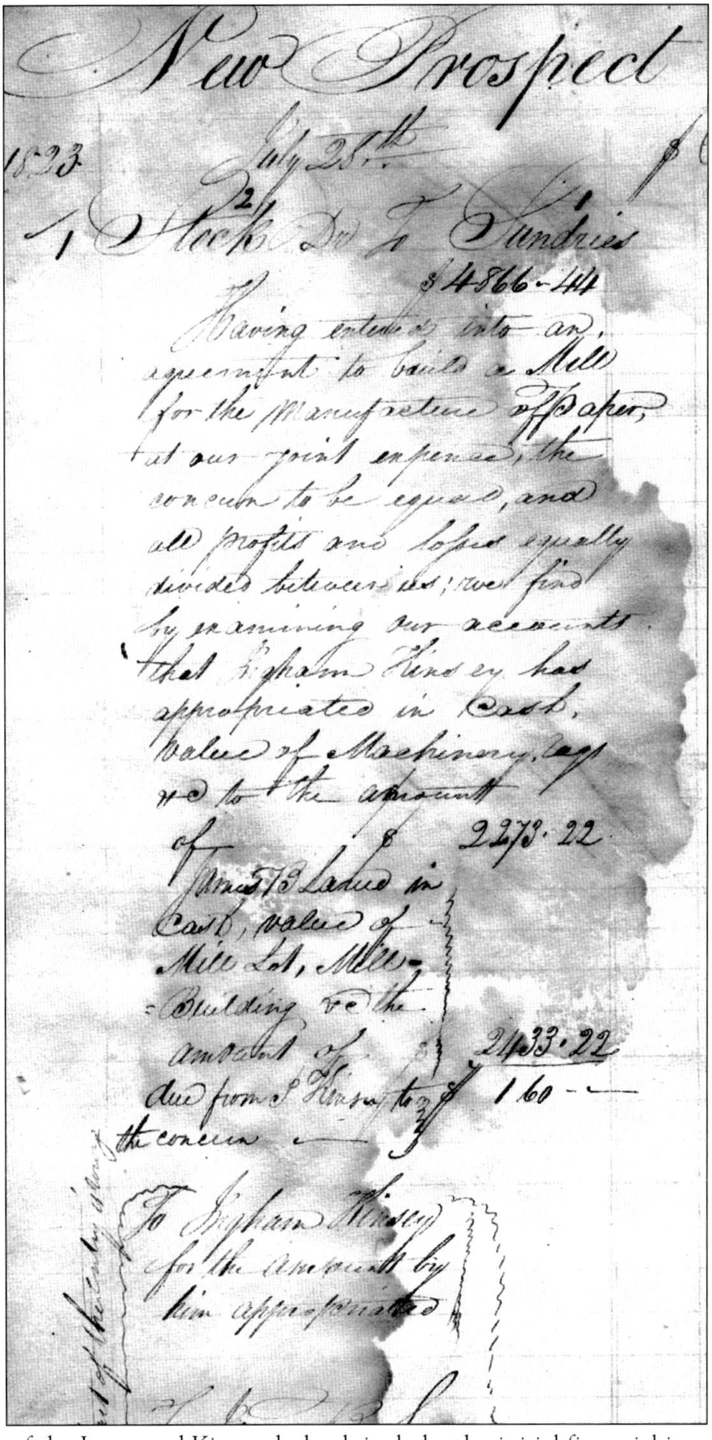

New Prospect

1823 July 25th

1 Stock Dr To Sundries

$4866.44

Having entered into an agreement to build a Mill for the Manufacture of Paper, at our joint expense, the concern to be equal, and all profits and losses equally divided between us; we find by examining our accounts that Ingham Kinsey has appropriated in Cash, value of Machinery, &c &c to the amount of $ 2273.22

James B Larue in Cash, value of Mill Lot, Mill-Building &c the amount of $ 2433.22

due from I Kinsey to the concern $ 160 —

To Ingham Kinsey for the amount by him appropriated

The first page of the Larue and Kinsey daybook includes the initial financial investments made by both Kinsey and Larue, totaling some $4,866.44. It appears that this partnership ended in 1829, but the mill continued to be operated by Larue alone until 1835, when he put it up for sale in an advertisement. It is further believed that Larue sold the mill to John White in 1837.

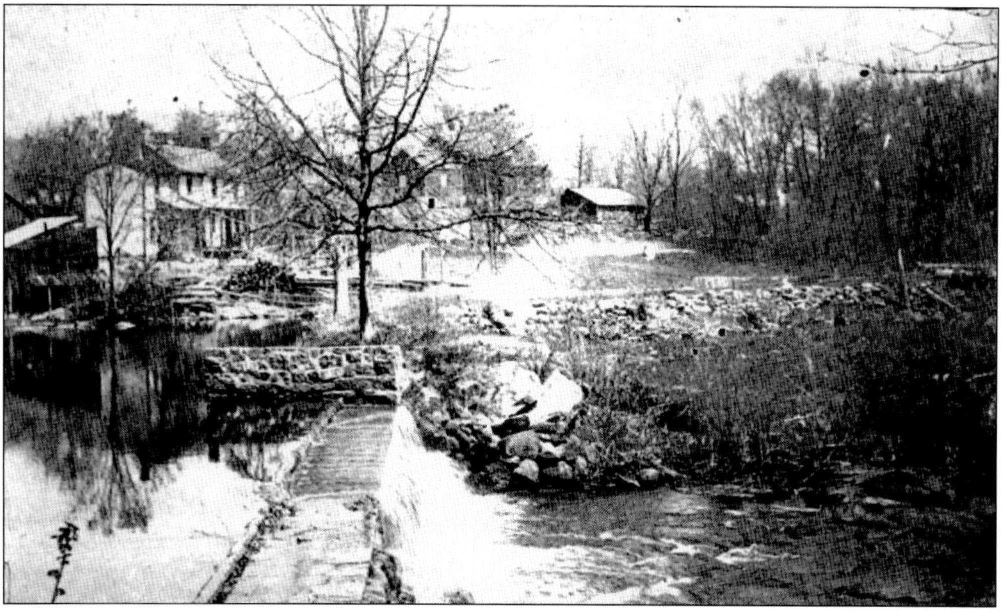

The White paper mill burned in 1857. It was rebuilt, only to burn again in 1876. It was rebuilt once more, although it reemerged as a sawmill. This photograph shows the White complex, including the tenant house, a multiple dwelling for mill workers. Also seen is Koole's Pond and the dam adjacent to the mill.

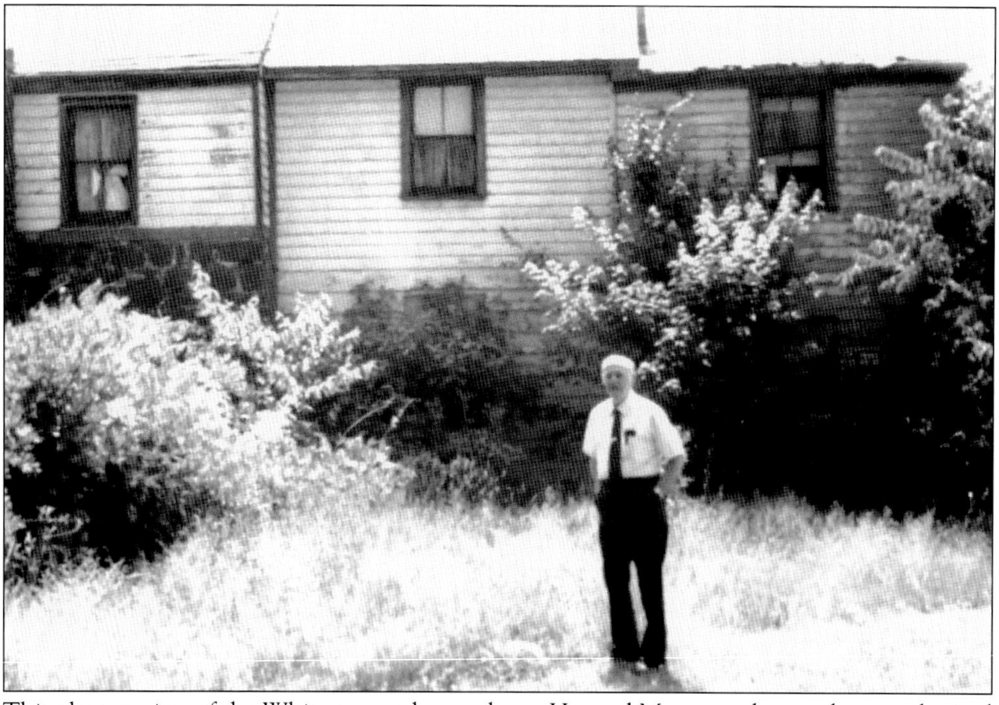

This closeup view of the White tenant house shows Howard Morgan, who was born and raised in the house. Three generations of his family lived and worked in this mill area also called the hollow. The tenant house was on the National Register of Historic Places but was razed by the Northwest Bergen County Utilities Authority in 1985.

Two

The Iron Horse Doesn't Stop Here

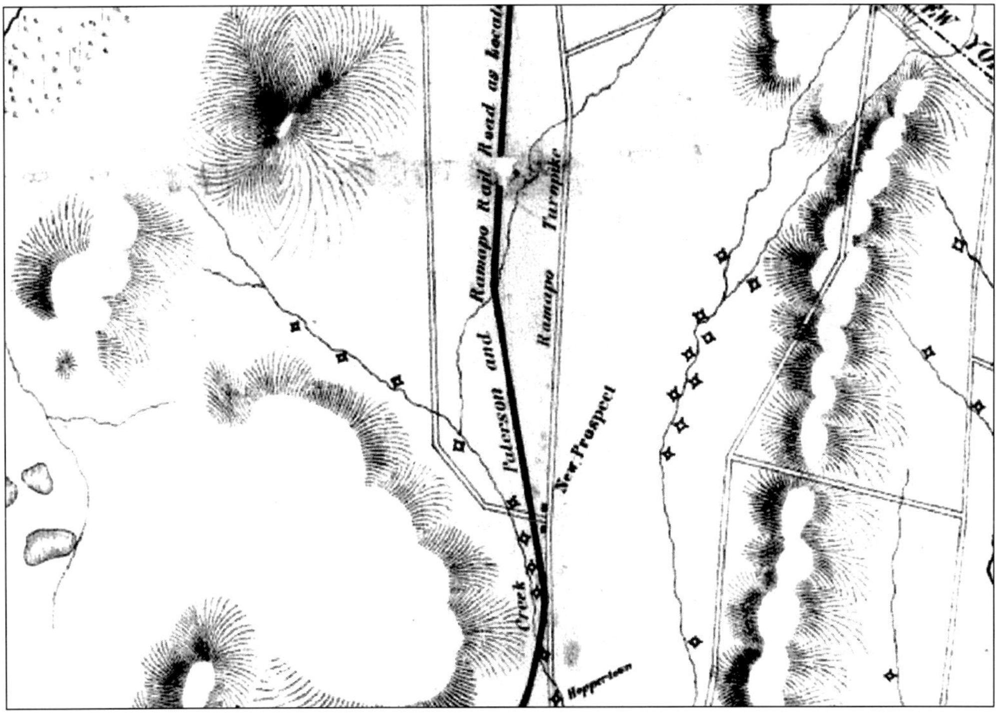

The Paterson and Ramapo Railroad was constructed from Paterson to the outskirts of Suffern, New York, in 1848. Combined with the Paterson and Hudson River Railroad (completed a few years earlier), it created a link between the Erie Railroad at Suffern to the Paterson and Hudson River Railroad ferry terminal in Jersey City. This map was created by civil engineer John W. Allen (for whom Allendale is named) in 1847. The nearest depot stop on the railroad closest to present-day Waldwick was at the Rosencrantz cotton mill complex, south of the Hermitage.

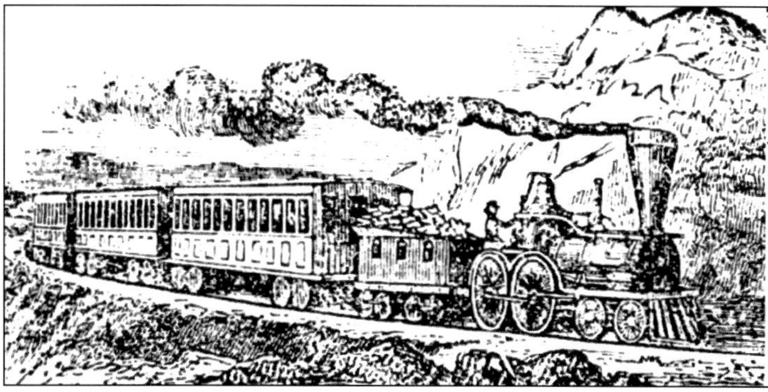

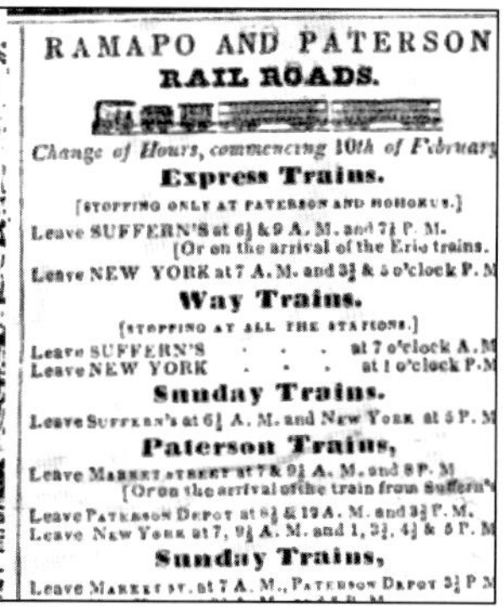

RAMAPO AND PATERSON
RAIL ROADS.

Change of Hours, commencing 10th of February

Express Trains.

[STOPPING ONLY AT PATERSON AND HOHOKUS.]

Leave SUFFERN'S at 6½ & 9 A. M. and 7½ P. M.
[Or on the arrival of the Erie trains.
Leave NEW YORK at 7 A. M. and 3½ & 5 o'clock P. M

Way Trains.

[STOPPING AT ALL THE STATIONS.]

Leave SUFFERN'S . . . at 7 o'clock A. M
Leave NEW YORK . . . at 1 o'clock P. M

Sunday Trains.

Leave SUFFERN'S at 6½ A. M. and NEW YORK at 5 P. M

Paterson Trains,

Leave MARKET STREET at 7 & 9½ A. M. and 8 P. M
[Or on the arrival of the train from Suffern's
Leave PATERSON DEPOT at 6½ & 12 A. M. and 3½ P. M.
Leave NEW YORK at 7, 9½ A. M. and 1, 3½, 4½ & 5 P. M

Sunday Trains,

Leave MARKET ST. at 7 A. M., PATERSON DEPOT 3½ P. M

This is an early engraving said to be the infamous reverse curve on the railroad just south of Wyckoff Avenue. Next to it is a schedule of the Paterson and Ramapo Railroad from 1852.

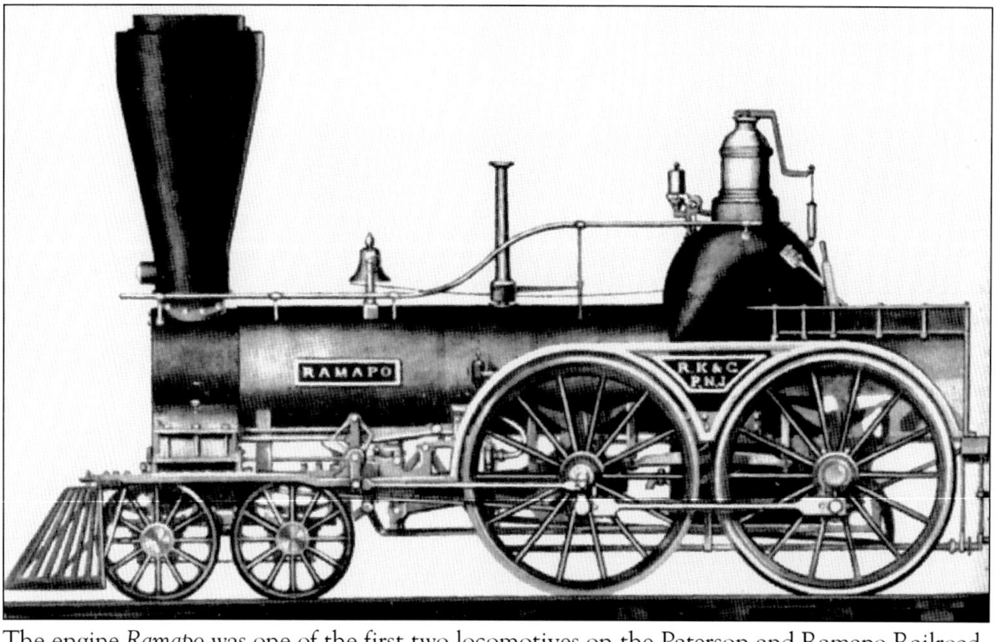

The engine *Ramapo* was one of the first two locomotives on the Paterson and Ramapo Railroad.

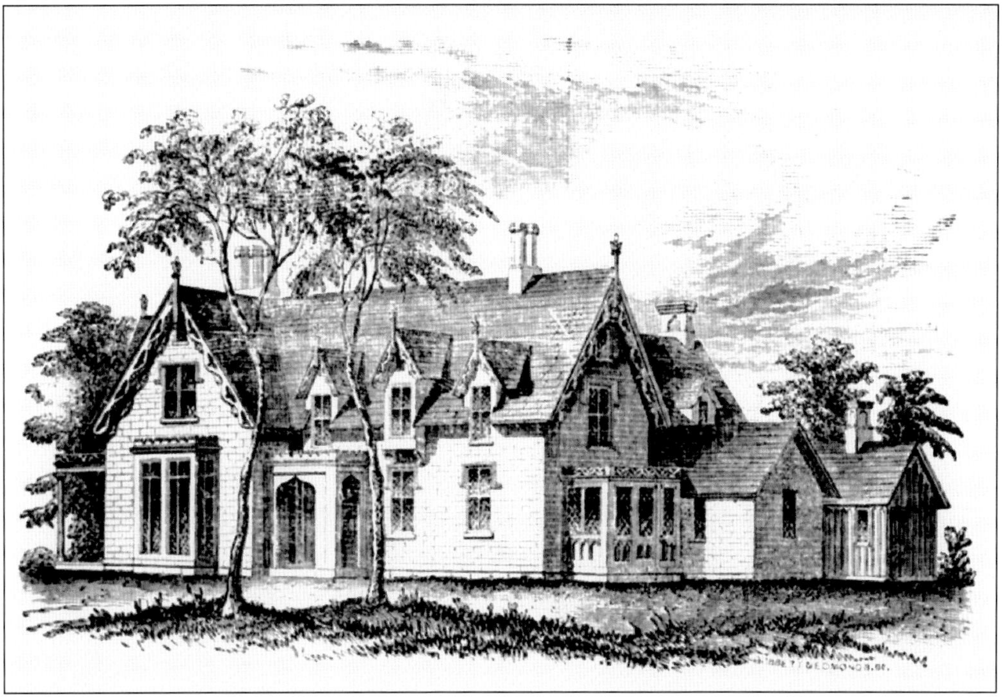

The Waldwic Cottage is more commonly known as the Hermitage. The Hermitage was extensively remodeled in the 1840s by architect William Ranlett. The name given to this renovated country home played a critical role in 1885, when Hermitage resident Elizabeth Rosencrantz suggested the name of the new railroad depot at New Prospect be called Waldwick.

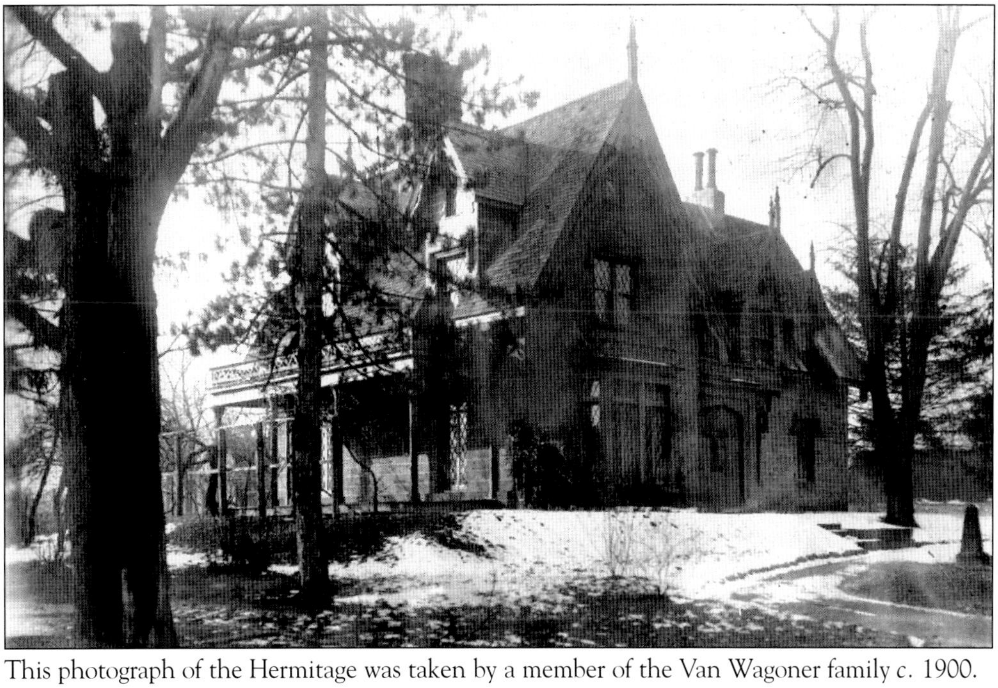

This photograph of the Hermitage was taken by a member of the Van Wagoner family *c.* 1900.

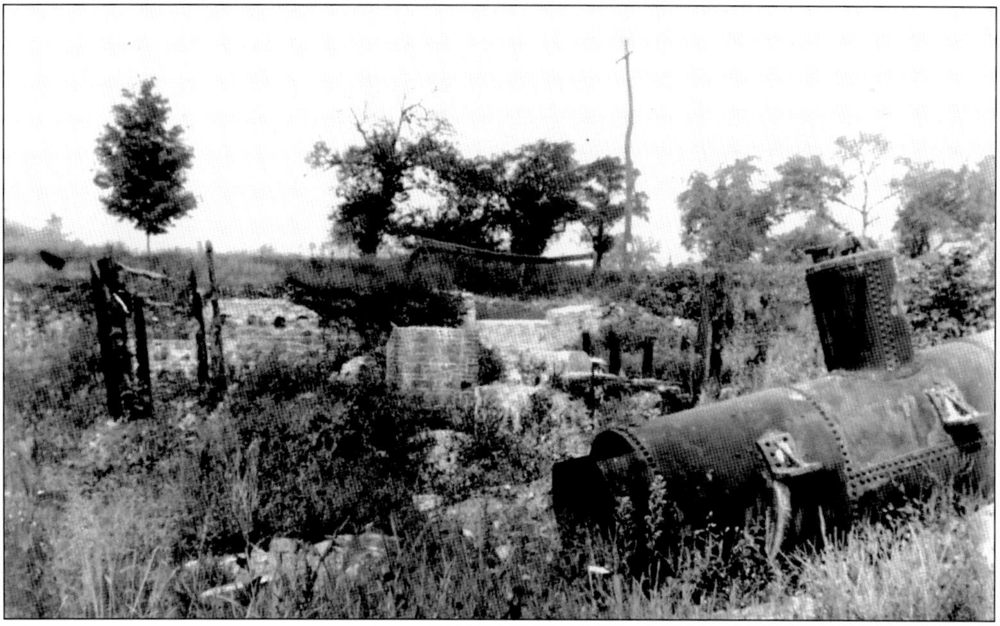

These are the ruins of Charles White's paper twine mill, located at Hopper Avenue and West Prospect Street. Established prior to 1860, it was producing 15 to 20 barrels a day by the time of the Civil War. The plant ceased operations sometime in the late 1890s. Shortly afterwards, it was burned by vagrants who perished in the blaze. White's Pond, which is still in existence, was created for this factory. The Waldwick municipal pool now occupies the site.

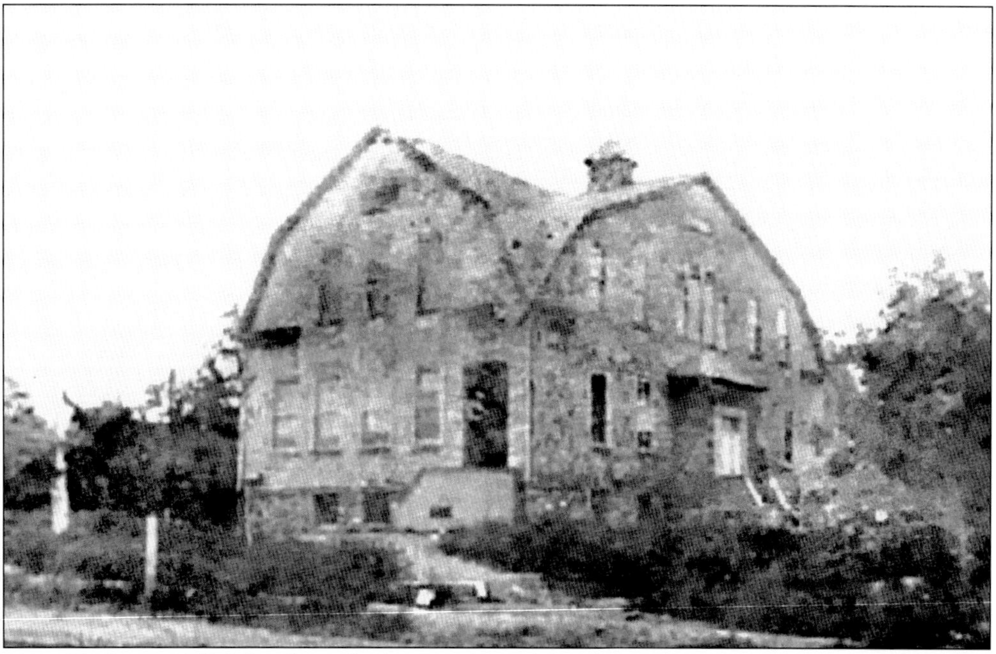

The old Union Hill School was built in 1859 and was located on the north side of Wyckoff Avenue just west of the Waldwick and Wyckoff border. It served students who lived in the western portion of present-day Waldwick. Other students went to the "little red schoolhouse" in Allendale.

This is a receipt from H.H. Goetschius, a local blacksmith whose shop was located on the southeast side of the Ho-Ho-Kus Brook along Wyckoff Avenue. Goetschius also served as a constable and tax collector.

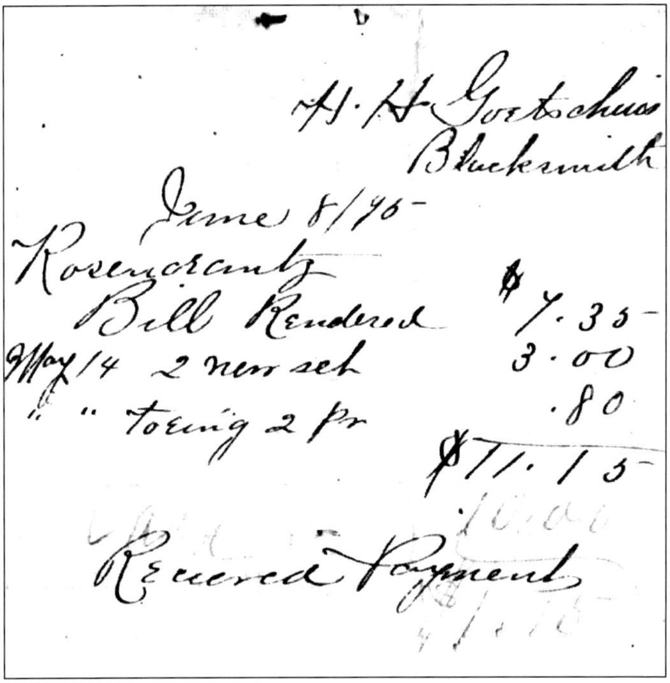
H. H. Goetschius
Blacksmith
June 8/96-
Rosencrantz
Bill Rendered $7.35-
May 14 2 new set 3.00
" " toeing 2 pr .80
$11.15-
Received Payment

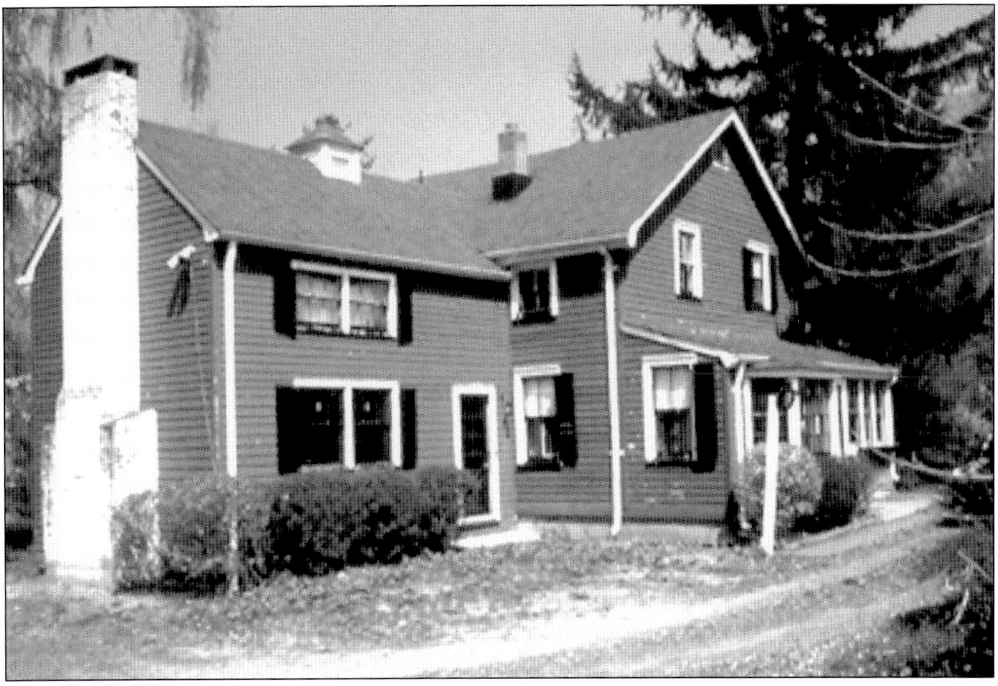

The Goetschius home also served as his blacksmith shop. It was built prior to 1870, and it has also been known as the Garretson house.

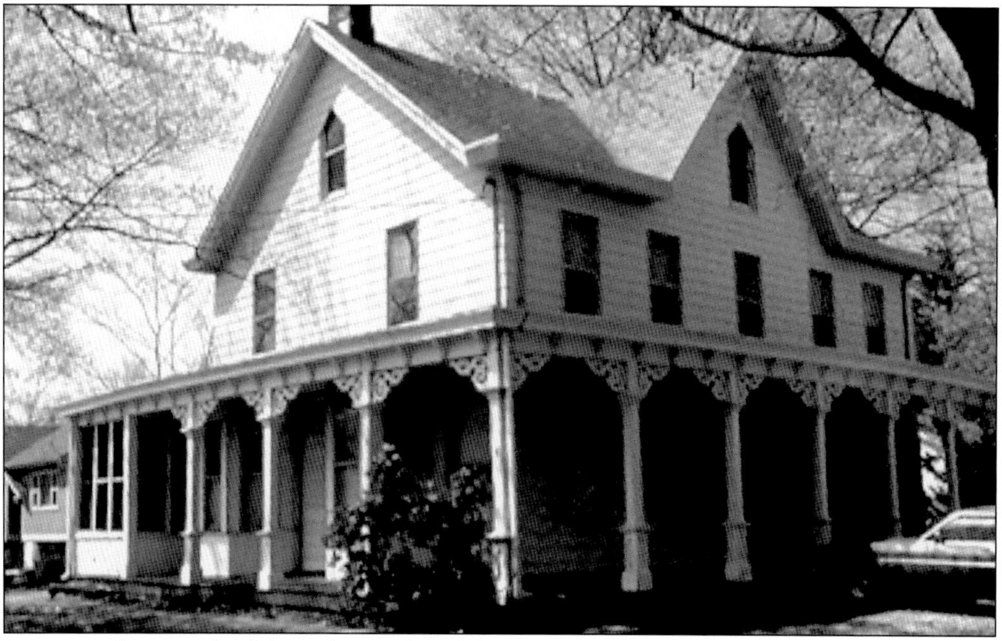

Seen is a photograph of the White-Babcock house at 16 White's Lane. The house dates from at least the 1850s, and it was occupied by the Matthew White family near the family's paper mill operations.

OFFICERS AND MEN OF NEW JERSEY

NO.	NAME.	RANK.	COM. OR ENROLLED.	MUST'D IN.	PERIOD	MUST'D OUT.	REMARKS.
1	Cornelius D. Ackerman	Corporal....	Sept. 1, '62	Sept. 22, '62	9 Mos.	June 25, '63	
2	Albert G. Hopper.......	"	"	"	"	"	Corp. Nov. 1, '62.
3	William D. Meeker.....	"	"	"	"	"	Corp. Nov. 1, '62.
4	Theodore Bamper.......	"	"	"	"	"	
5	Garret C. Hopper........	"	"	"	"	"	Corp. Nov. 1, '62.
6	John A. Boyd............	"	"	"	"	"	Corp. March 8, '63; transferred from Co. A, Feb. 1, '63.
7	John J. Meyers..........	"	"	"	"	"	Corp. March 8, '63.
8	John Harrop.............	"	"	"	"	"	Corp. March 8, '63.
1	Peter Ackerman.........	Musician...	"	"	"	"	
2	Henry L. Hopper.......	"	"	"	"	"	
1	Isaac P. Finch..........	Wagoner...	"	"	"	"	
1	Abrams, Elias...........	Private......	"	"	"	"	
2	Abrams, Henry.........	"	"	"	"	"	
3	Acker, John..............	"	"	"	"	"	Corp. Sept. 1, '62; Private Nov. 1, '62.
4	Aller, Henry T..........	"	"	"	"	"	
5	Banta, Thomas T........	"	"	"	"	"	
6	Bartholf, Peter...........	"	"	"	"	"	
7	Bartholf, Stephen D...	"	"	"	"	"	Corp. Sept. 1, '62; Private Nov. 1, '62.
8	Boyd, James.............	"	"	"	"	"	Transferred from Co. A, Feb. 1, '63.

Company B, Twenty-second Regiment.

NO.	NAME.	RANK.	COM. OR ENROLLED.	MUST'D IN.	PERIOD	MUST'D OUT.	REMARKS.
1	Abraham Van Emburgh	Captain.....	Sept. 2, '62	Sept. 22, '62	9 Mos.	....	Promoted Lieut. Col. Feb. 11, '63.
2	Benjamin Z. Van Emburgh..................	"	Feb. 21, '63	Mar. 2, '63	"	....	2d Lieut. Sept. 2, '62; Capt. vice Abraham Van Emburgh promoted; resigned April 13, '63.
3	Andrew Van Emburgh	"	May 18, '63	May 30, '63	"	June 25, '63	1st Serj. Sept. 1, '62; 1st Lieut. Feb. 21, '63; Capt. vice Benjamin Z. Van Emburgh resigned.
1	Jacob Z. Van Blarcom	1st Lieut..	Sept. 2, '62	Sept. 22, '62	"	....	Resigned Feb. 11, '63.
2	Charles Van Riper.....	"	May 18, '63	May 30, '63	"	June 25, '63	Serj. Sept. 1, '62; 2d Lieut. Feb. 21, '63; promoted 1st Lieut. vice Van Blarcom resigned.
1	Thomas Eckerson.......	1st Serj......	Sept. 1, '62	Sept. 22, '62	"	"	Serj. Sept. 1, '62; 1st Serj. March 8, '63.

This is a roster of Company B of the 22nd New Jersey Regiment during the Civil War. Most of the men from this area were in Company B or D, including local resident Henry L. Hopper, who enlisted and became a musician.

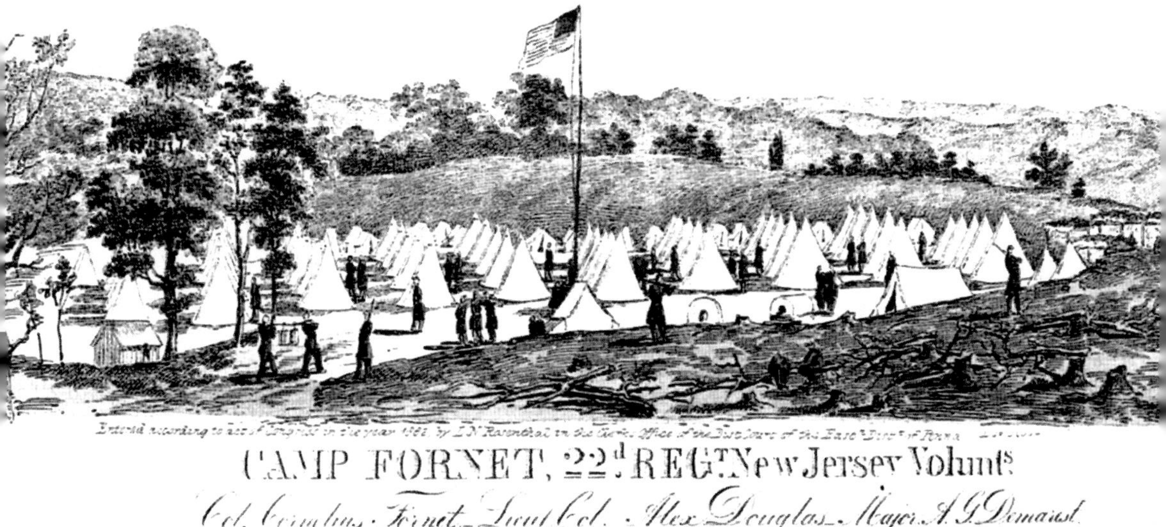

This is a view of a campground of the 22nd New Jersey Regiment. The regiment was under the leadership of Col. Cornelius Fornet. The men of this area had been drilling constantly under the direction of Capt. Abraham Van Emburgh of Company B. When the day of September 22, 1863, dawned for their departure from New Jersey, they gathered in the guard room of the local drill hall, where Rev. E.T. Corwin gave them a farewell sermon and gave each man a Bible to take with him. From the hall they marched down to the depot at the Ho-Ho-Kus station to catch the train to Trenton. Captain Van Emburgh had an order from the governor of New Jersey for free passage. The stationmaster refused the order. The captain immediately gave the order to block the tracks with railroad ties. When the train arrived, the men boarded, except for four men. The stationmaster relented, and the four men pulled aside the ties. As the order was given to proceed, a loud cheer went up from the assembled crowd and the troops were off. The regiment saw limited action at the Battle of Chancellorsville. They were mustered out on June 25, 1863.

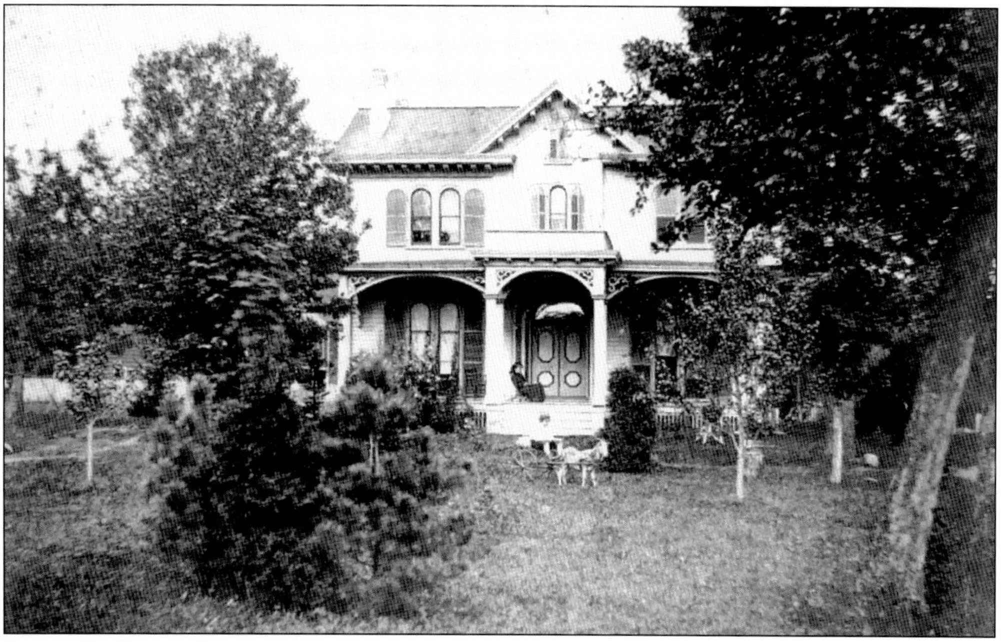

Pictured riding in his goat cart is Henry G. Ackerman. His mother, Jane Ryerson Ackerman, watches from the porch in this 1870s photograph. The house was built in the mid-1860s near the location of the original Ackerman homestead. John T. Ackerman sought out the best plans of the day to build the house, and he drove a wagon all the way to Rochester to obtain the best lumber available.

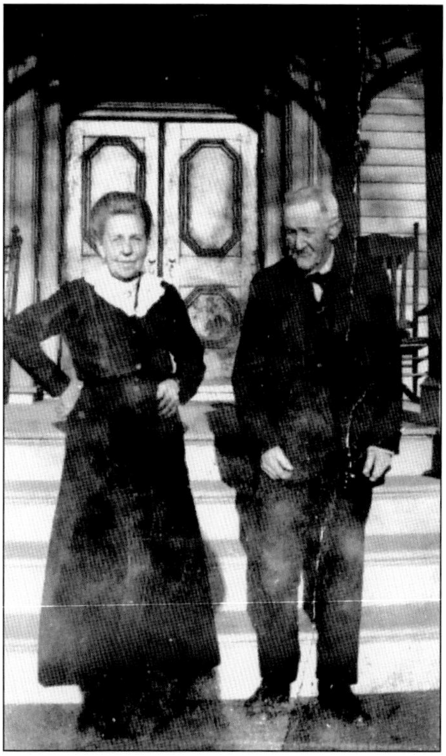

John T. and Jane Ackerman stand on their front porch on West Saddle River Road.

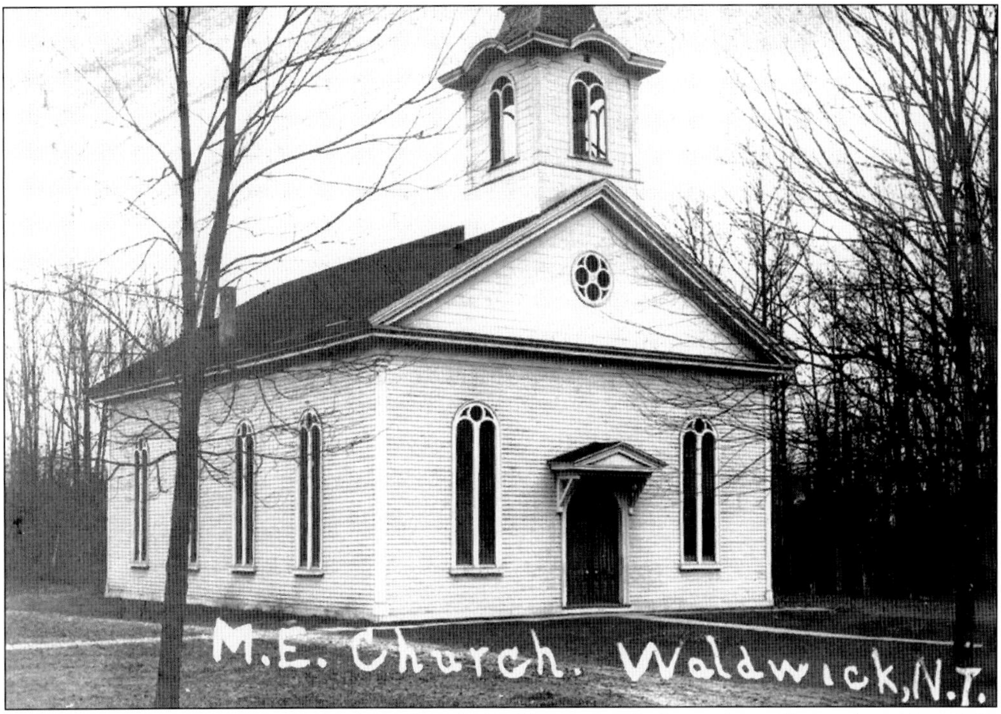

The third (and current) Methodist church building was dedicated on December 15, 1867. Church members paid $8,000 for this building on the east side of Franklin Turnpike at Wyckoff Avenue.

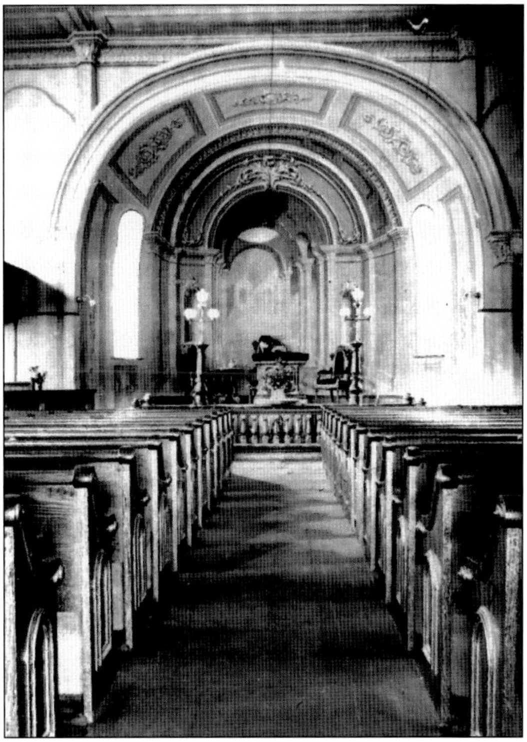

The interior of the church is shown prior to renovations in 1908.

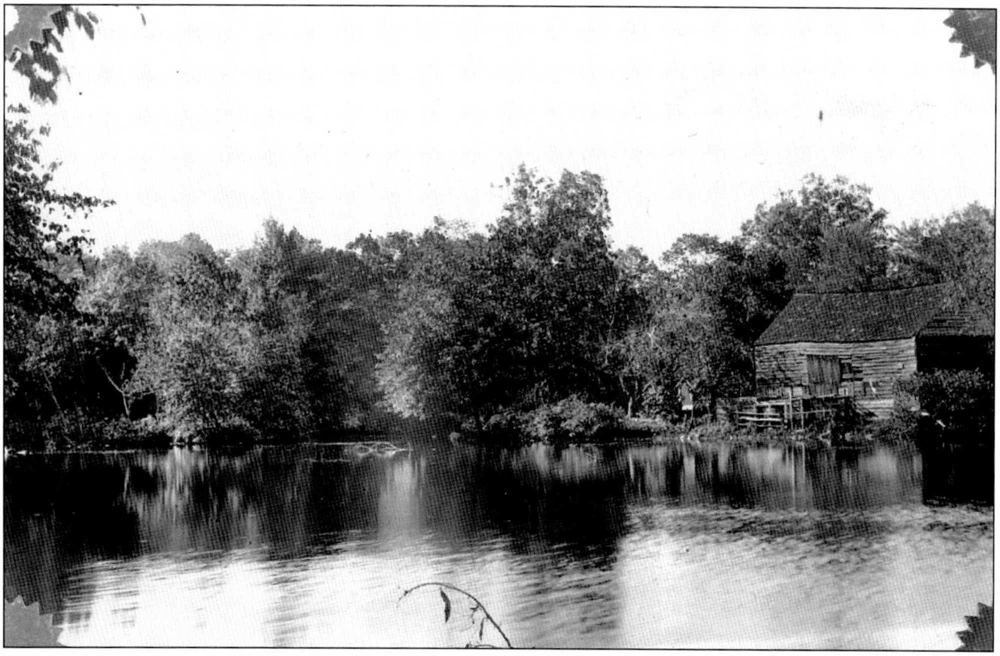

This view of Koole's Pond shows the sawmill on the opposite shore. The Koole family resided in the hollow and became longtime friends of the Hermitage's Rosencrantz family.

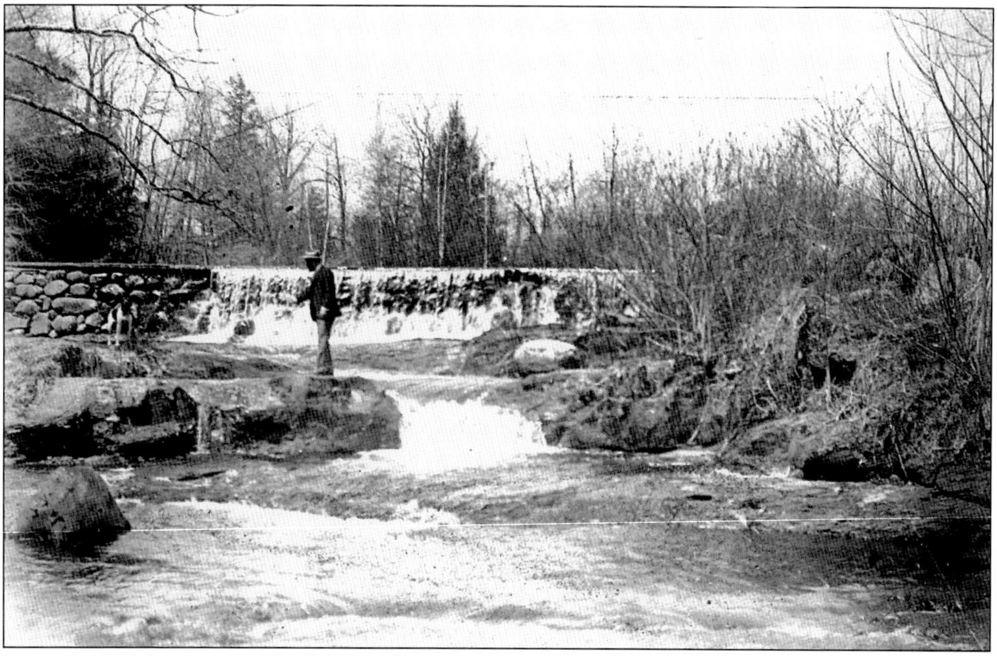

This sawmill dam was at Koole's Pond.

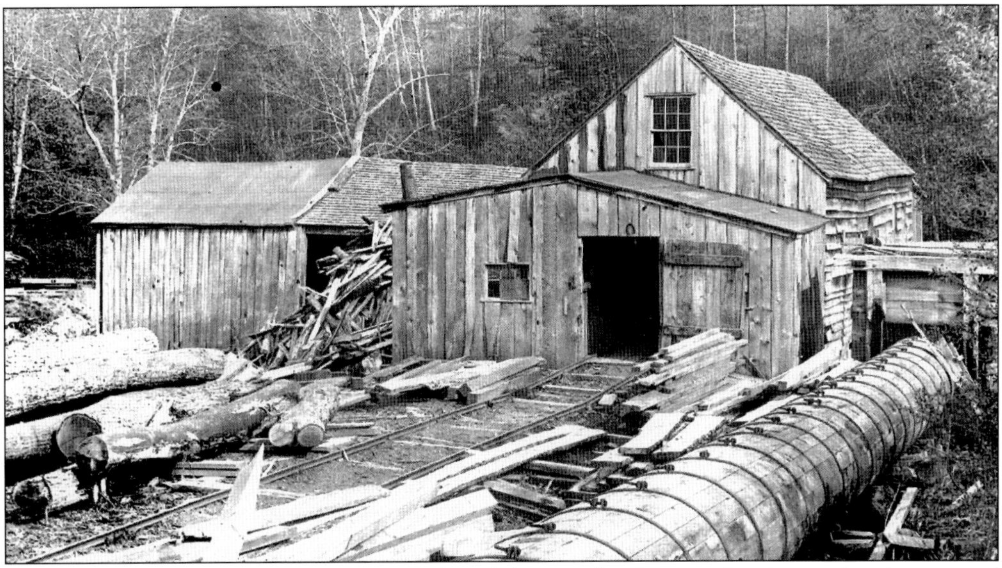

This sawmill was operated by Matthew White (along with a Bamper family member for a period of time) on the site of the original White paper mill. They produced 3,000 railroad ties in a week's time in 1878.

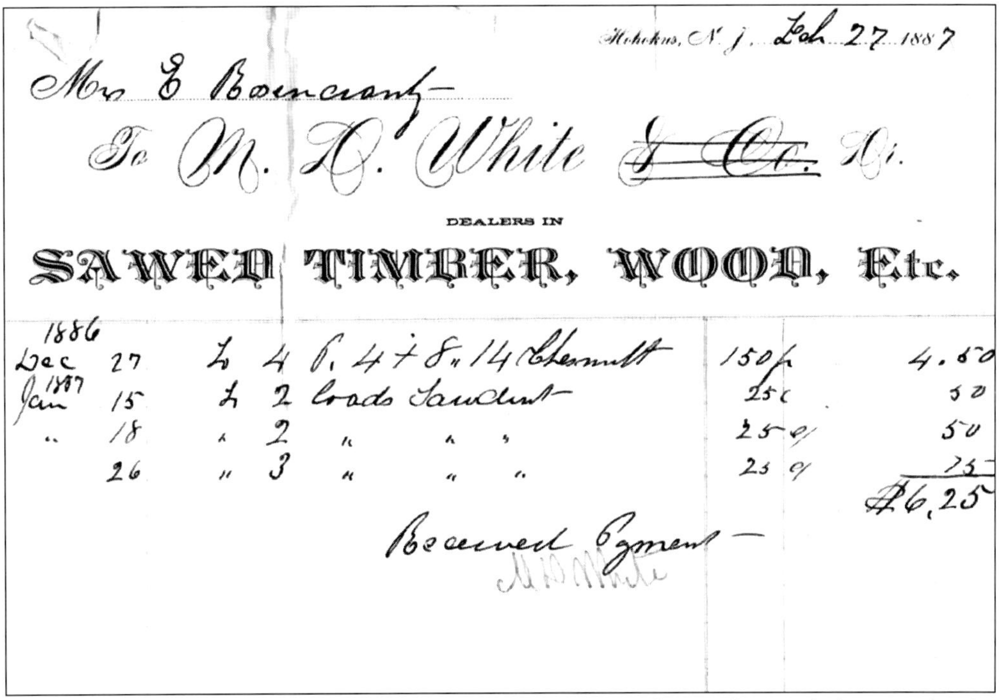

Hohokus, N.J., Feb 27 1887

Mrs E Rosencrantz

To M. D. White ~~& Co.~~ Dr.

DEALERS IN

SAWED TIMBER, WOOD, Etc.

1886 Dec	27	To 4 6, 4 + 8 " 14 Chestnut	150 ft	4.50
1887 Jan	15	" 2 loads Sawdust	25 ¢	50
..	18	" 2 " " "	25 ¢	50
	26	" 3 " " "	25 ¢	75
				$6.25

Received Payment —

M D White

Seen here is a receipt of the M.D. White lumber company for sawdust and chestnut for the Rosencrantz family.

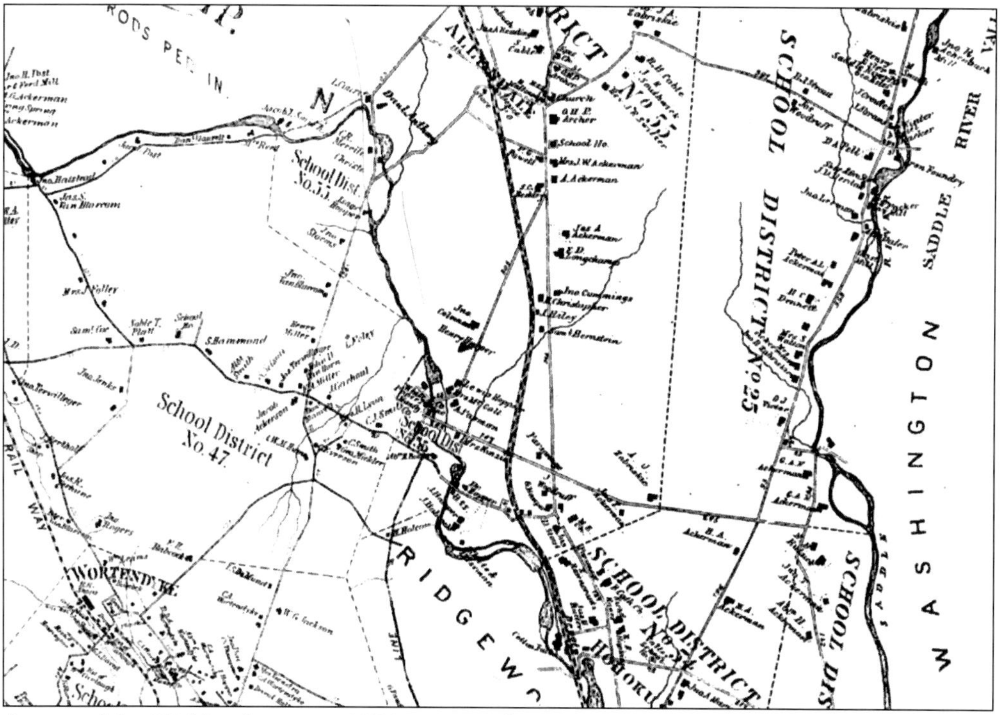

A map of the Waldwick area in 1876 portrays the various mills and homes that are indicated by name.

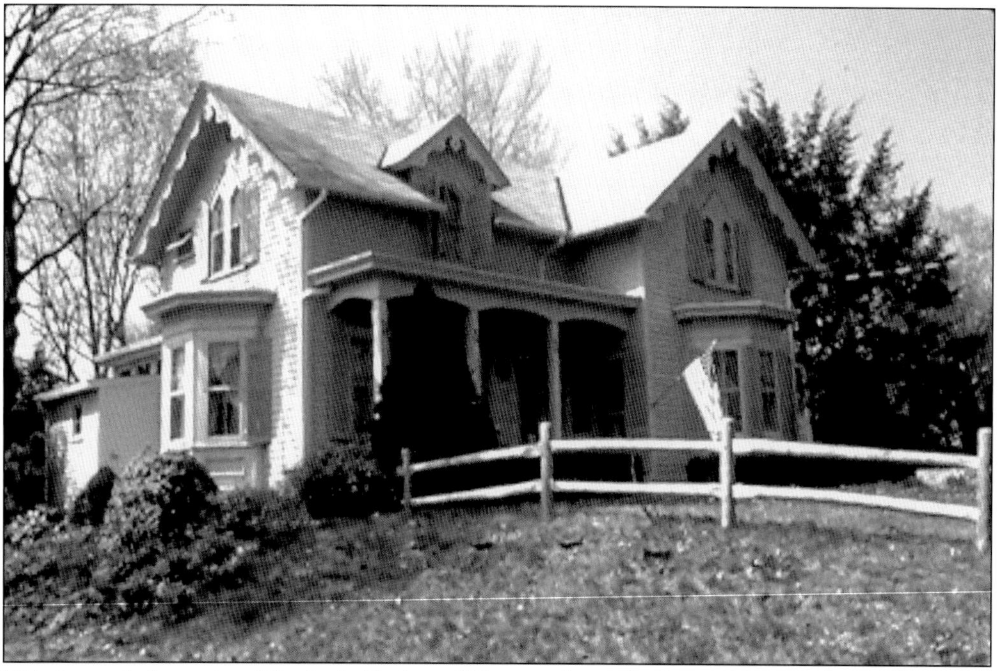
This home belonged to Elizabeth Higham White and was built in 1867 on the south side of Wyckoff Avenue, next to Monroe Street. She was the daughter of John and Mabelle White, who took over the Larue paper mill in 1837. The house stayed in family until 1927.

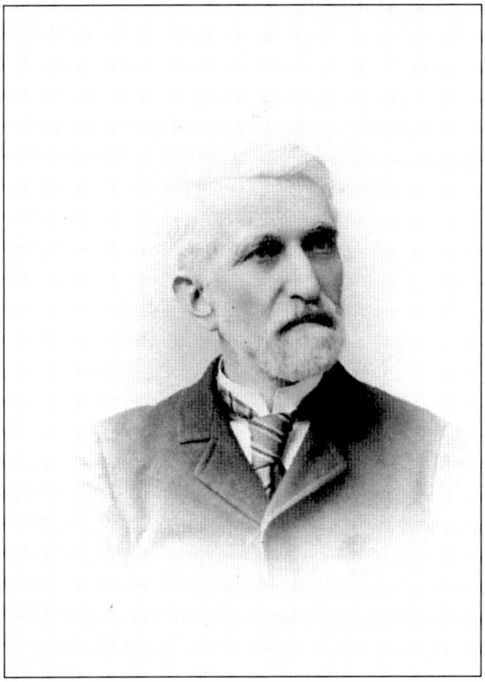

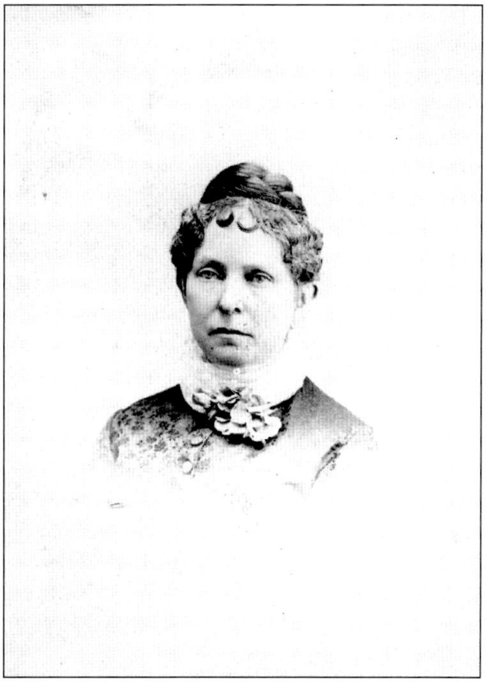

Orville and Metta Victor came to this area from Ohio and settled into a stately home on West Saddle River Road just north of current Bergen Avenue and Sheridan Avenue intersection. Orville was well known for his published history of the Civil War and his magazine editing, and Metta was a prolific pulp novel author.

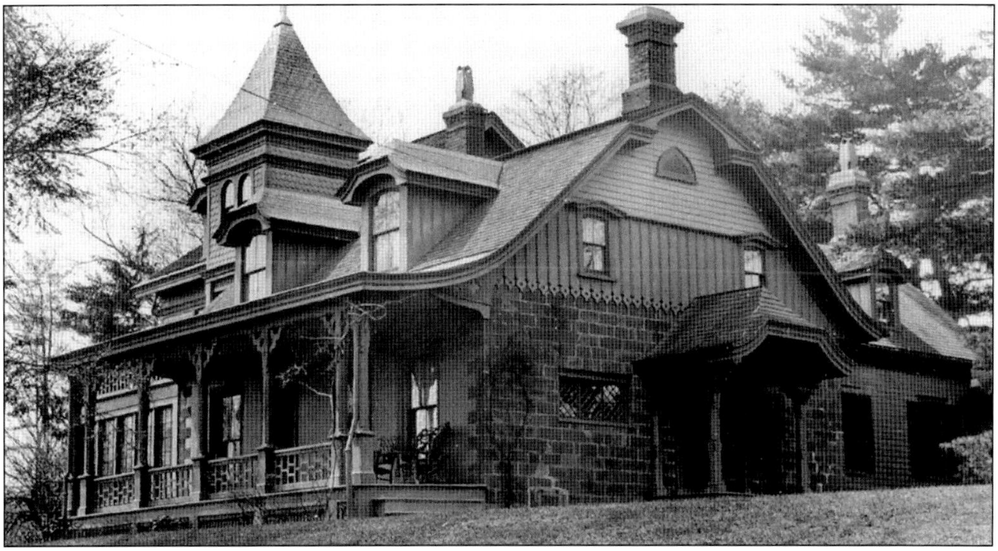

Seen is the Orville house, on West Saddle River Road in present-day Saddle River. It was originally built by a D. Hopper and owned by the Victors throughout the late 1800s. It was subsequently sold to the R.A. Adams family.

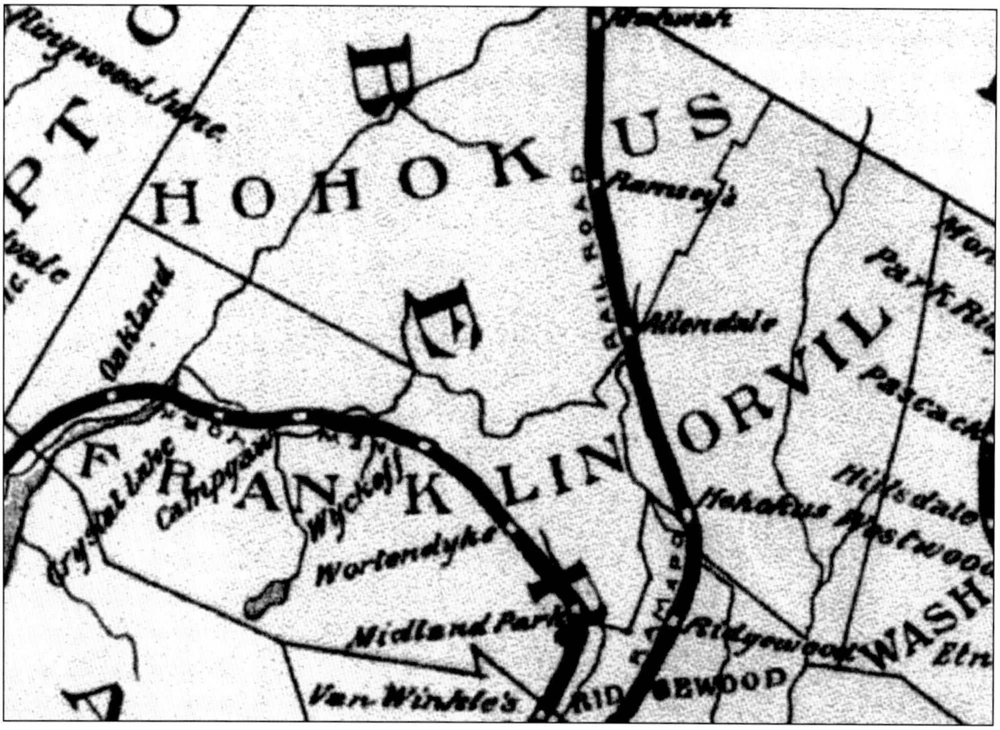

In 1885, a decision was made to split up the large township of Ho-Ho-Kus and a portion of Washington Township into smaller entities including a new Orvil Township, named in honor of Orville Victor. This new Orvil Township, as shown on this map, included the area encompassing present-day Allendale, Saddle River, Upper Saddle River, Waldwick, Montvale, and Woodcliff Lake.

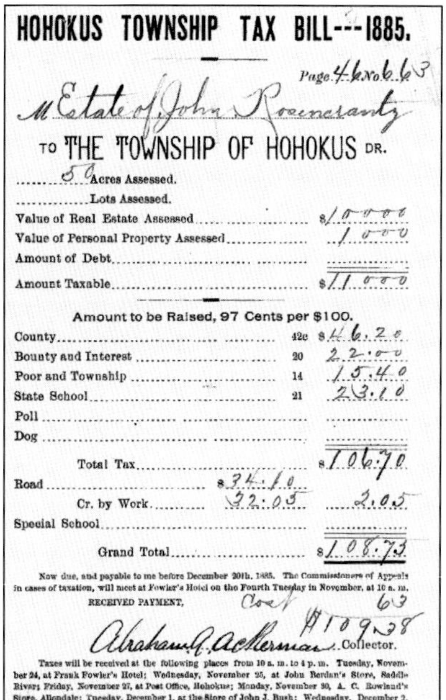

HOHOKUS TOWNSHIP TAX BILL---1885.

Page 46 No 663

M Estate of John Rosencrantz

TO THE TOWNSHIP OF HOHOKUS DR.

59 Acres Assessed.
Lots Assessed.

Value of Real Estate Assessed		$10000
Value of Personal Property Assessed		1000
Amount of Debt		
Amount Taxable		$11000

Amount to be Raised, 97 Cents per $100.

County	42c		$46.20
Bounty and Interest	20		22.00
Poor and Township	14		15.40
State School	21		23.10
Poll			
Dog			
Total Tax			$106.70
Road		$34.10	
Cr. by Work		32.05	2.05
Special School			
Grand Total			$108.75

Now due, and payable to me before December 20th, 1885. The Commissioners of Appeals in cases of taxation, will meet at Fowler's Hotel on the Fourth Tuesday in November, at 10 a. m.

RECEIVED PAYMENT, Cost 63

$109.38

Abraham A. Ackerman Collector.

Taxes will be received at the following places from 10 a. m. to 4 p. m. Tuesday, November 24, at Frank Fowler's Hotel; Wednesday, November 25, at John Berdan's Store, Saddle River; Friday, November 27, at Post Office, Hohokus; Monday, November 30, A. C. Rowland's Store, Allendale; Tuesday, December 1, at the Store of John J. Bush; Wednesday, December 2, at the Hotel of Andrew H. Hagerman; Thursday, December 17, at Frank Fowler's Hotel, Ramseys.

P. O. RAMSEYS. ABRAHAM A. ACKERMAN, Collector.

This is an 1885 Ho-Ho-Kus tax bill for the Hermitage. It was the last bill for the Rosencrantz family from Ho-Ho-Kus Township prior to becoming Orvil Township.

Three

ALL ABOARD, WALDWICK

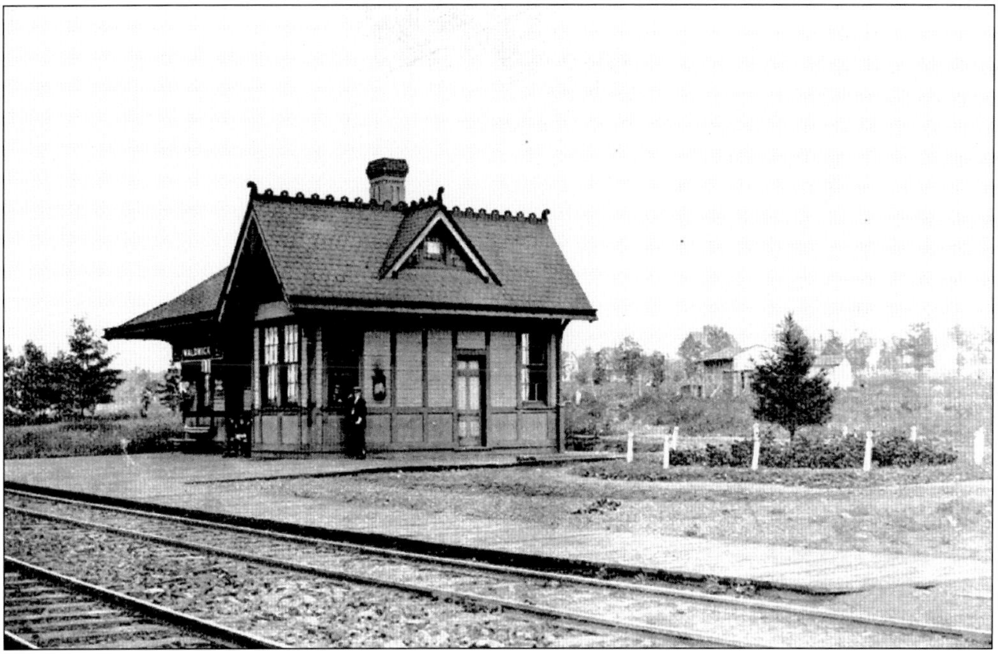

The railroad depot is shown as it appeared in 1887, recently built on land donated by Orvil Township resident Peter Bogert. Local residents paid subscriptions to have the station built by the Erie Railroad.

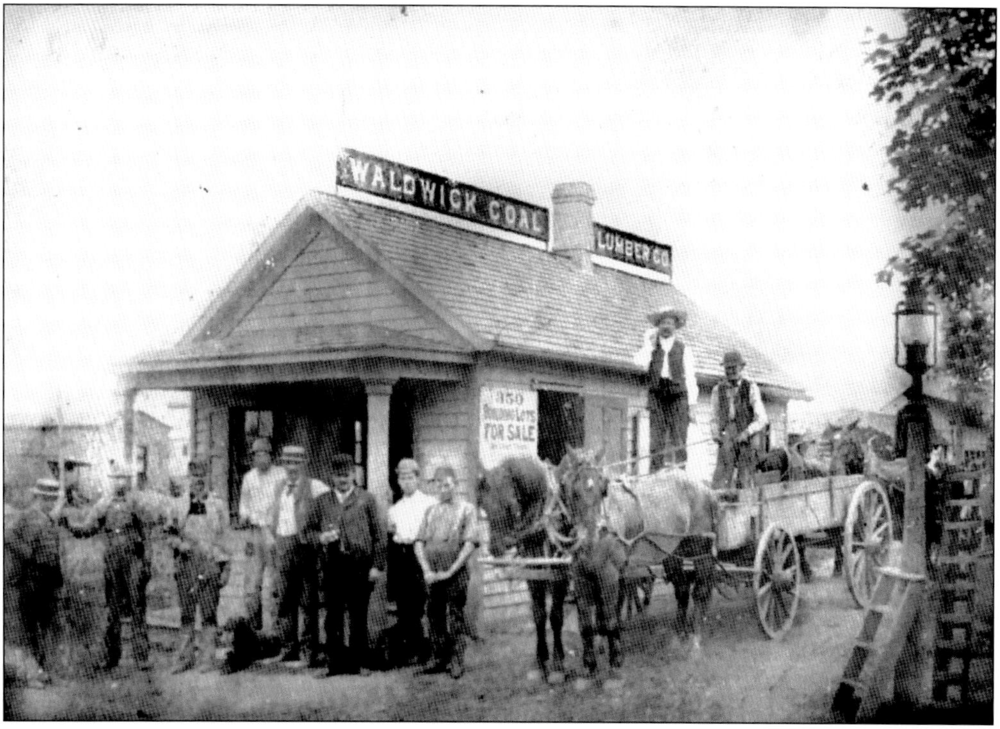

The Waldwick Coal and Lumber Company was likely created soon after the opening of the new Waldwick station. This photograph is believed to have been taken in the 1890s.

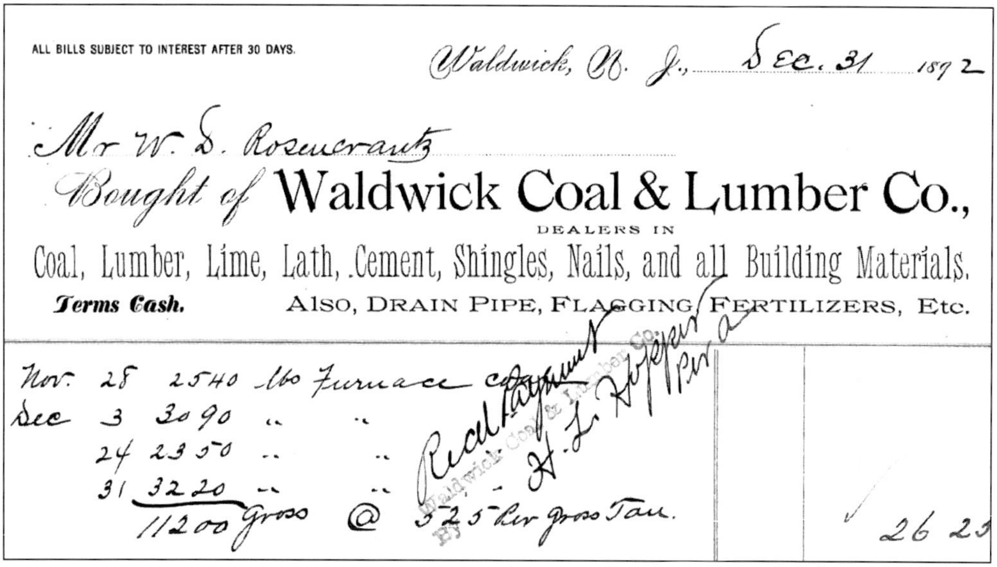
ALL BILLS SUBJECT TO INTEREST AFTER 30 DAYS.

Waldwick, N. J., Dec. 31 1892

Mr W. D. Rosencrantz

Bought of Waldwick Coal & Lumber Co.,

DEALERS IN

Coal, Lumber, Lime, Lath, Cement, Shingles, Nails, and all Building Materials.

Terms Cash. ALSO, DRAIN PIPE, FLAGGING, FERTILIZERS, Etc.

Nov. 28	2540 lbs Furnace coal			
Dec 3	3090 " "			
24	2350 " "			
31	3220 " "			
	11200 Gross @ 525 Per gross Ton.			26 25

Recd Payment
Waldwick Coal & Lumber Co.
By H. L. Hopper
Per a

This 1892 receipt reflects the booming construction business in the rapidly growing town. It is signed by Henry L. Hopper, a principal in the company and a prominent resident. He was the son of Louis Hopper and was a musician in Company B of the 22nd New Jersey Regiment. He later became a Republican committeeman of Orvil Township.

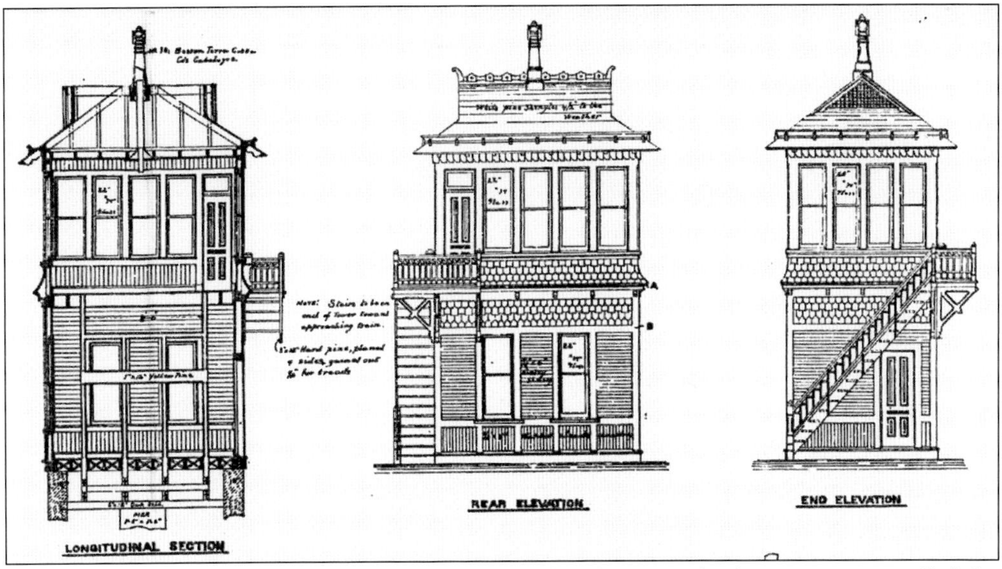

These are plans for the switching tower at Waldwick. The tower, built in 1888, controlled the track switches in the large rail yard that was created in 1890. The station and this switching tower were added to the National Register of Historic Places in 1977 and 1987, respectively.

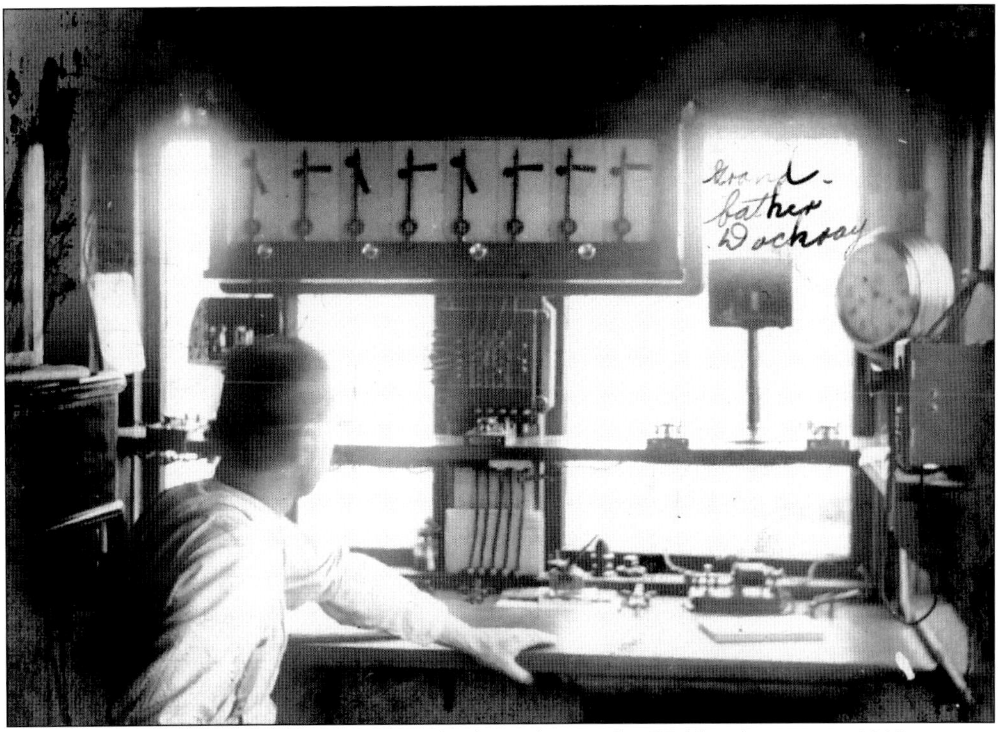

Joe Dockray was a Waldwick resident and telegrapher in the Waldwick tower in 1902.

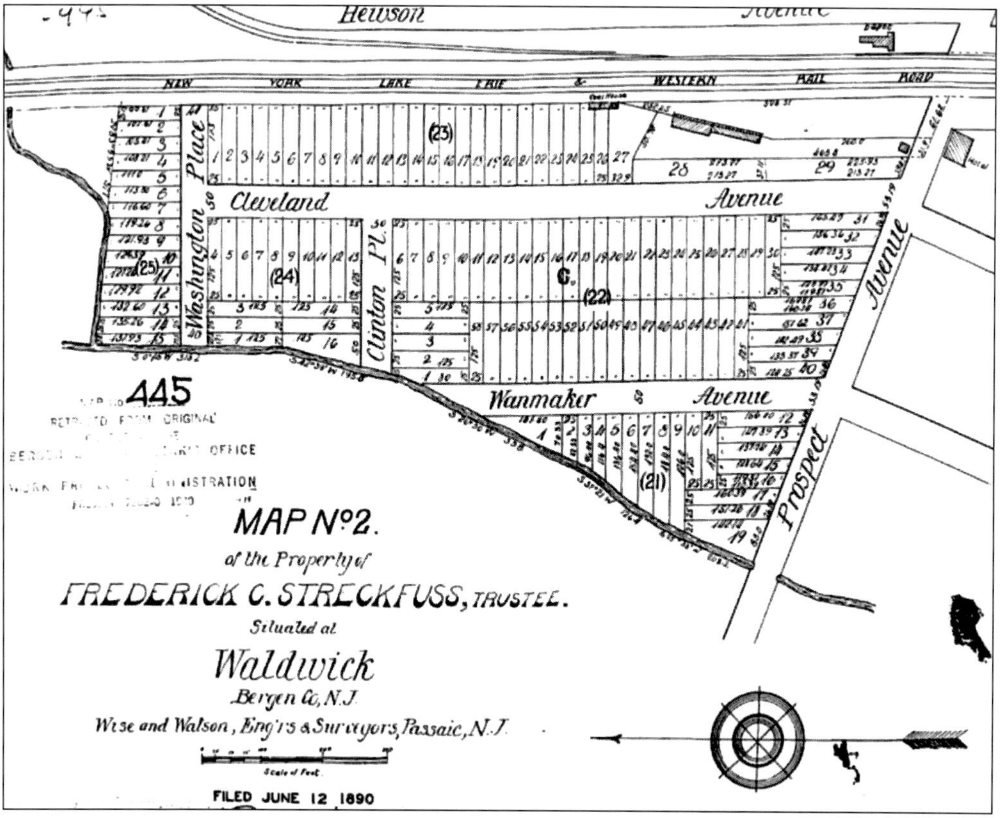

This is a copy of the Frederick C. Streckfuss map created in 1889. The map shows only a portion of his vast landholdings. In the late 1890s, he owned the area bounded by Franklin Turnpike on the east, the Smoches Vol Creek on the west, and Wyckoff Avenue on the south. Note the hotel, which was built in August 1890 and owned by Frank Wagner.

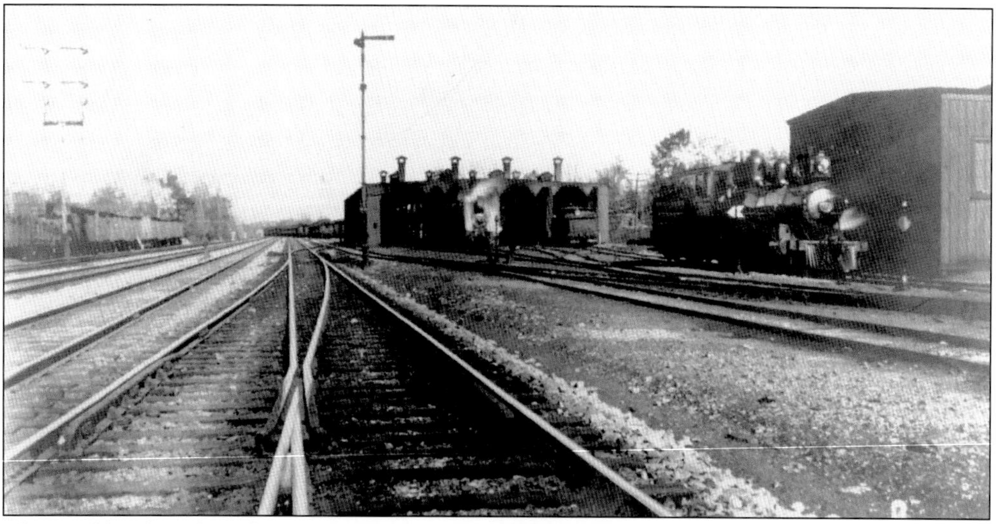

The Waldwick rail yard was a busy place in the late 19th century. Here, steam trains were watered and commuter trains stored for their morning run to Jersey City. Locomotives were turned around here as well, using the wye located opposite the tower.

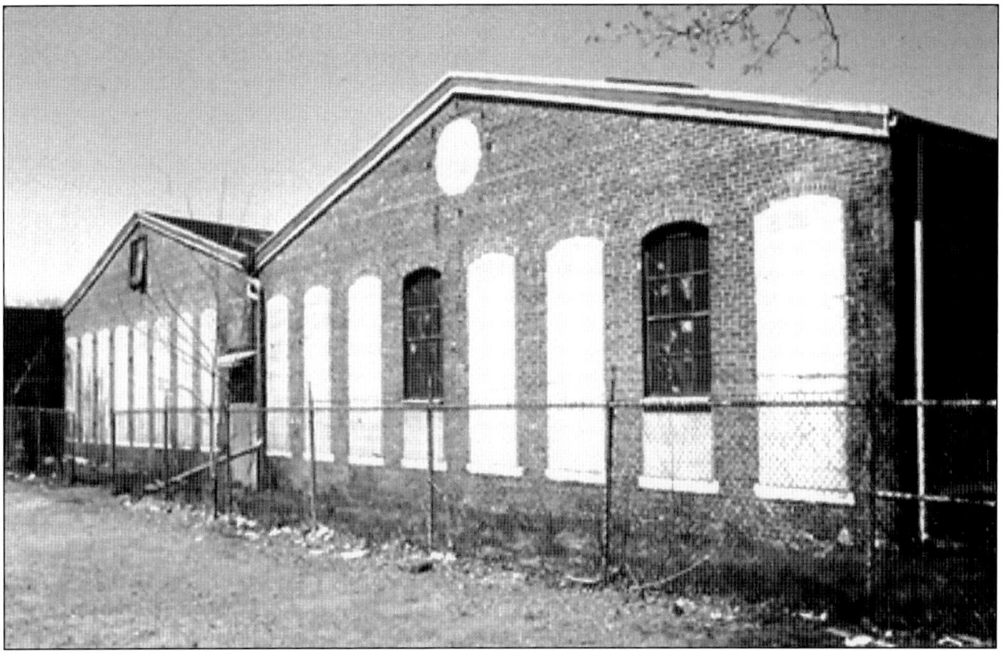

John A. Post started a silk mill on the site of the "Hankey" Hopper gristmill in 1891. He started with 12 hands, and by 1899, he had nearly 100 hands. Frederick Streckfuss became the secretary and treasurer in this incorporated business.

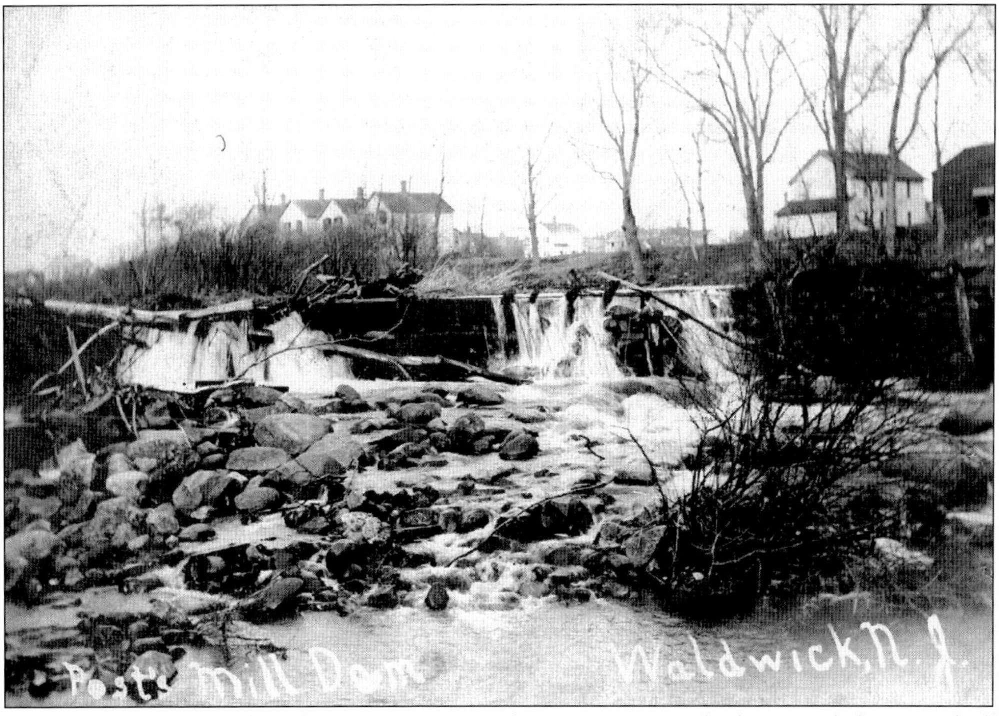

The Post Silk Mill pond on the Ho-Ho-Kus Brook is seen in a view looking north from Wyckoff Avenue. A common problem of the mills along the Ho-Ho-Kus Brook was dam breakage due to flooding.

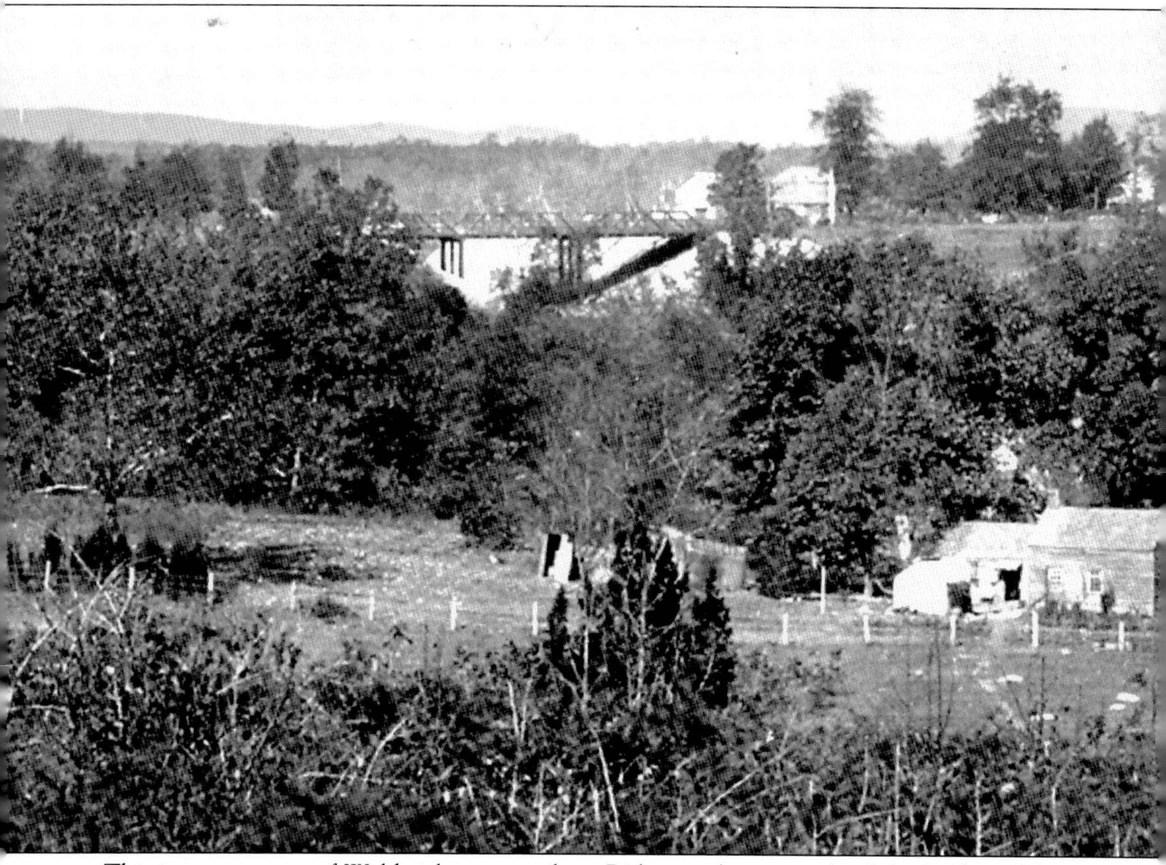

This is a panorama of Waldwick, as seen from Ridgewood, just south of the hollow. Of note is the replacement wooden truss bridge built across Wyckoff Avenue in 1891. Note the large

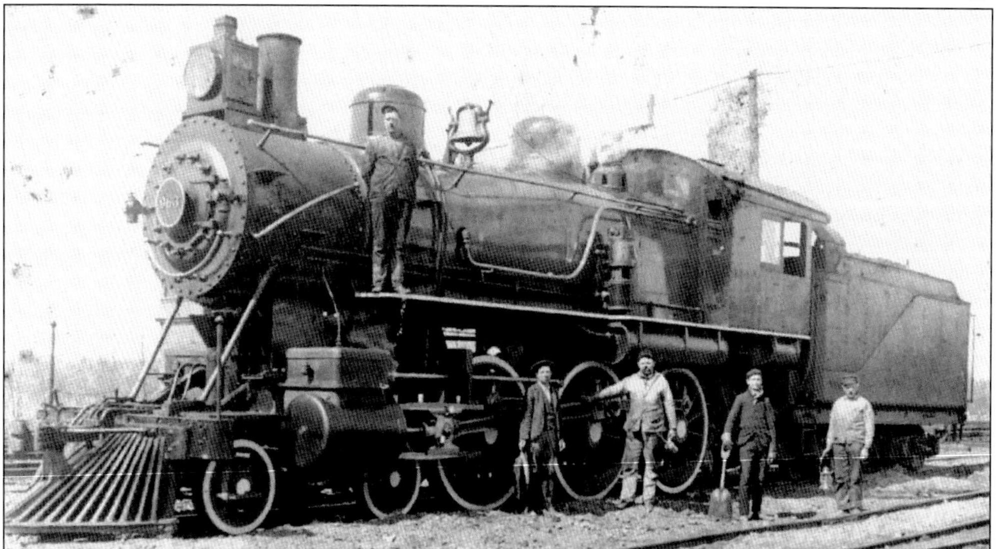

Seen in the Waldwick rail yard is a steam engine with its crew and their catch from the watering pond near the wye turnaround.

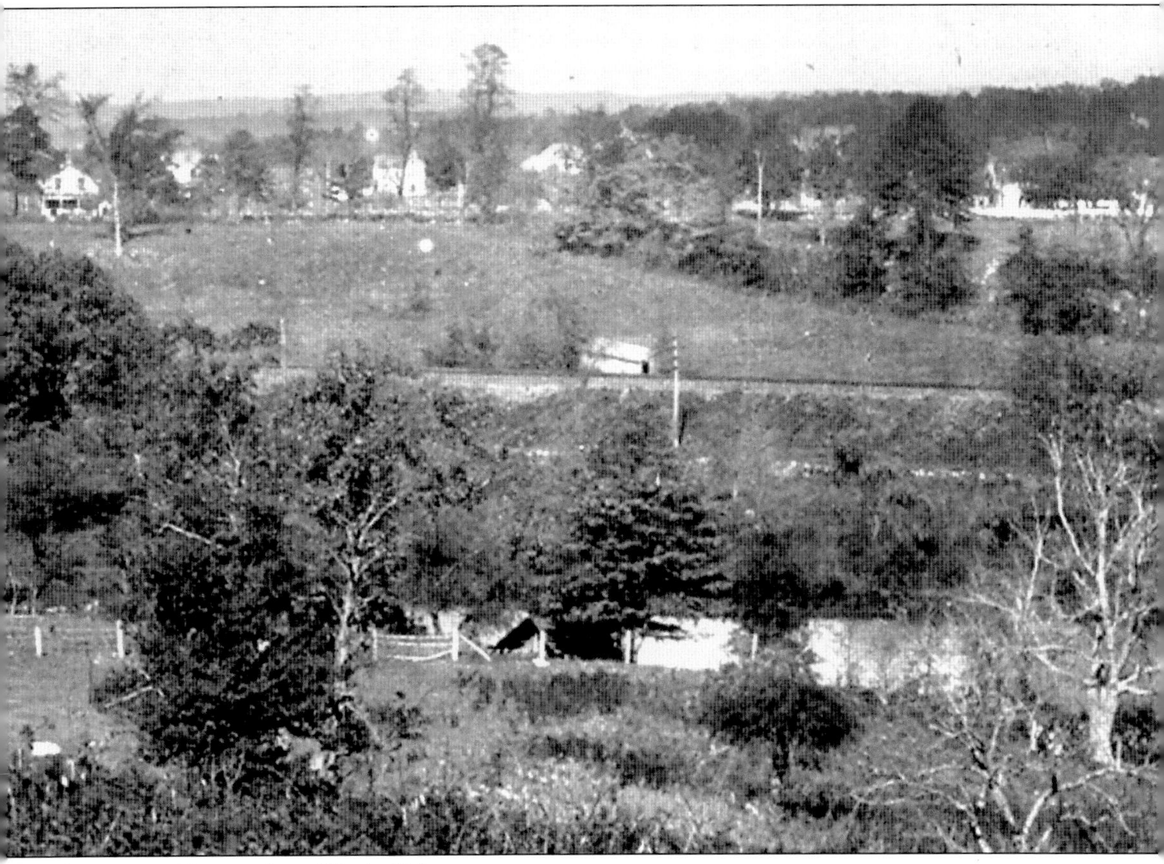

homes and barns along Wyckoff Avenue.

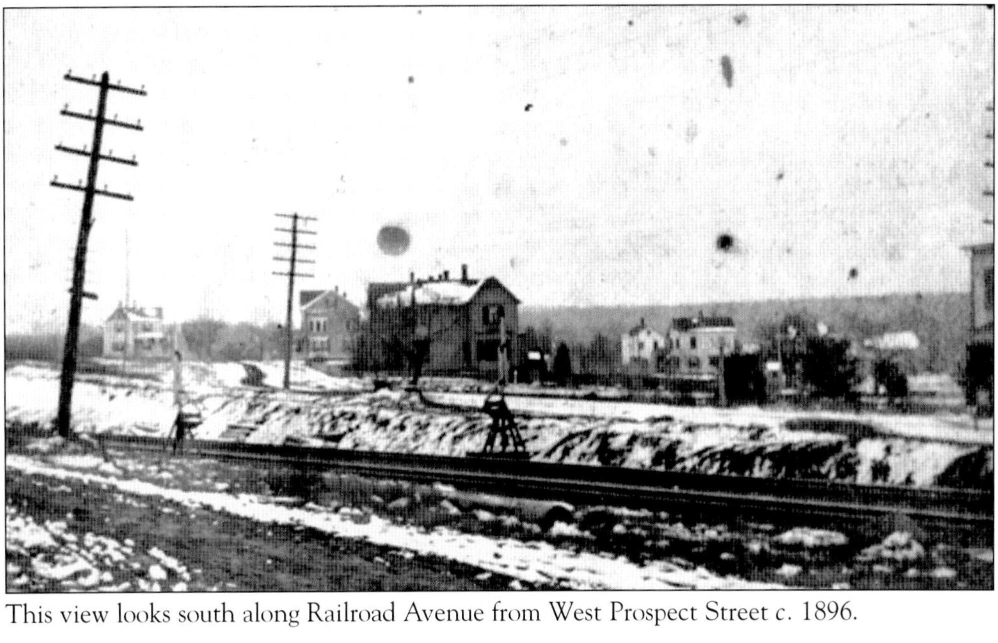

This view looks south along Railroad Avenue from West Prospect Street c. 1896.

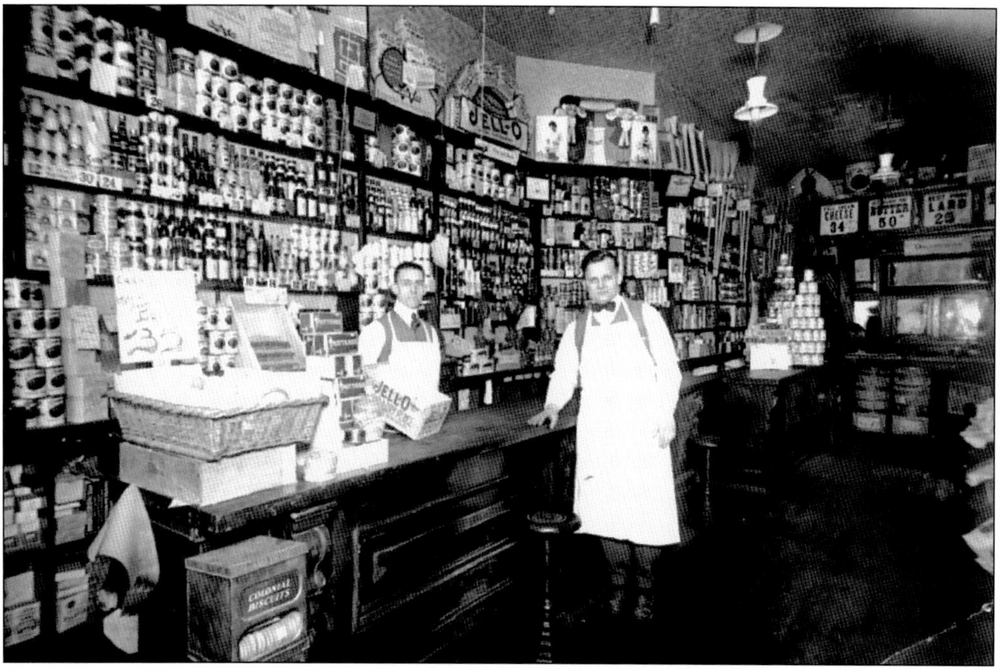

One of several businesses on West Prospect Street was the Oughton grocery store. This business was started in 1881, moving to the Streckfuss Building (as seen in this photograph) in 1891.

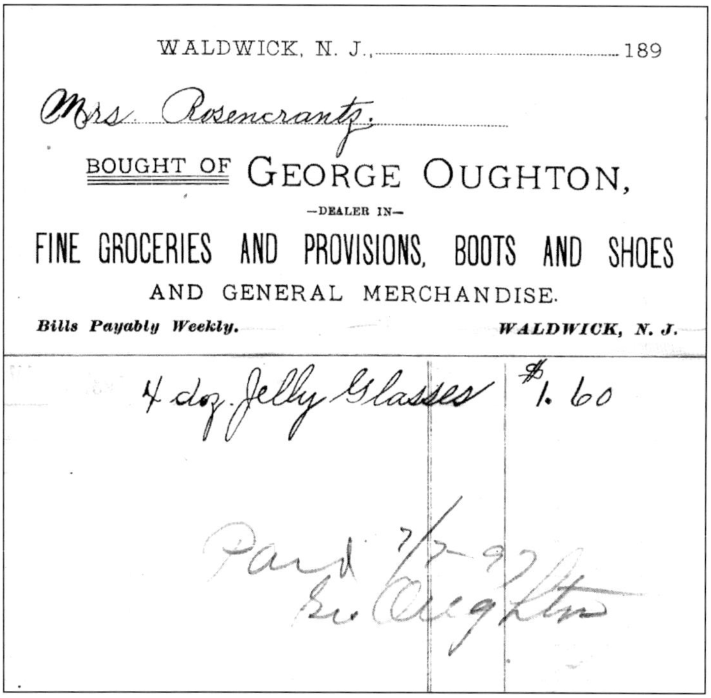

WALDWICK, N. J., ... 189

Mrs. Rosencrantz.

BOUGHT OF GEORGE OUGHTON,

—DEALER IN—

FINE GROCERIES AND PROVISIONS, BOOTS AND SHOES

AND GENERAL MERCHANDISE.

Bills Payably Weekly. *WALDWICK, N. J.*

4 doz. Jelly Glasses	$1.60

Paid 7/7-97
G. Oughton

Seen is an Oughton receipt from 1897. Oughton also ran the local post office as well.

Oughton's delivery wagon is seen in this *c.* 1908 photograph.

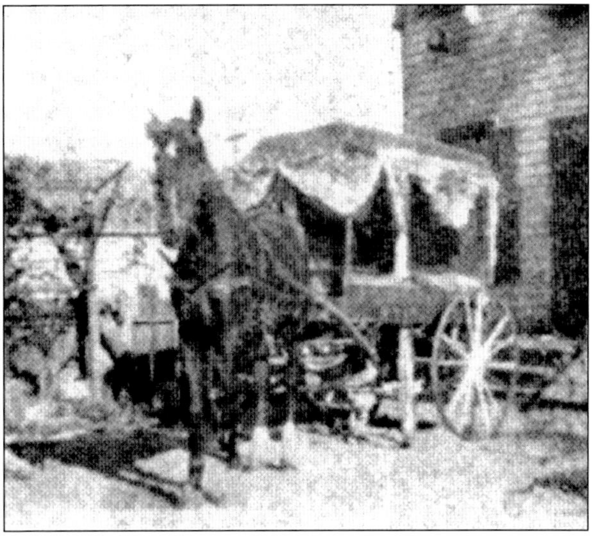

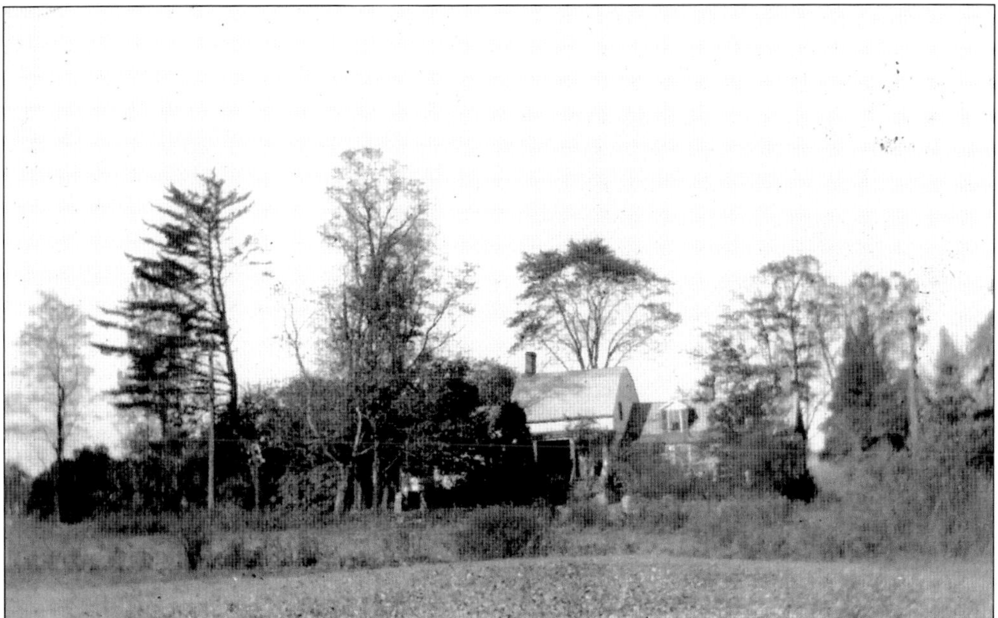

The Van Wagoner house, on the north side of Wyckoff Avenue near Monroe Street, was probably built in early 1800s. Benjamin Brundred (B.B.) Van Wagoner and his family moved into the house in 1891. This was also the former home of the Captain Potter and Abraham Bender families. The Bender family ran an ornamental wax flower business during the 1870s and 1880s, a very popular form of art at that time. The factory (also known as the glass house) was located on the east side of this home.

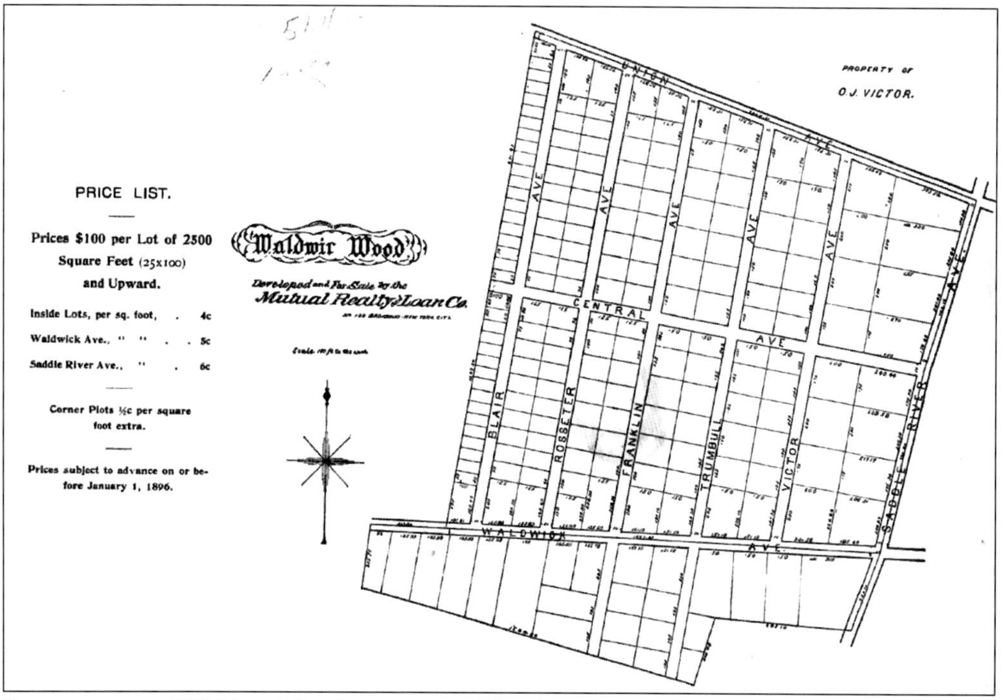

Seen is a map of Waldwic Woods, a proposed development on the eastern slope of Waldwick. It was never constructed.

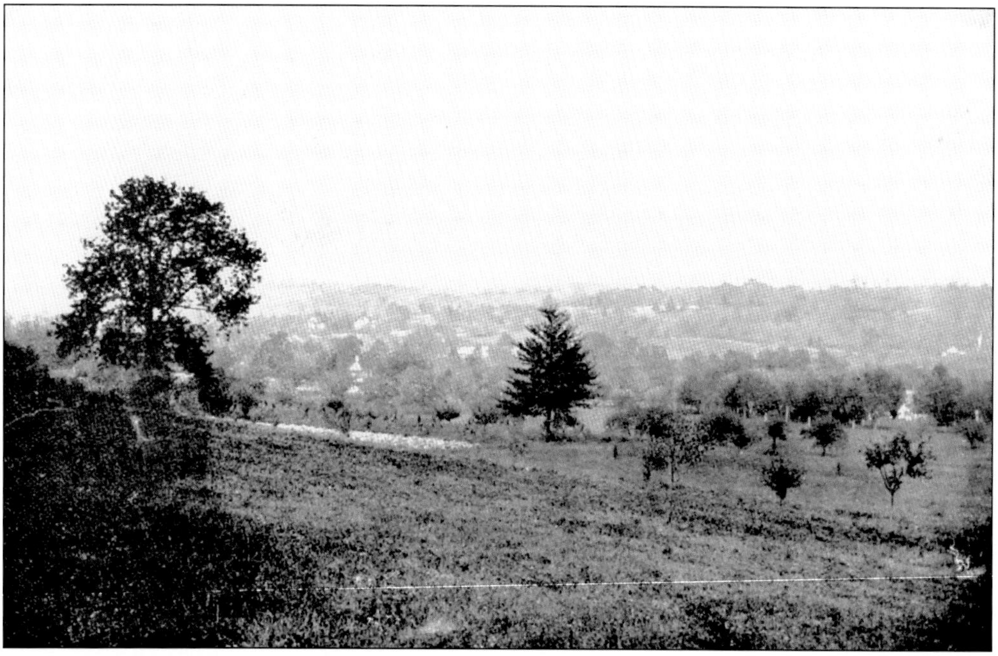

This panorama, from a pamphlet of the proposed Waldwick Woods development, looks east over the Saddle River Valley. A section of this view later became known as the Villa fields and was a popular sleigh-riding hill from the 1920s to the 1970s.

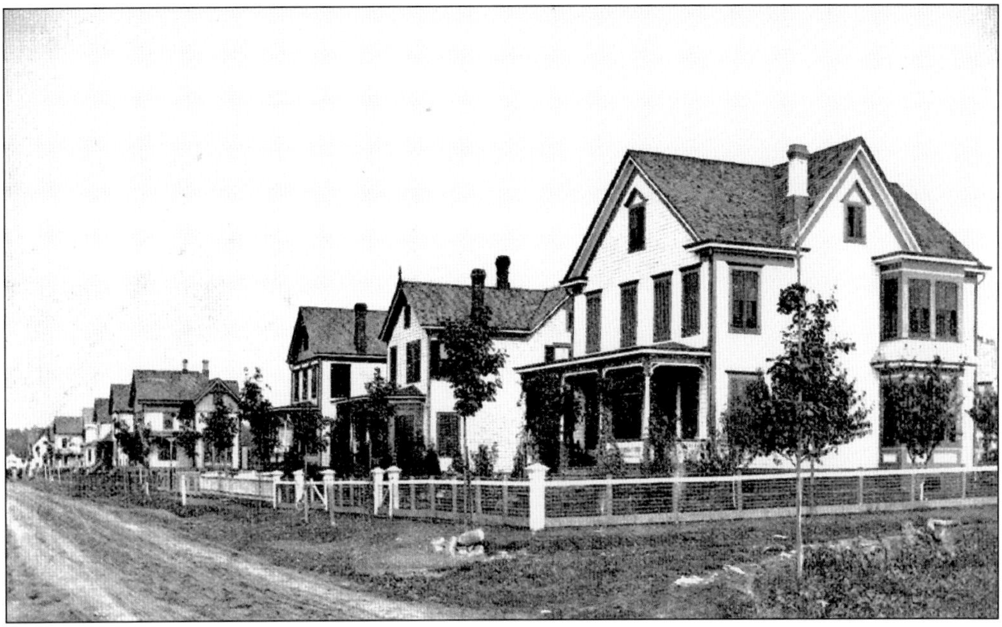

This view, looking south along Railroad Avenue (now Maple Avenue), shows the streetscape of newly constructed houses in the 1890s.

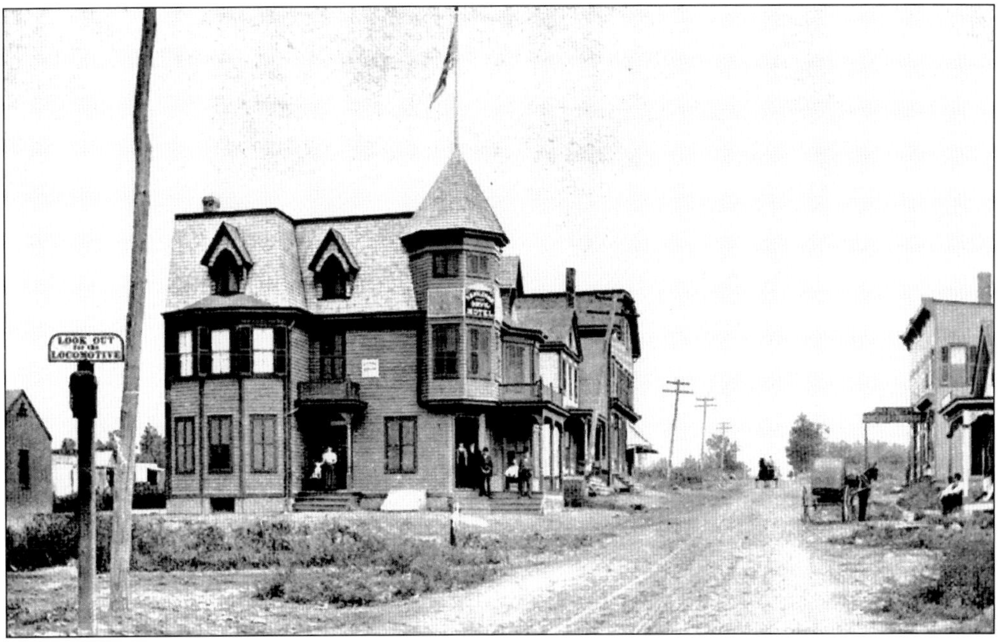

The Orvil House is one of the most photographed buildings of "old" Waldwick. It was built in 1894 by Horace Holcomb at the corner of West Prospect Street and Hewson Avenue. It still stands today in an altered form.

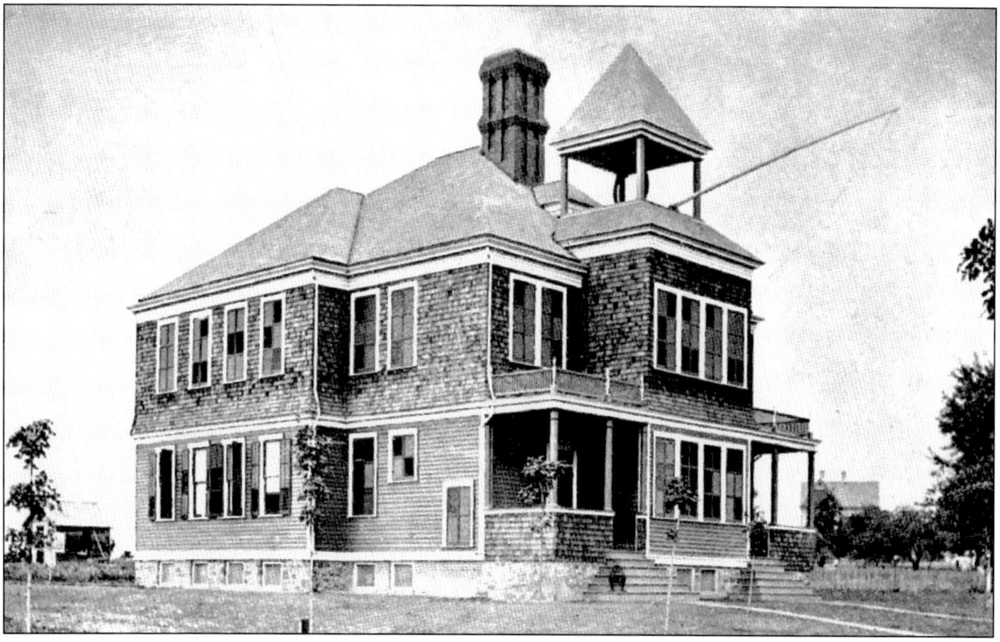

The new Waldwick School opened in 1895 at the northwest corner of Wyckoff and West Prospect Streets. Another earlier school had been built across the street sometime in the 1880s, replacing the use of the Bamper house's gun room as a classroom. The new school had two teachers—William MacKenzie, the principal, and Olive H. Seabury, his assistant. Their annual salaries were $675 and $400, respectively. Note the locomotive wheel used as a gong; a new bell was purchased a few years later through local fund-raising efforts.

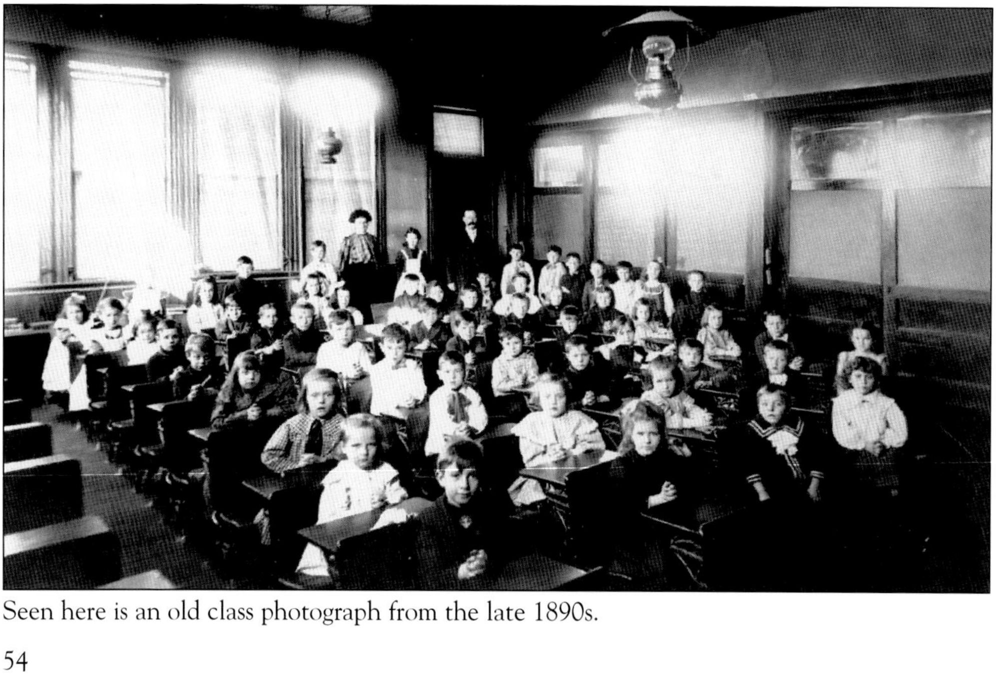

Seen here is an old class photograph from the late 1890s.

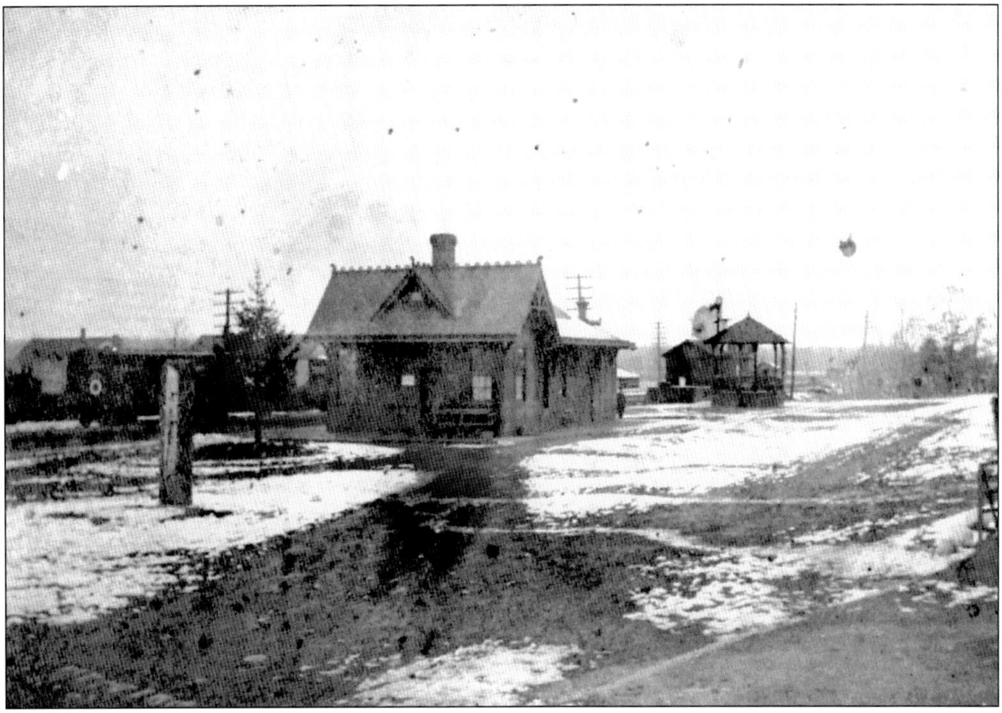

The Waldwick train station, with the freight depot and bandstand in the background, is seen in this *c.* 1896 photograph.

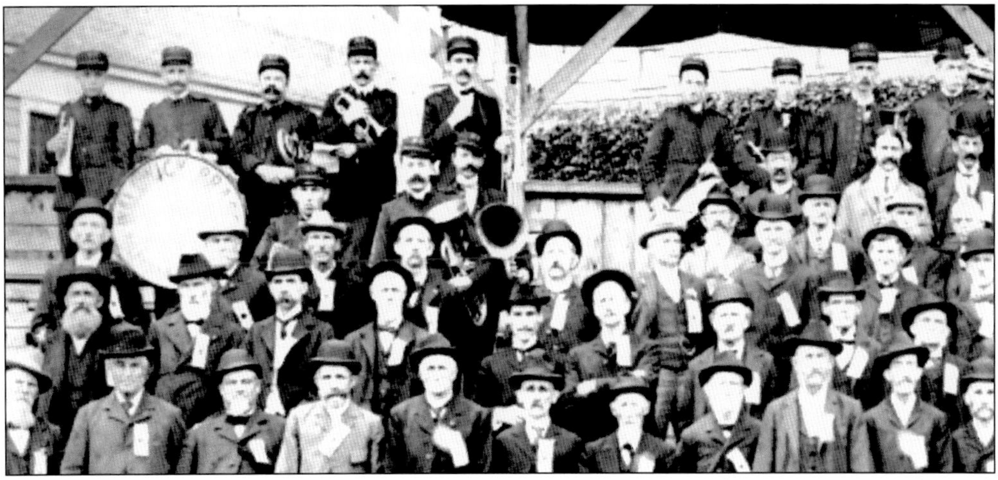

The Post Brass Band performed at a Civil War reunion of the 22nd Regiment in Englewood. The band was founded by John A. and Abraham J. Post in the early 1890s. They both played the cornet and were members of the local musicians union. They played at many local functions and at the bandstand on Tuesday and Thursday nights. In 1904, the bandstand was moved to West Prospect Street and Harrison Avenue.

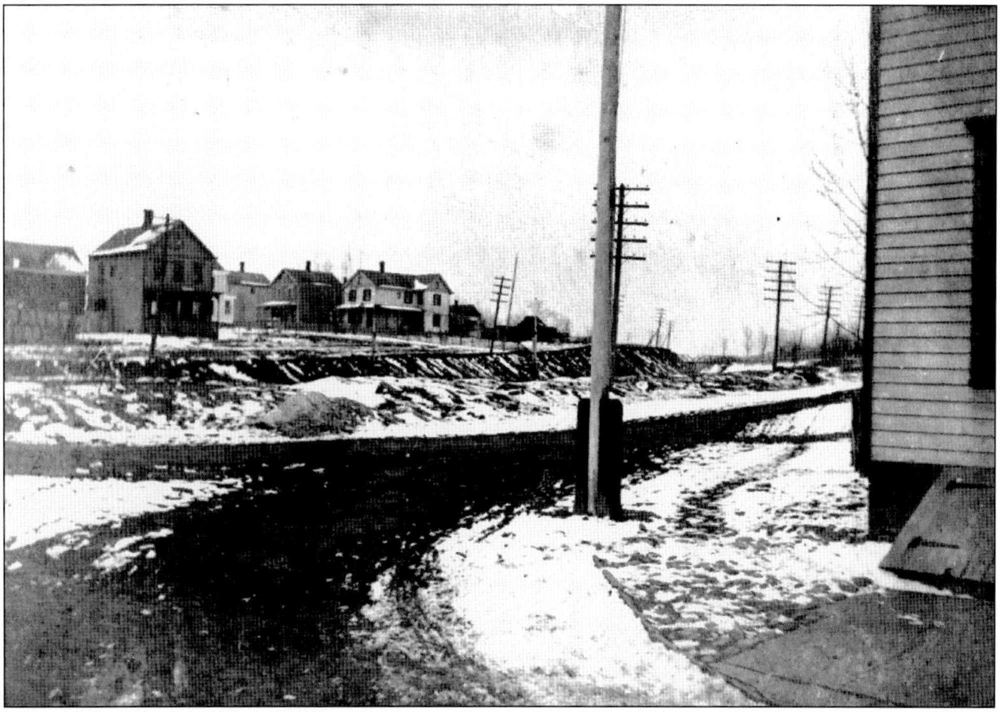

This view looks southeast down the tracks from the Waldwick station.

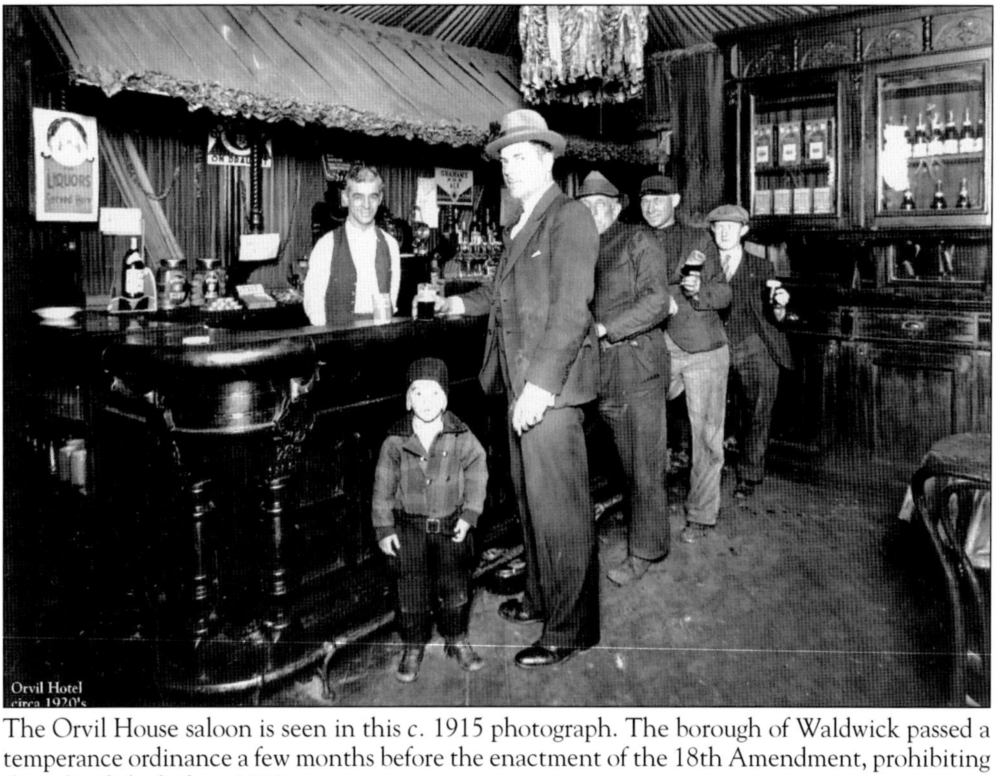

The Orvil House saloon is seen in this *c.* 1915 photograph. The borough of Waldwick passed a temperance ordinance a few months before the enactment of the 18th Amendment, prohibiting the sale of alcohol, in 1920.

John W. Quackenbush stands in front of his 1896 house on Franklin Turnpike opposite the end of Grove Street. He was married in 1891 to Annie Henion. Besides selling real estate and insurance, he was a Waldwick switching-tower telegrapher. Serving as an Orvil Township committeeman, he later became the first mayor of Waldwick in 1919.

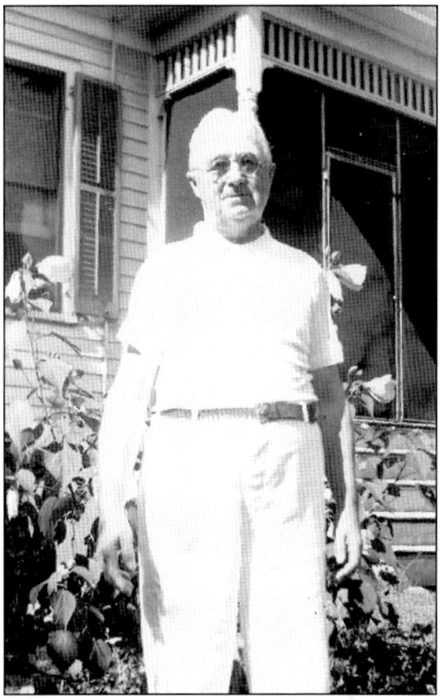

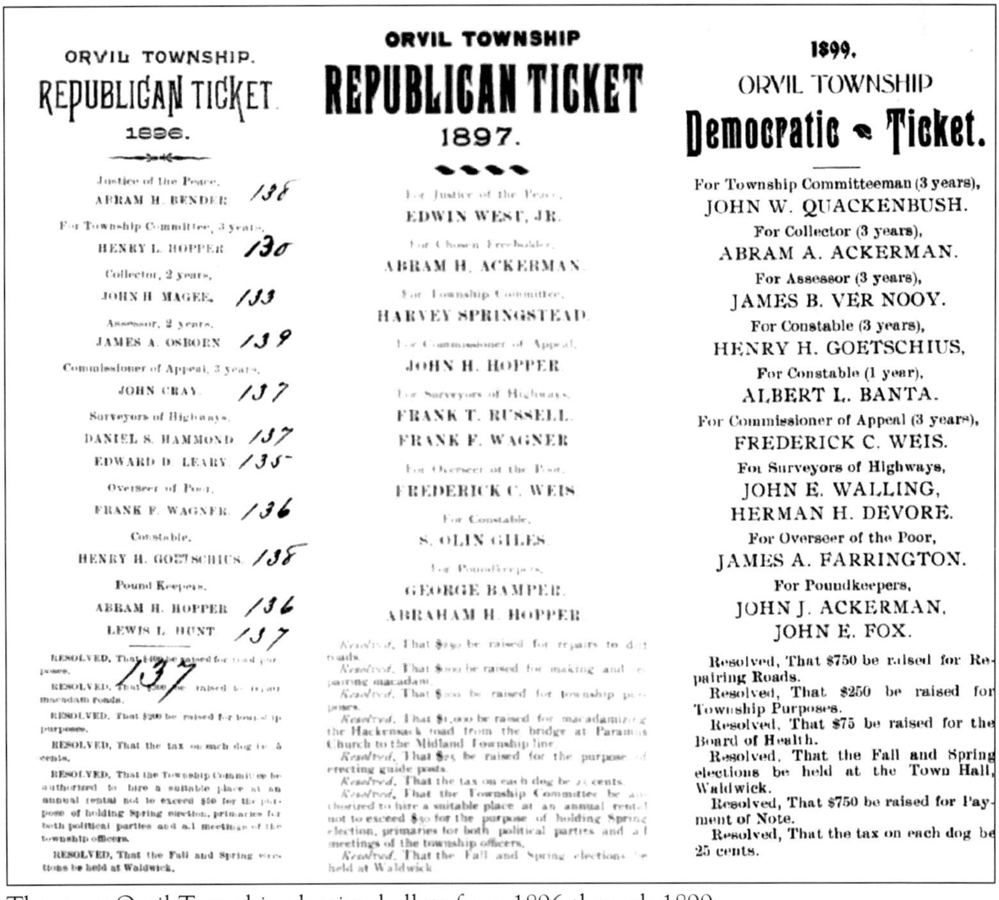

ORVIL TOWNSHIP.

REPUBLICAN TICKET

1896.

Justice of the Peace,
ABRAM H. BENDER 138

For Township Committee, 3 years,
HENRY L. HOPPER 130

Collector, 2 years,
JOHN H. MAGEE. 133

Assessor, 2 years,
JAMES A. OSBORN 139

Commissioner of Appeal, 3 years,
JOHN CRAY 137

Surveyors of Highways,
DANIEL S. HAMMOND 137
EDWARD D. LEARY 135

Overseer of Poor,
FRANK F. WAGNER 136

Constable,
HENRY H. GOETSCHIUS 138

Pound Keepers,
ABRAM H. HOPPER 136
LEWIS L. HUNT 137

137

RESOLVED, That [illegible] be raised for road purposes.

RESOLVED, That [illegible] be raised to repair macadam roads.

RESOLVED, That $200 be raised for township purposes.

RESOLVED, That the tax on each dog be [illegible] cents.

RESOLVED, That the Township Committee be authorized to hire a suitable place at an annual rental not to exceed $50 for the purpose of holding Spring election, primaries for both political parties and all meetings of the township officers.

RESOLVED, That the Fall and Spring elections be held at Waldwick.

ORVIL TOWNSHIP

REPUBLICAN TICKET

1897.

For Justice of the Peace,
EDWIN WEST, JR.

For Chosen Freeholder,
ABRAM H. ACKERMAN

For Township Committee,
HARVEY SPRINGSTEAD

For Commissioner of Appeal,
JOHN H. HOPPER

For Surveyors of Highways,
FRANK T. RUSSELL.
FRANK F. WAGNER

For Overseer of the Poor,
FREDERICK C. WEIS

For Constable,
S. OLIN GILES

For Poundkeepers,
GEORGE BAMPER.
ABRAHAM H. HOPPER

Resolved, That $[illegible] be raised for repairs to dirt roads.

Resolved, That $[illegible] be raised for making and repairing macadam.

Resolved, That $[illegible] be raised for township purposes.

Resolved, That $1,000 be raised for macadamizing the Hackensack road from the bridge at Paramus Church to the Midland Township line.

Resolved, That $[illegible] be raised for the purpose of erecting guide posts.

Resolved, That the tax on each dog be [illegible] cents.

Resolved, That the Township Committee be authorized to hire a suitable place at an annual rental not to exceed $[illegible] for the purpose of holding Spring election, primaries for both political parties and all meetings of the township officers.

Resolved, That the Fall and Spring elections be held at Waldwick.

1899.

ORVIL TOWNSHIP

Democratic Ticket.

For Township Committeeman (3 years),
JOHN W. QUACKENBUSH.

For Collector (3 years),
ABRAM A. ACKERMAN.

For Assessor (3 years),
JAMES B. VER NOOY.

For Constable (3 years),
HENRY H. GOETSCHIUS,

For Constable (1 year),
ALBERT L. BANTA.

For Commissioner of Appeal (3 years),
FREDERICK C. WEIS.

For Surveyors of Highways,
JOHN E. WALLING,
HERMAN H. DEVORE.

For Overseer of the Poor,
JAMES A. FARRINGTON.

For Poundkeepers,
JOHN J. ACKERMAN,
JOHN E. FOX.

Resolved, That $750 be raised for Repairing Roads.

Resolved, That $250 be raised for Township Purposes.

Resolved, That $75 be raised for the Board of Health.

Resolved, That the Fall and Spring elections be held at the Town Hall, Waldwick.

Resolved, That $750 be raised for Payment of Note.

Resolved, That the tax on each dog be 25 cents.

These are Orvil Township election ballots from 1896 through 1899.

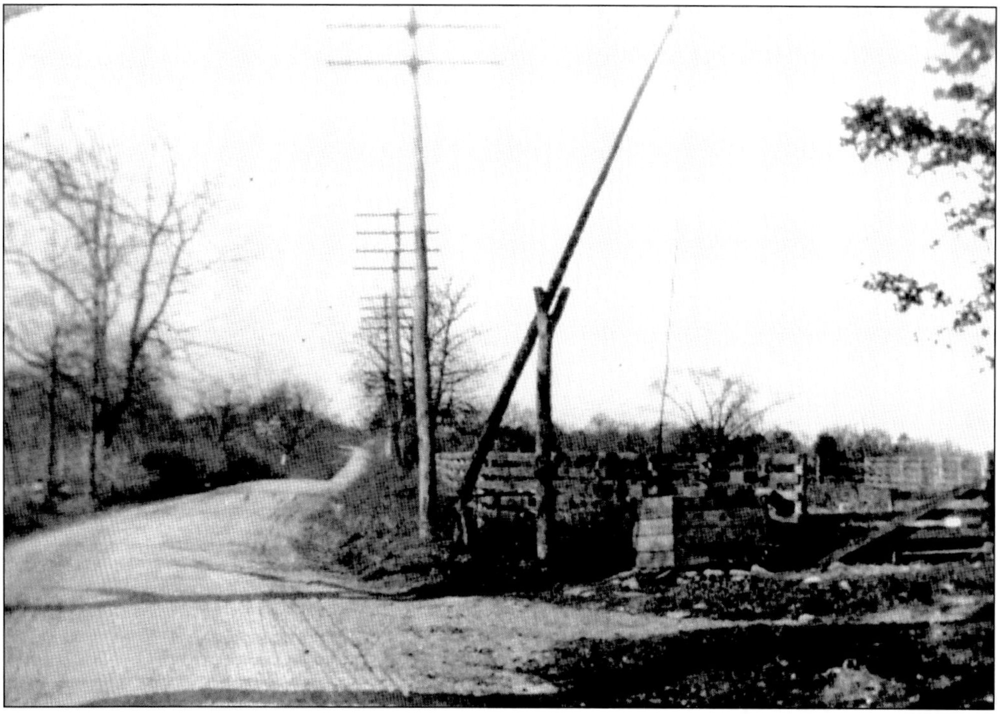

The well sweeps of Wyckoff Avenue were located adjacent to the Cornelius Smith house. This well and another behind the house were famous throughout the area. Descendant John Y. Smith was a farmer and dairyman.

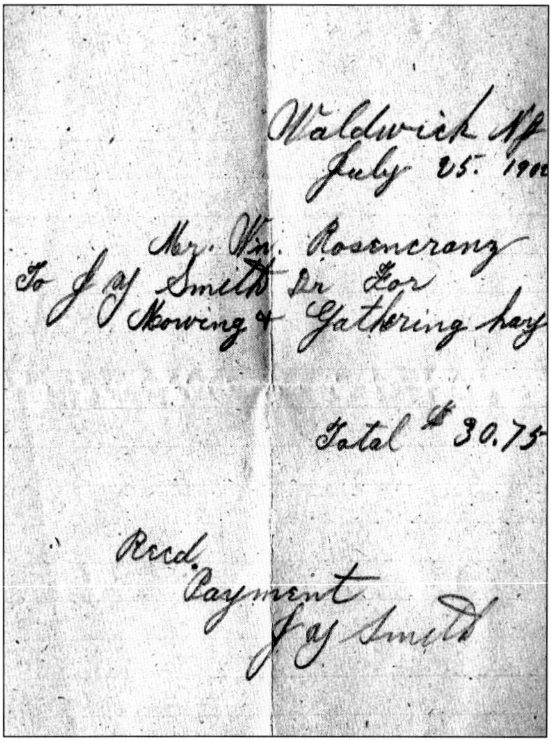

Waldwick NJ
July 25. 190

Mr. Wm. Rosencranz
To J Y Smith Dr For
Mowing & Gathering hay

Total $ 30.75

Recd.
Payment
J Y Smith

A Smith receipt for hay delivered to the Rosencrantz family is seen here.

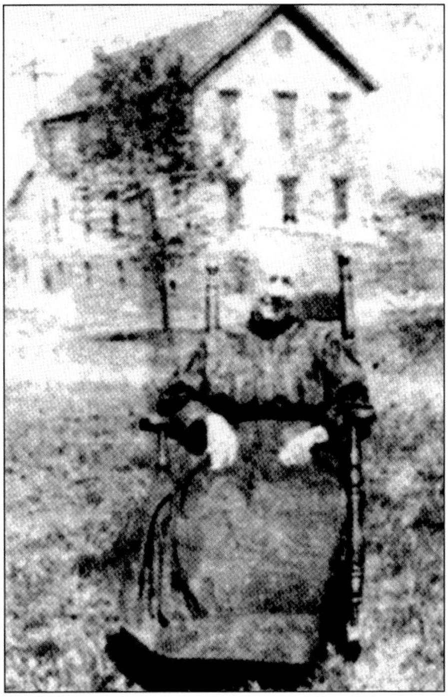

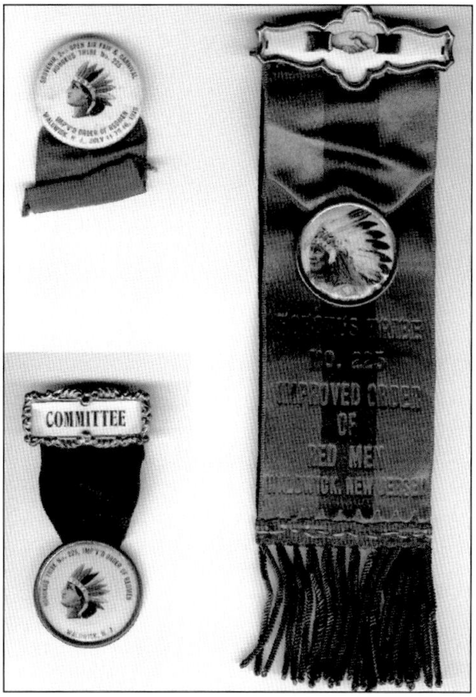

Left: Kate Morgan sits in front of the Redmen's Hall. The Loyal Order of the Redmen was a fraternal organization located on Cleveland Avenue. Kate was the Morgan family matriarch during the early 1900s. *Right:* The ribbon from the Loyal Order of the Redmen is seen here. This organization held dances, socials, and other activities. Local residents used it as a meeting place for both Orvil Township and the borough of Waldwick.

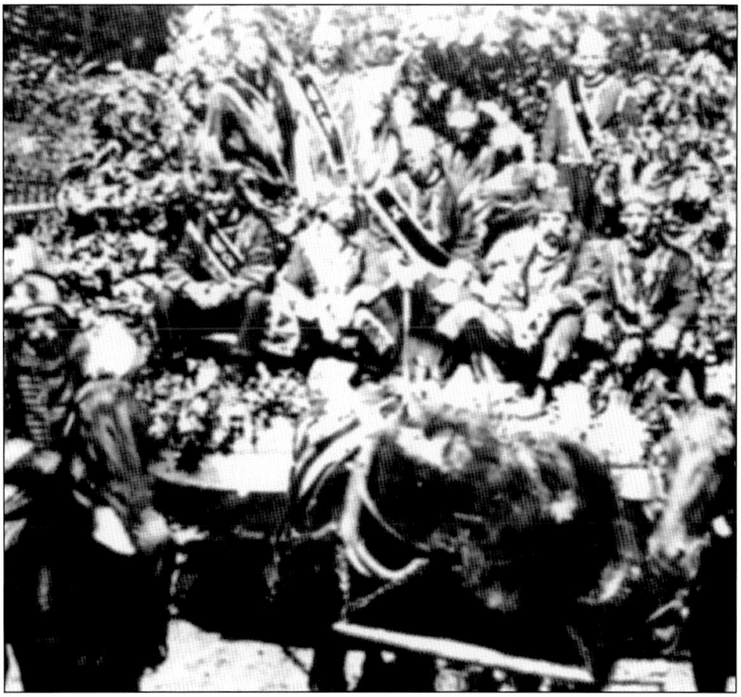

Redmen participate in a parade in Ramsey in 1910.

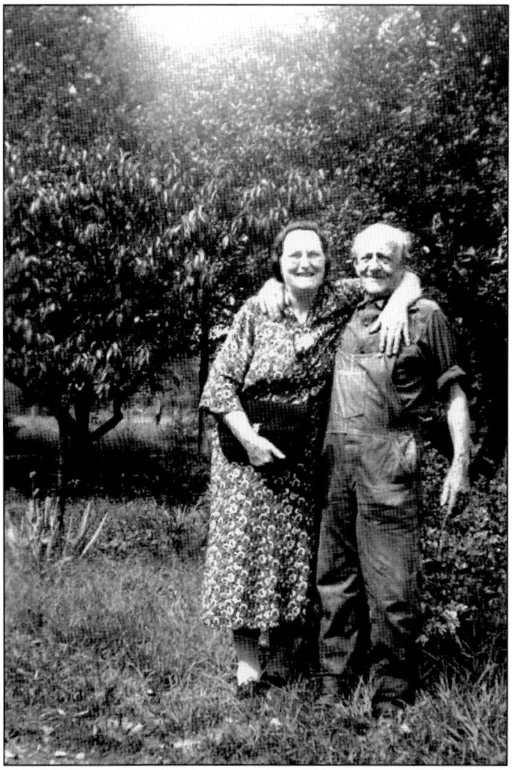

John, Kate Morgan's son, and Sarah Morgan are pictured on the Morgan farm on Smith Street in the 1930s.

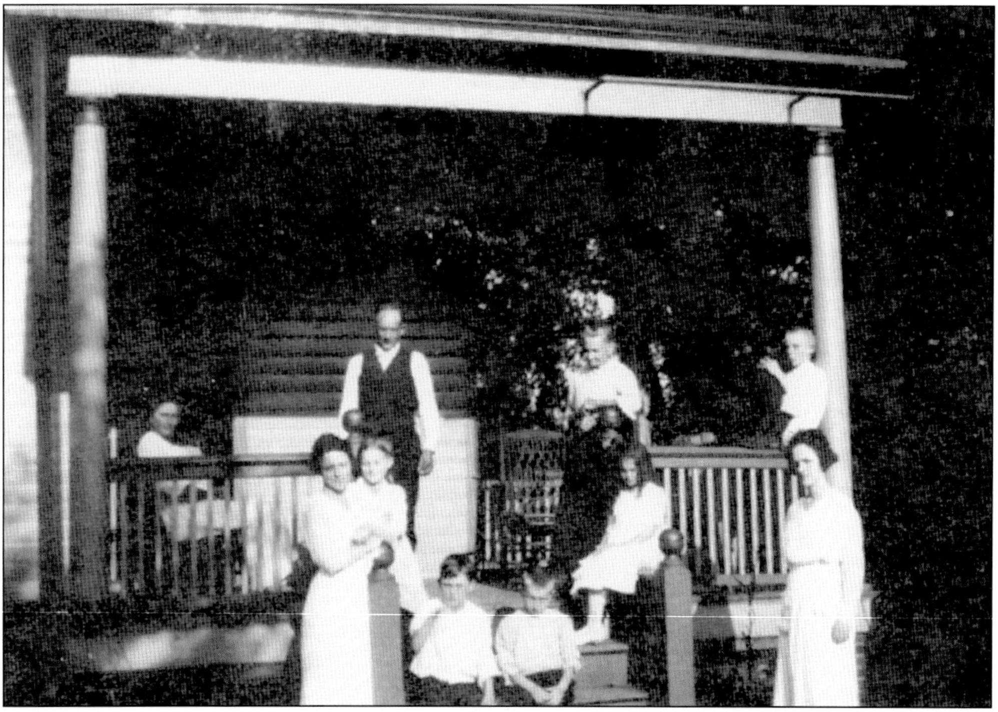

Members of the John Morgan family are seen on the front porch of their home on Smith Street in the late 1920s.

St. Luke's Roman Catholic Church was located on Franklin Turnpike opposite the Hermitage. Built in 1869, many people from Waldwick attended services at this house of worship. It burned in 1948 and was rebuilt in the following years.

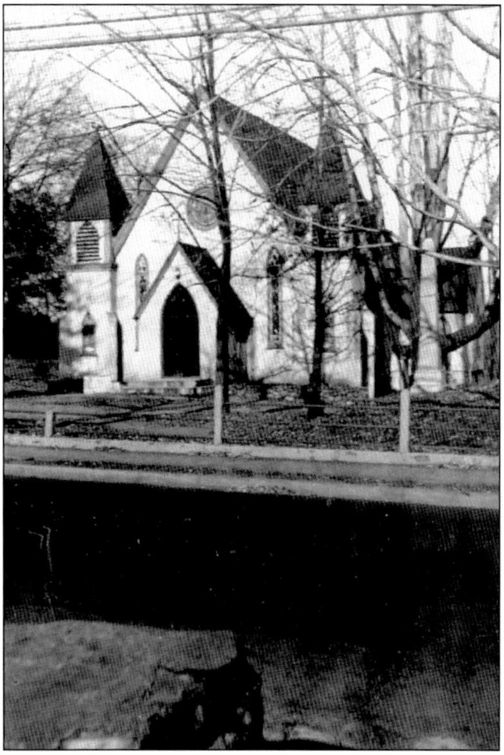

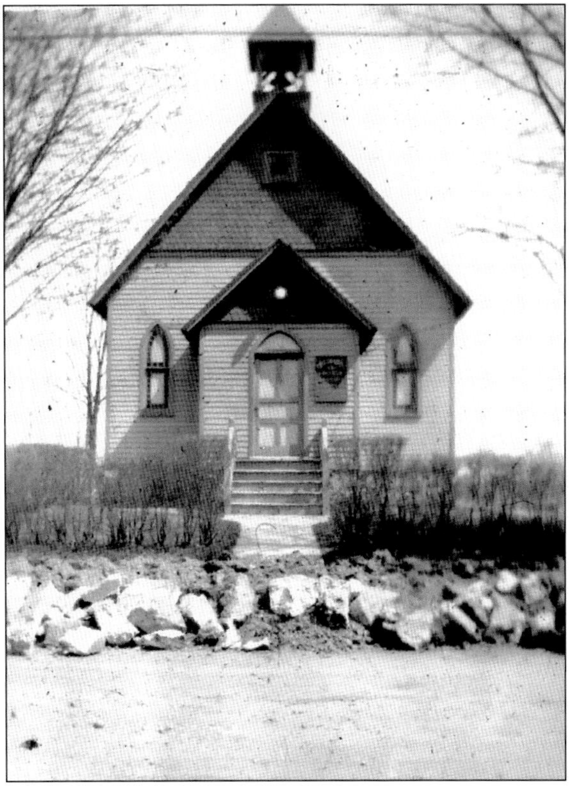

The Baptist church on West Prospect and Smith Streets was built in 1901. It later became the First Reformed Church. Today, it is the Knights of Columbus Hall.

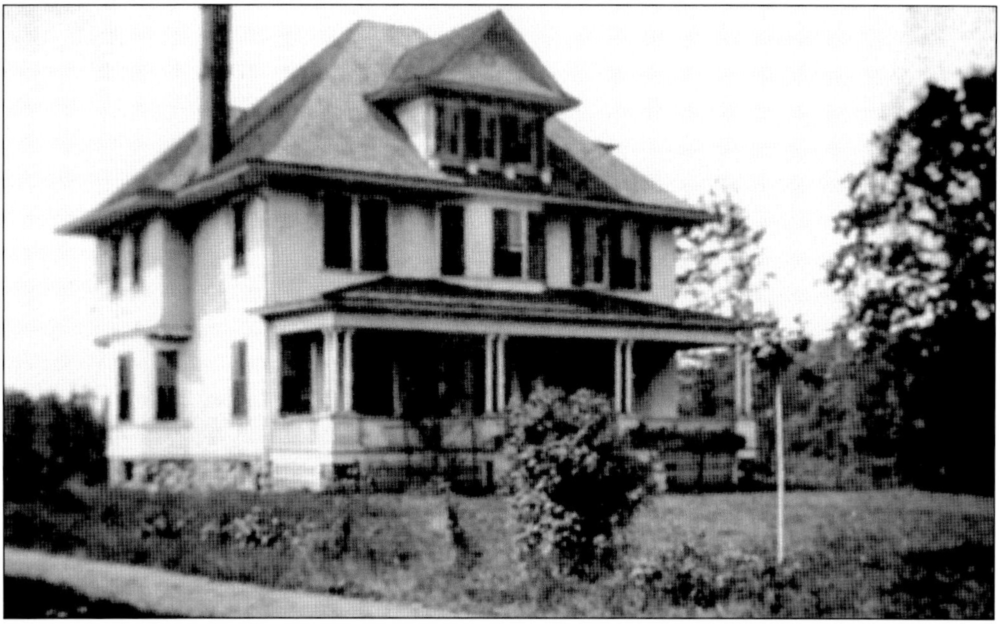

Seen is the Henry G. Ackerman farmhouse, located on the south side of East Prospect Street between present-day Richard Drive and Nordham Street. In 1902, it was built to house his growing farm family.

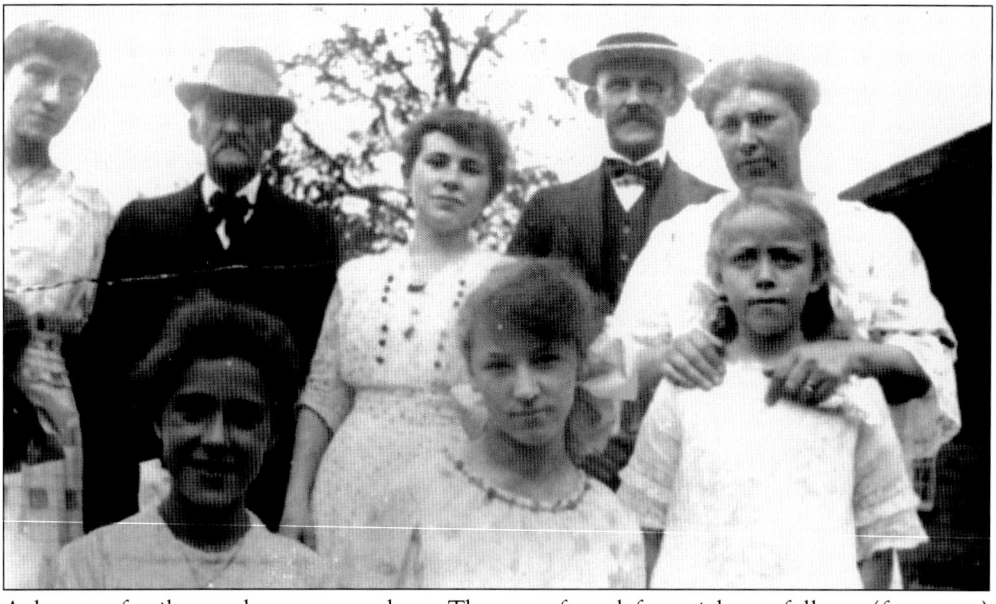

Ackerman family members are seen here. They are, from left to right, as follows: (front row) unidentified, Hazel, and Elizabeth; (back row) unidentified, John T., unidentified, Henry G., and Lizzie.

Lizzie Ackerman tends to peach baskets at the Ackerman house. Herman Ackerman drove the harvest of peaches by wagon to market in Paterson. He carried a pistol to protect himself for the ride home from thieves at the Goffle in present-day Hawthorne.

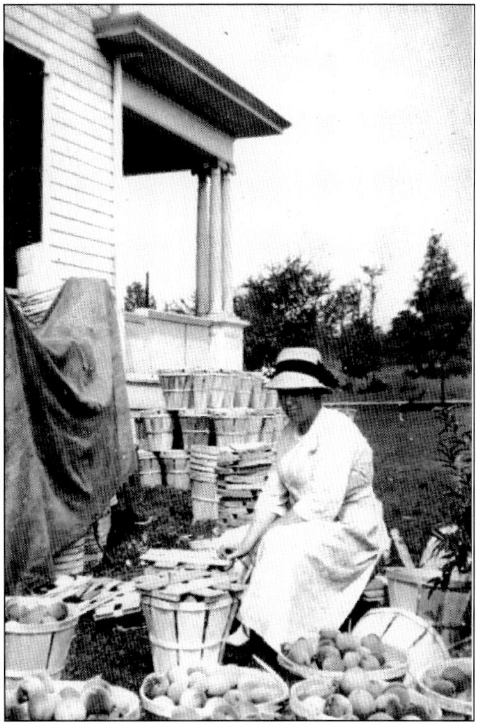

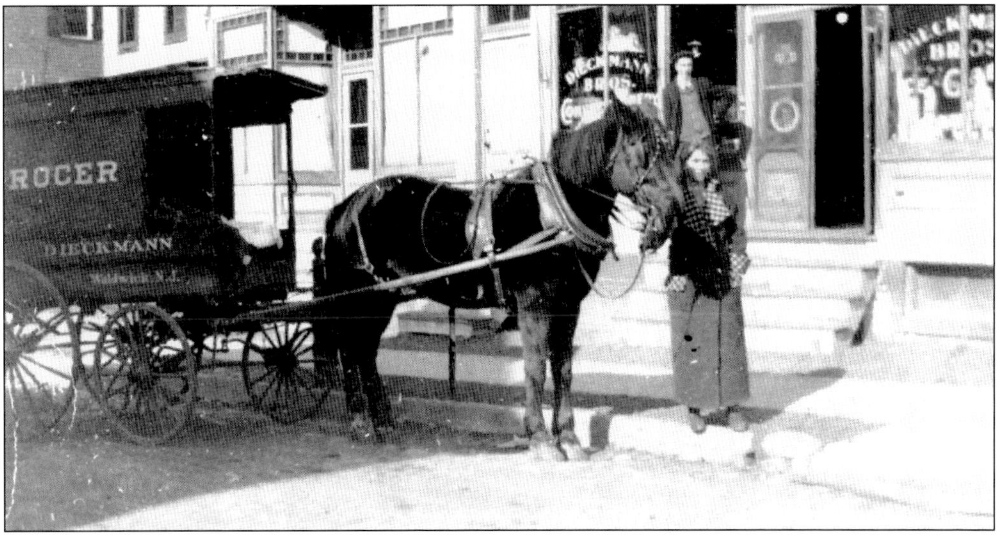

Seen is Henry Dieckman's dry goods store on West Prospect Street. He ran the store and made grocery deliveries in the Waldwick area from 1900 to the late 1920s. His son Charley began working for his father as a clerk *c.* 1910. Charley took over the store in the early 1920s. He later rented out his store and opened a large cider mill directly behind it. The store burned in the late 1930s.

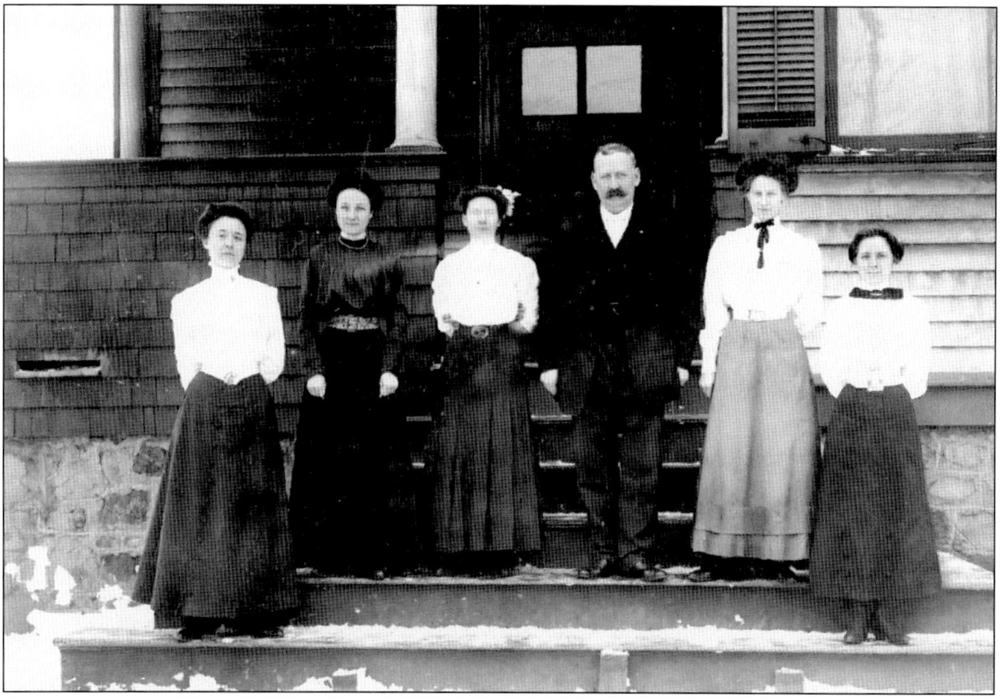

Faculty of the Waldwick School are seen in this 1903 photograph. They are, from left to right, Julia A. Traphagen, ? Monroe, ? Parsons, principal S.E. Barnes, ? Tatton, and ? Quackenbush.

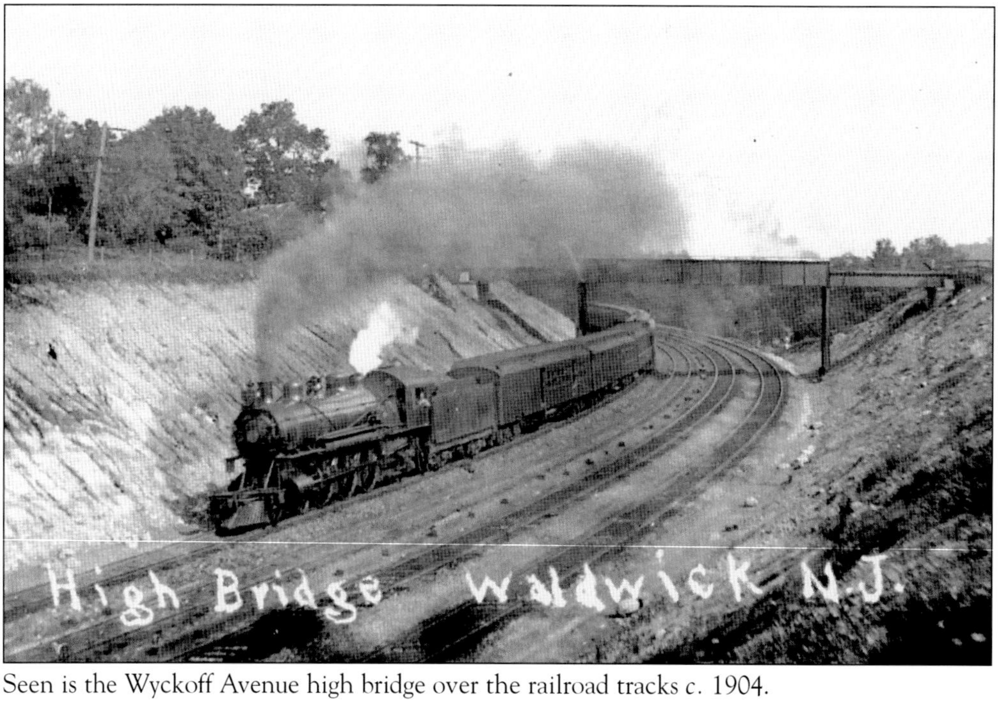

Seen is the Wyckoff Avenue high bridge over the railroad tracks c. 1904.

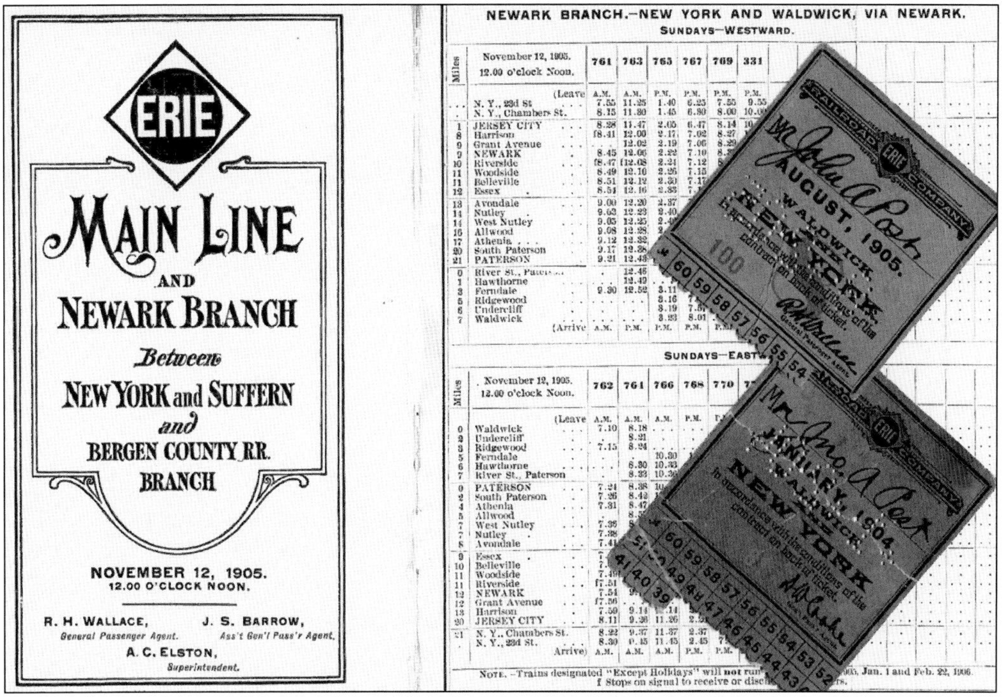

A 1905 Erie Railroad schedule indicates Waldwick as the end of the commuter line. Next to it are several monthly tickets from local businessman John Post.

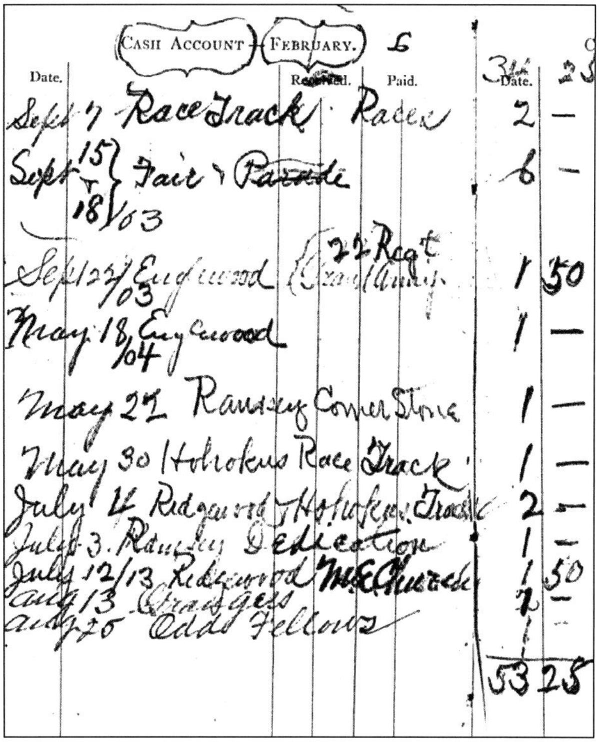

A page of the Post Brass Band date book lists performances from 1903. Of note is the September 22, 1903 date that indicates a performance in Englewood for the 40th reunion of the 22nd New Jersey Regiment. Abraham J. Post was the bandleader.

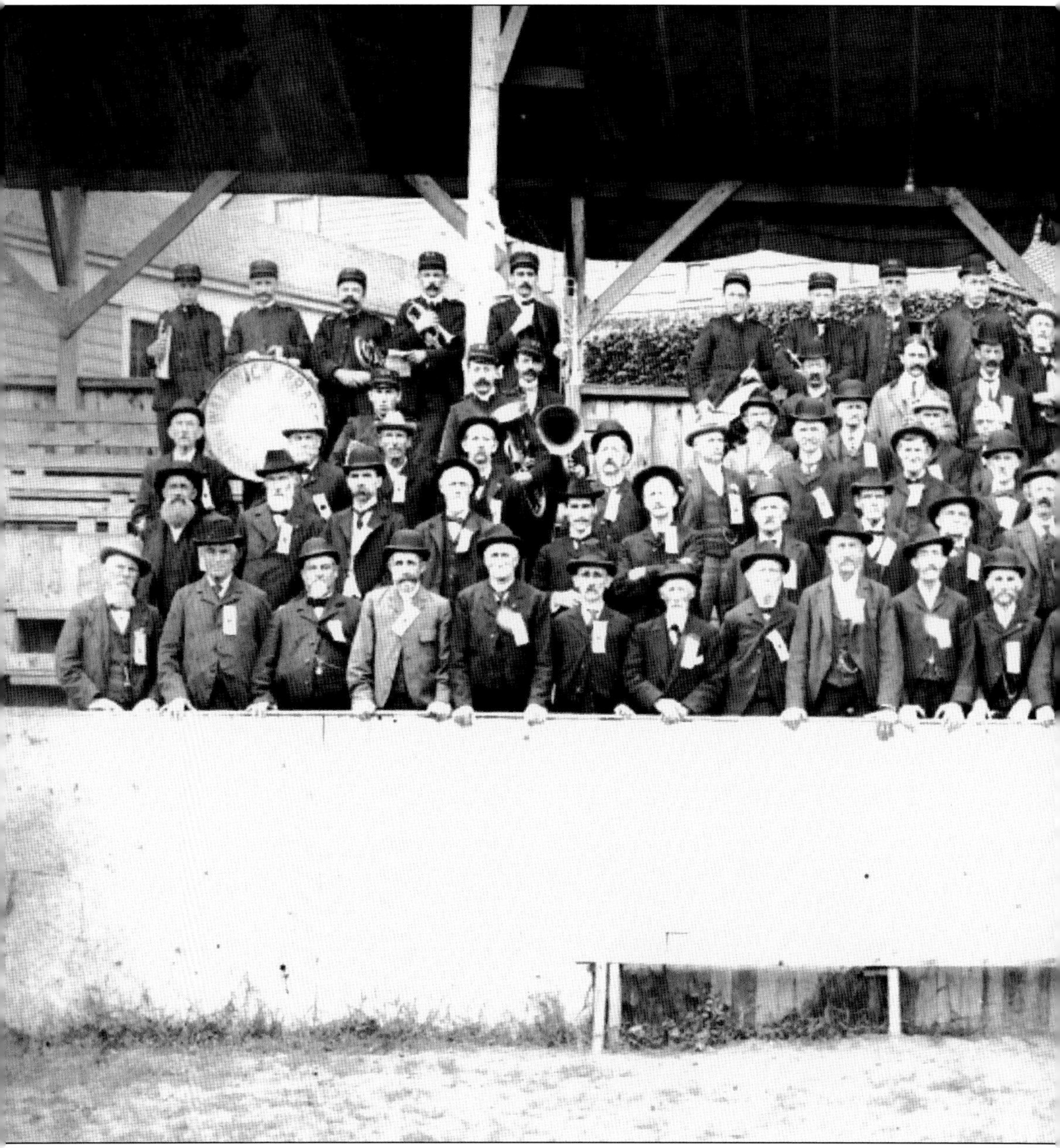

The Post Brass Band played at the 40th reunion of the 22nd New Jersey Regiment of the Grand

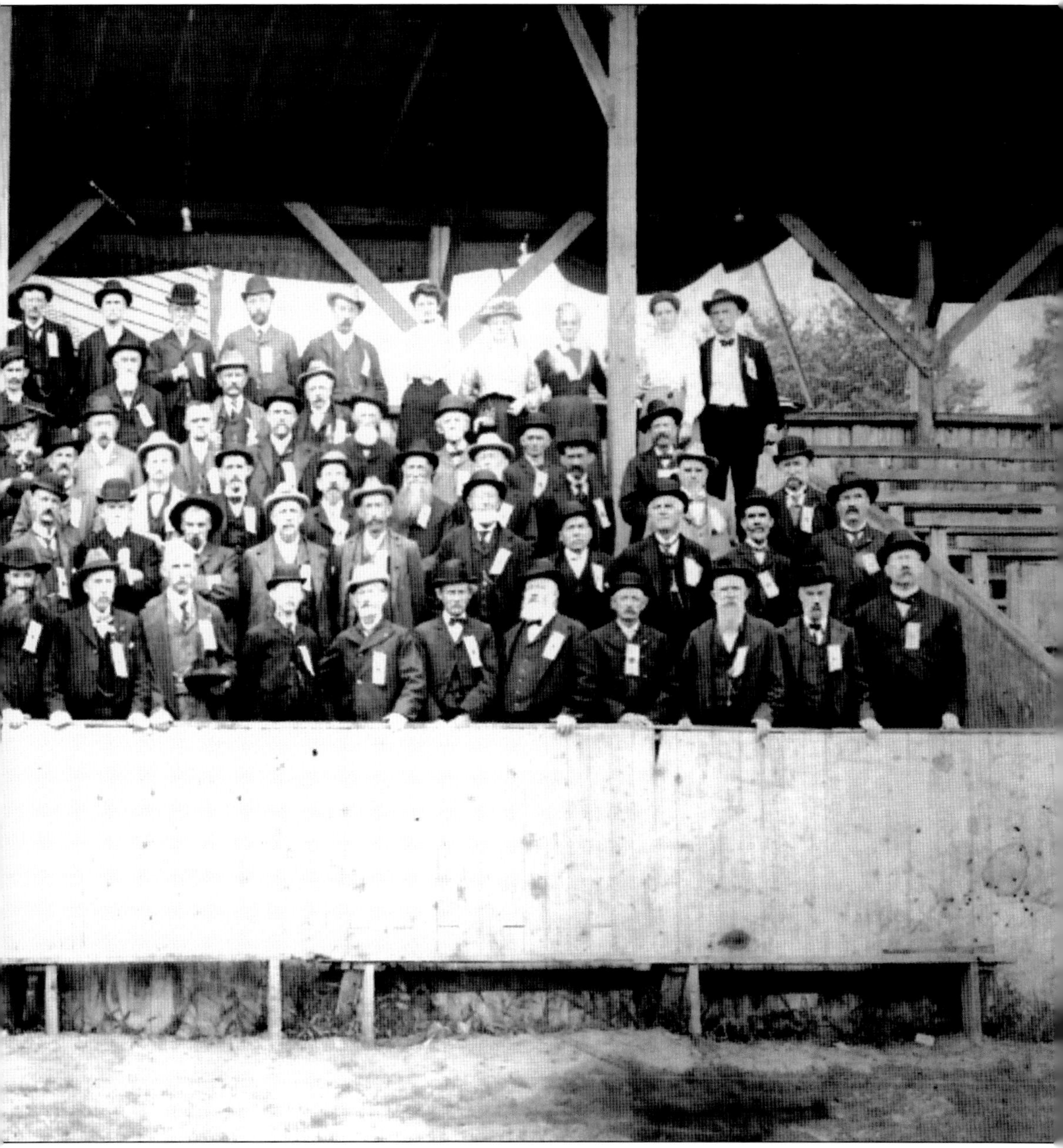

Old Army. The reunion was held in Englewood with a large picnic in the afternoon.

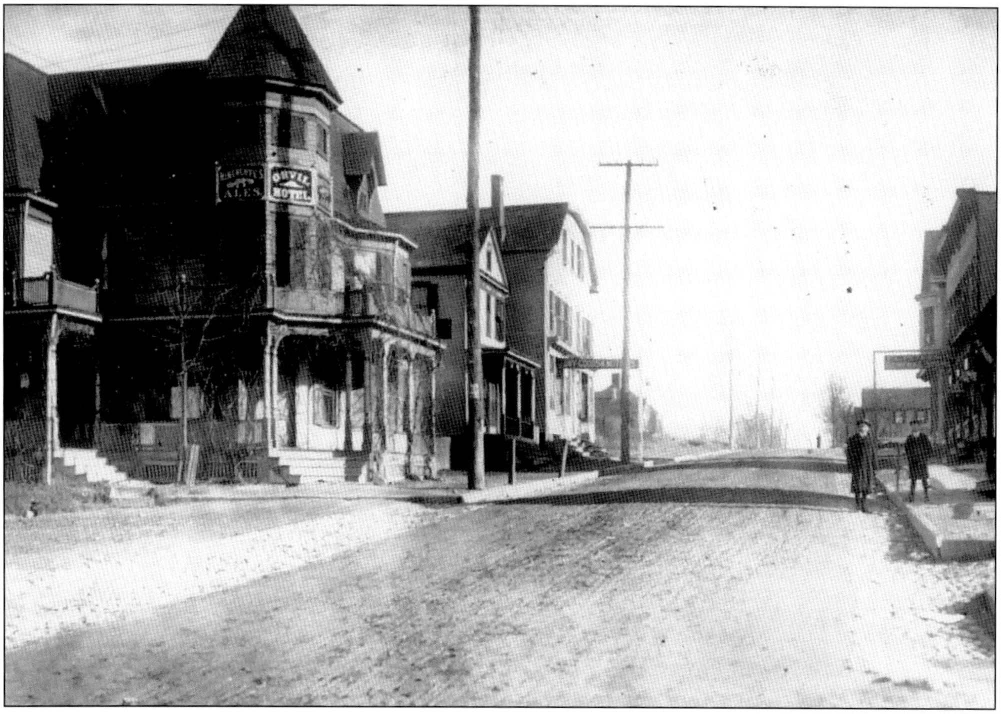

This streetscape, looking east along West Prospect Street with Peterson's general store on the right, was taken *c.* 1900. In 1908, F.L. Peterson became the postmaster, succeeding George Oughton.

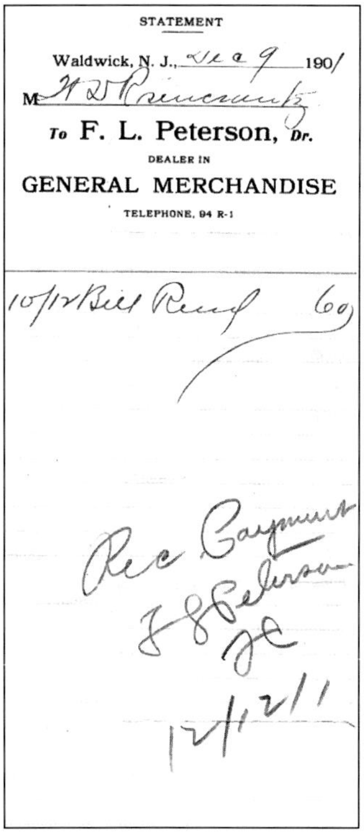

STATEMENT

Waldwick, N. J., Dec 9 1901

M

To F. L. Peterson, *Dr.*

DEALER IN

GENERAL MERCHANDISE

TELEPHONE, 94 R-1

10/12 Bill Rend 60

Rec Payment
F L Peterson
12/12/1

A receipt from F.L. Peterson's store is seen here.

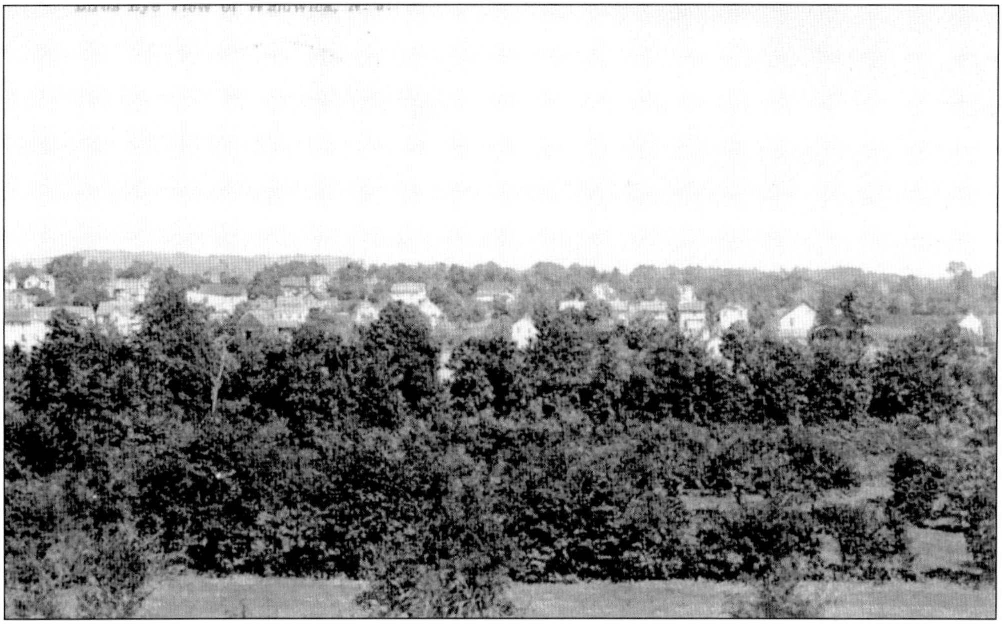

This bird's-eye view of downtown Waldwick toward Franklin Turnpike was taken from the area of the Smith farm along Wyckoff Avenue in 1906.

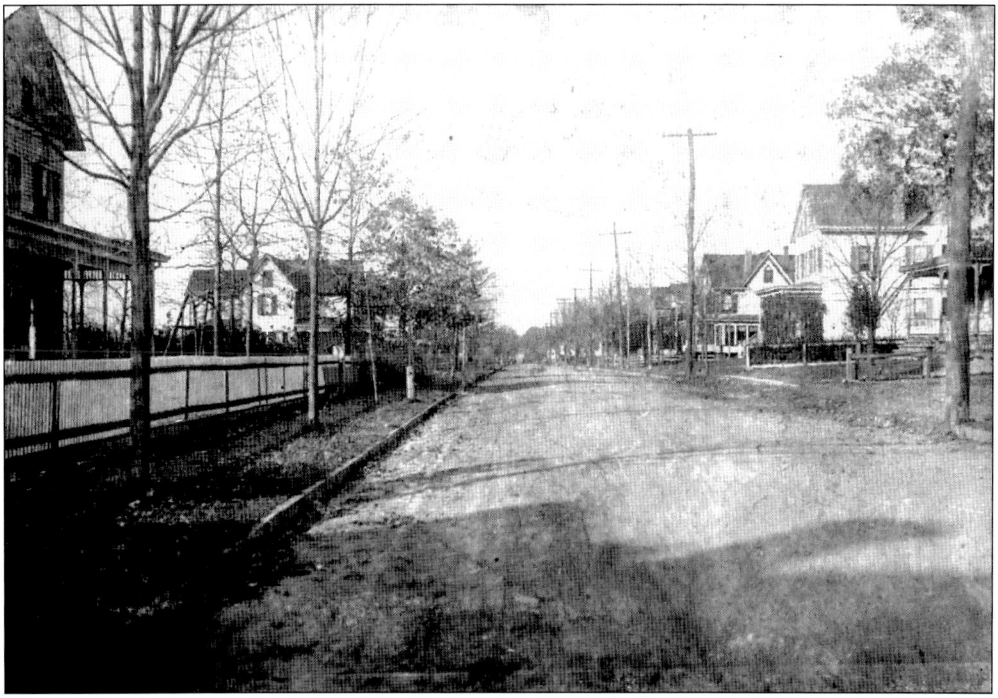

This view of Franklin Turnpike looks north from near Waldwick Avenue.

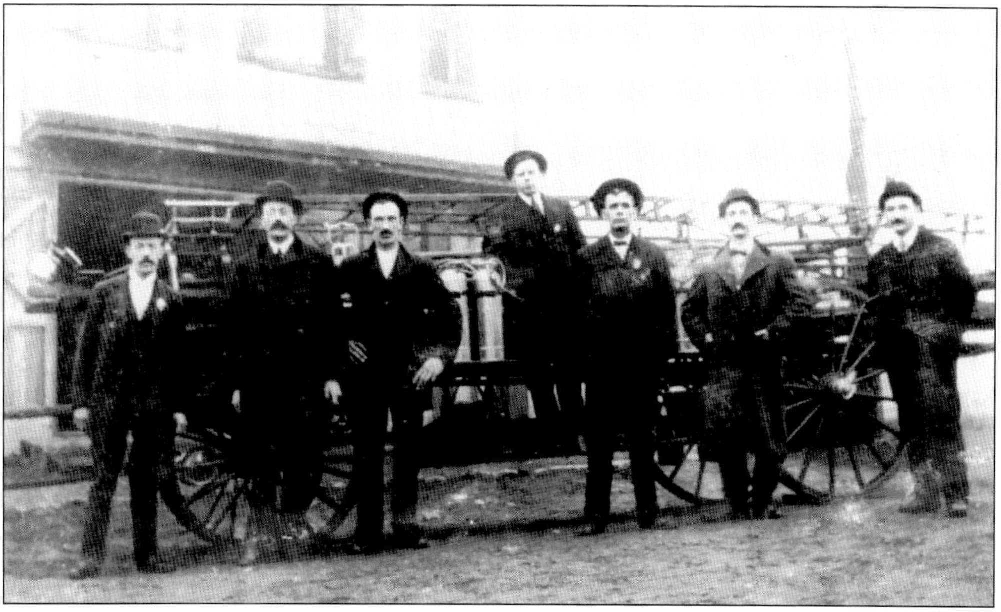

This is the earliest known image of the Waldwick Fire Department. It was taken soon after the department's formation in May 1907. In front of the horse-drawn ladder truck are, from left to right, Peter Fluer, Louis Terhune, Henry Dieckman, Daniel J. Mackerly, Charles Hull, Erskine D. Hook (the fire chief), and Charles Phitzner.

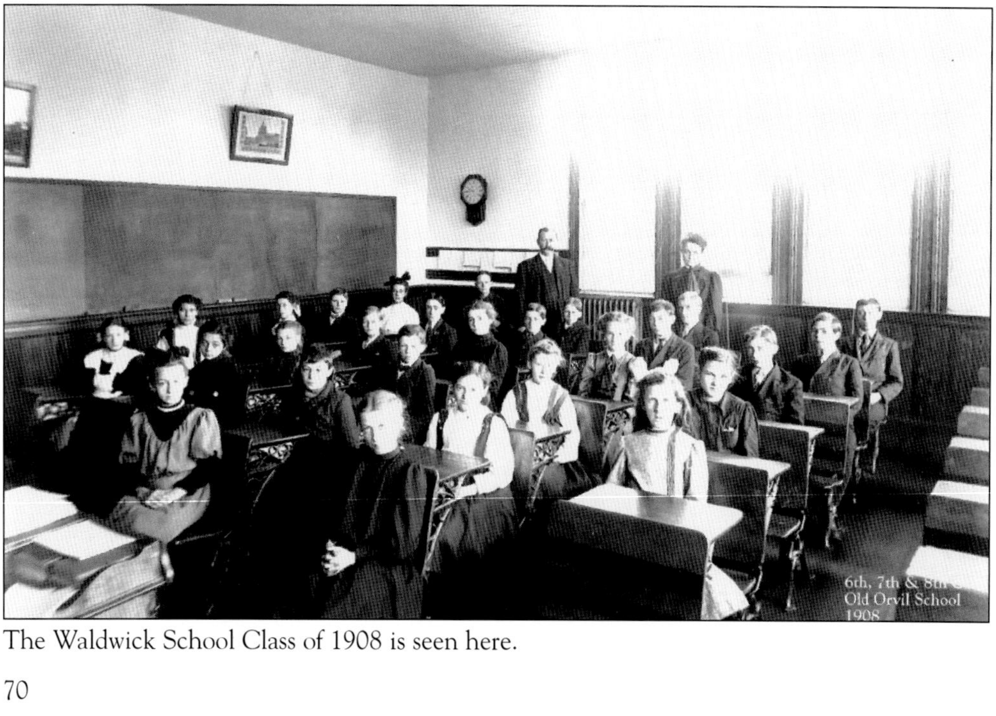

The Waldwick School Class of 1908 is seen here.

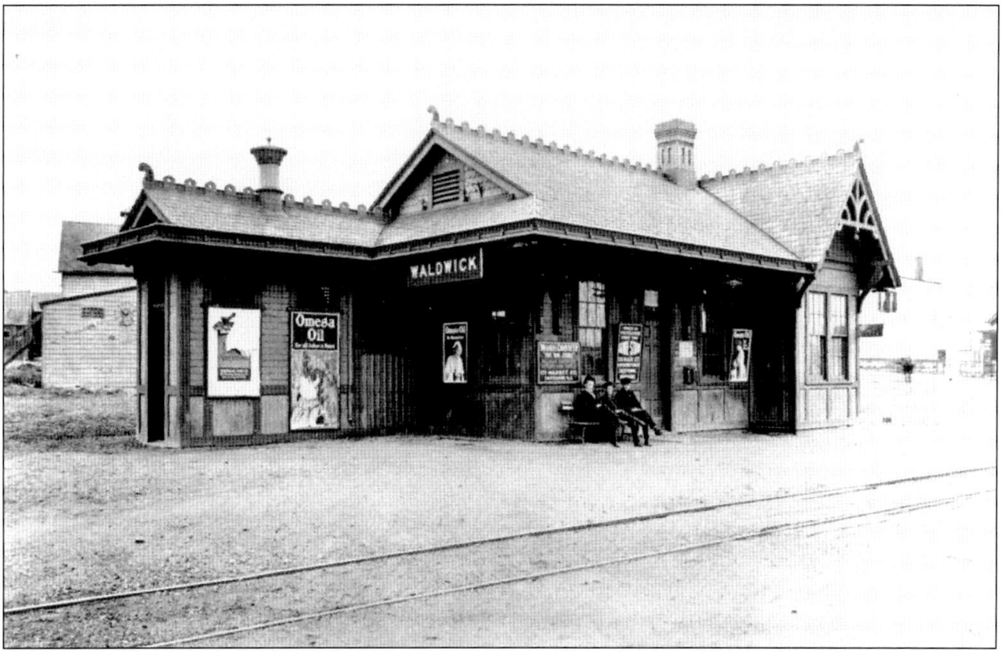

The Waldwick station is seen in this 1908 view. Waldwick and its train station became famous in the poem "The Twelve-Forty-Five," written by internationally acclaimed poet Joyce Kilmer, a resident of Mahwah. One stanza reads: "Subtly and certainly I feel / That Glen Rock welcomes us to her, / And silent Ridgewood seems to stir, / And smile because she knows the train, / Has brought her children back again, / We carry people home — and so, / God speeds us wheresoe'er we go, / Hohokus, Waldwick, Allendale, / Lift sleepy heads to give us hail."

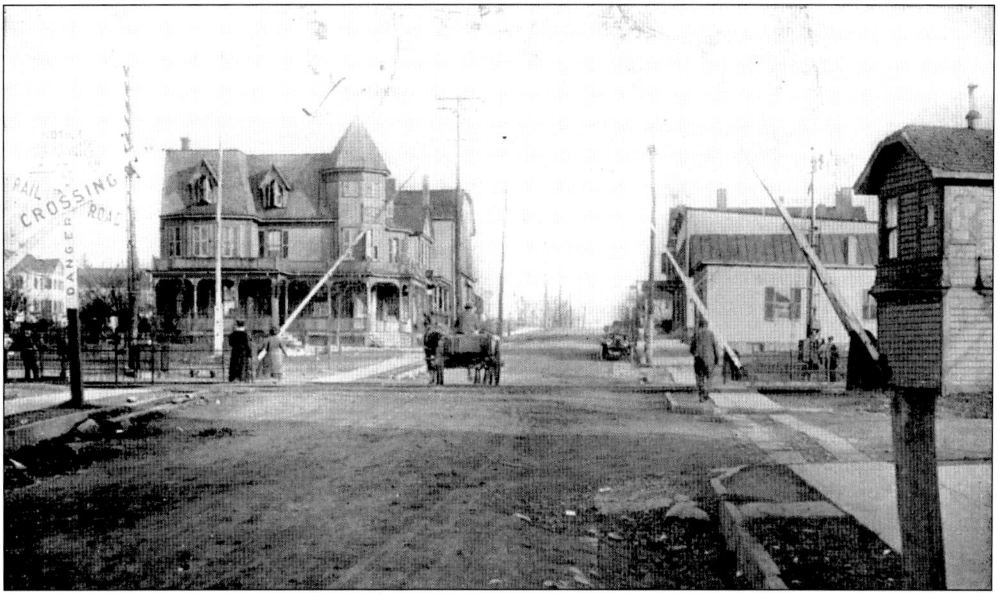

This view looks east across the railroad tracks along West Prospect Street. Note the gatehouse on the right and the Orvil House on the left.

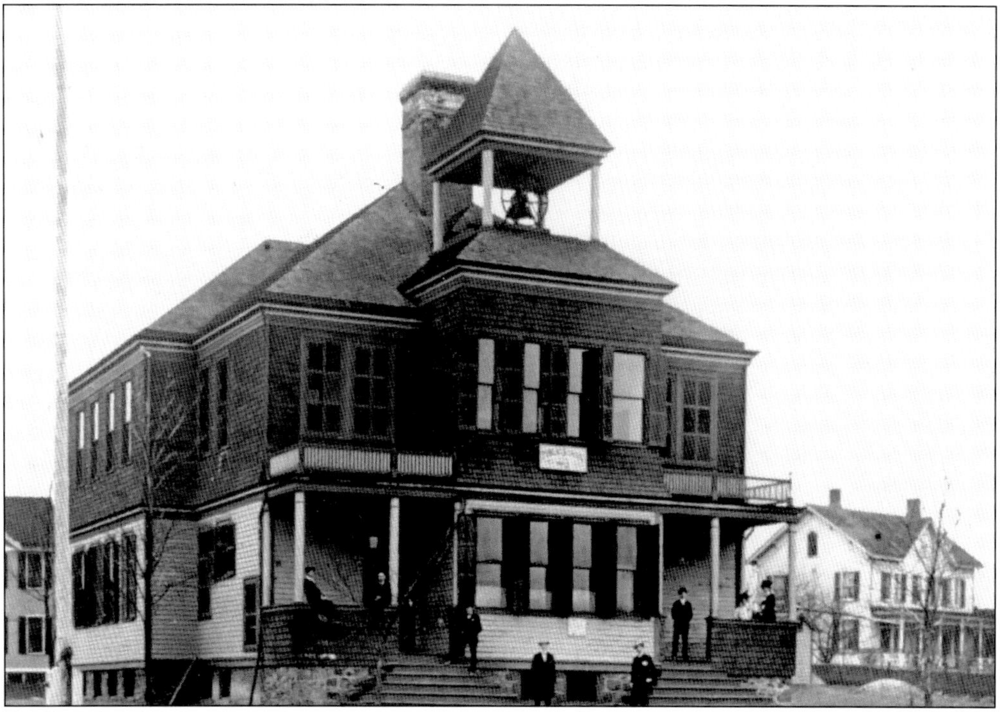

Waldwick School No. 2 is seen in this 1910 photograph. The number of the Waldwick School within Orvil Township was changed three times over the period from 1895 to 1910. A building addition to the rear of the school was made in 1912.

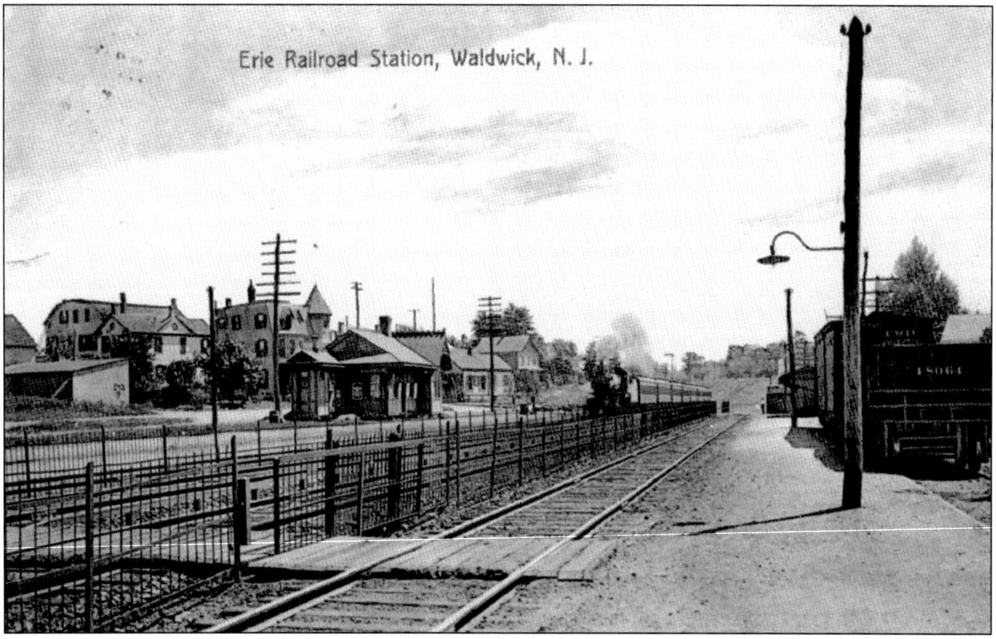

A view of the Waldwick station from the north shows a steam train pulling into town. This photograph dates from *c.* 1910.

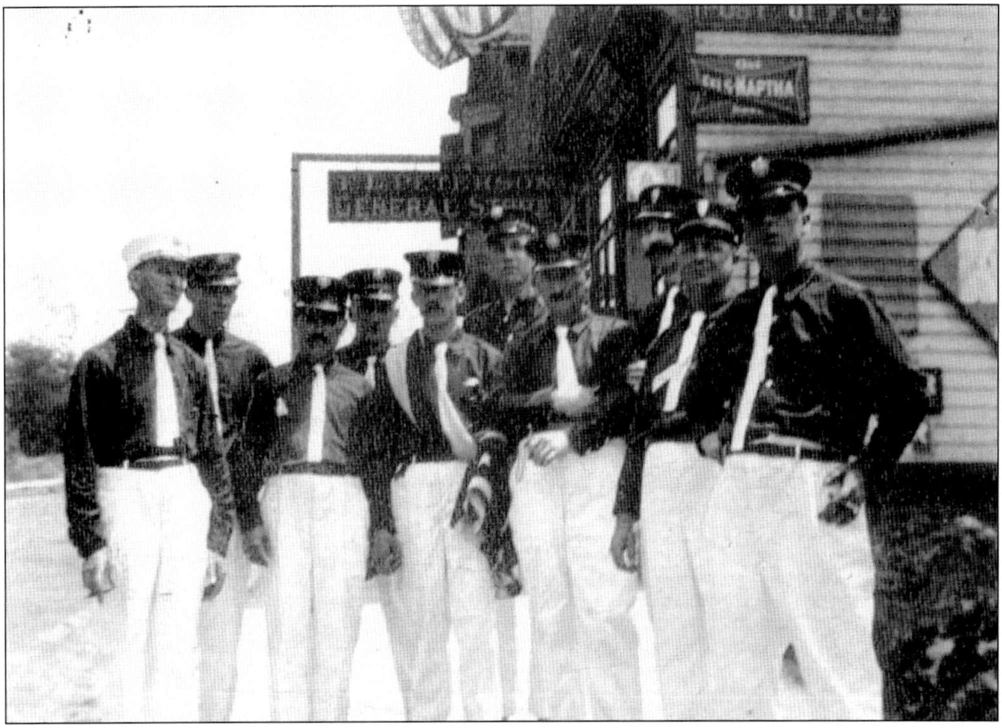

Waldwick firemen are assembled near Peterson's store after a parade *c.* 1910.

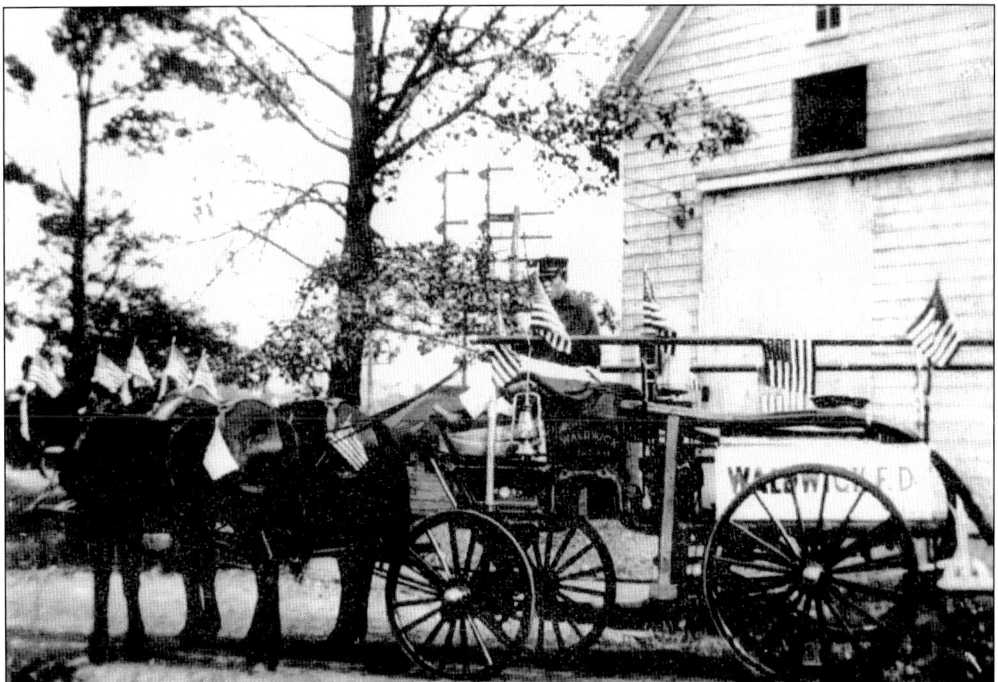

This photograph of the second horse-drawn fire engine was probably taken on the day of the parade above. Firemen used several private barns in the center of town to store the apparatus over the years prior to the construction of the municipal building.

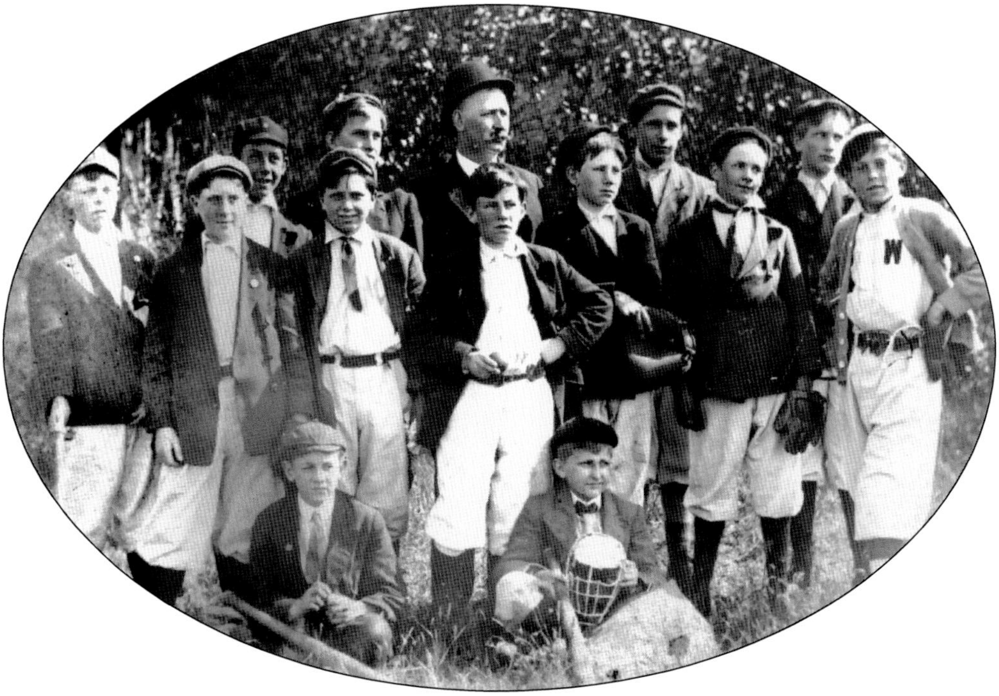

S.E. Barnes, the school principal, poses with the Waldwick baseball team. From left to right are the following: (front row) unidentified and Harold Hook; (middle row) unidentified, Edward Bamper, Phil Wagner, Edward Abbott, William Shuart, John Washer, and unidentified; (back row) Harold Monroe, unidentified, S.E. Barnes, Harold Lampe, and Edward Phitzner.

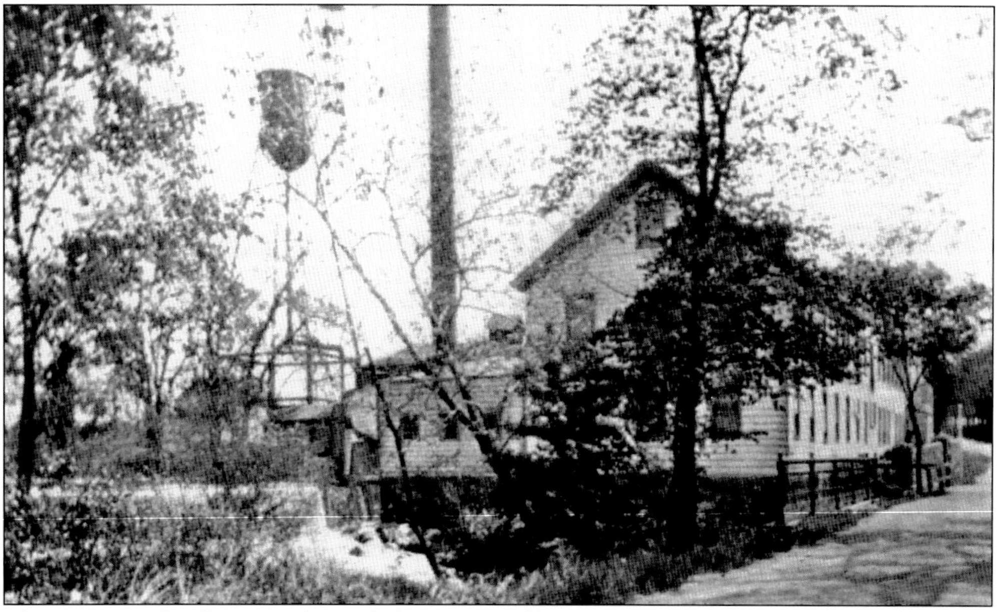

The Ramapo Bleachery was located along Wyckoff Avenue at Wanamaker Avenue. It was the site of many previous mills, including a gristmill and the Margroff Mill.

Seen here is an advertisement from Sears, Roebuck and Company for a prefabricated home that was delivered by rail. The six-room house cost $1,288.

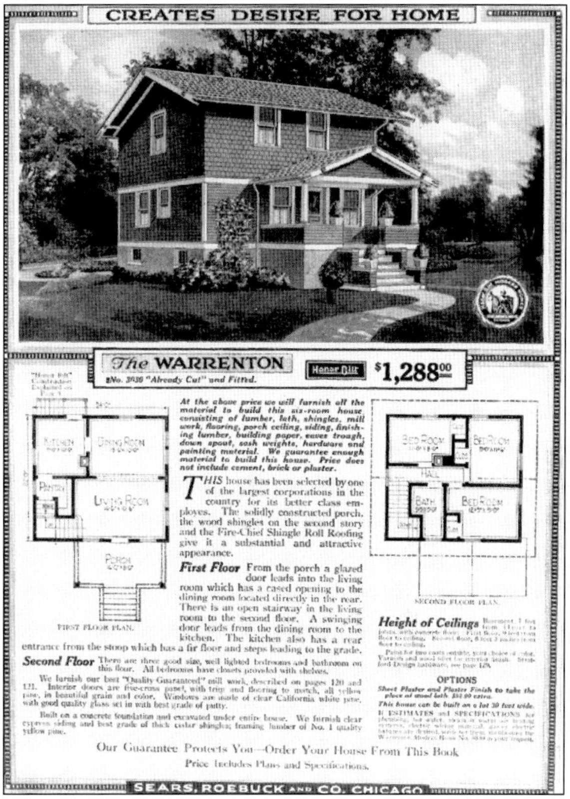

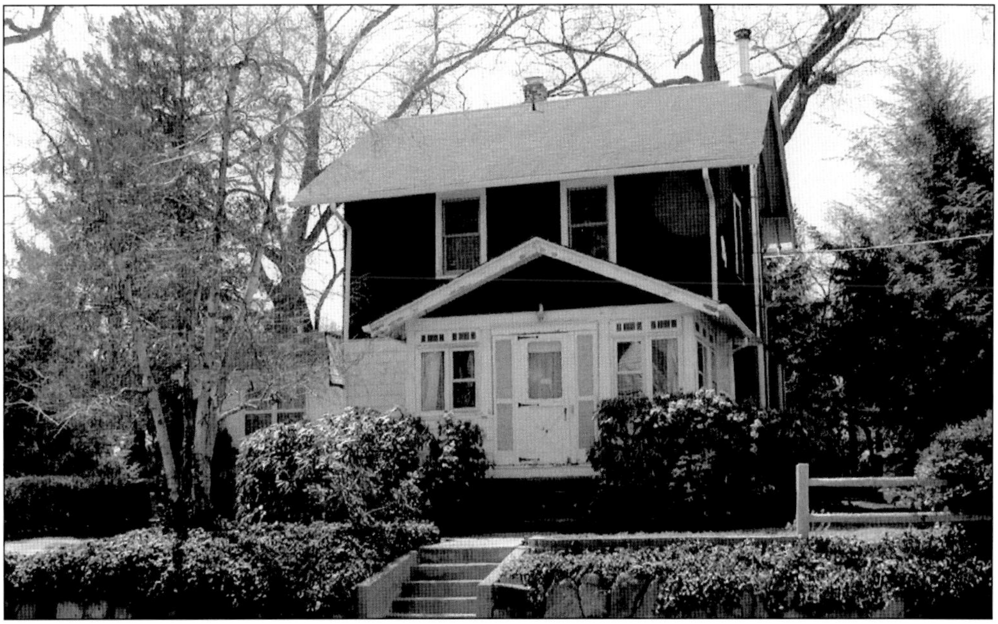

A Sears Warrenton model home still exists at 44 Bergen Avenue.

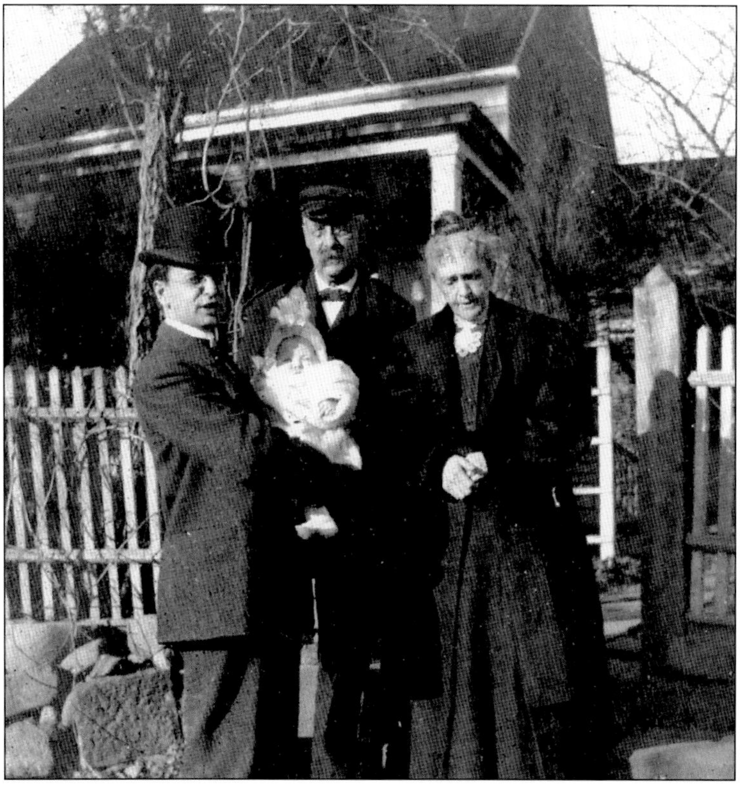

Van Wagoner family members seen here are, from left to right, Addison (holding Helen), B.B., and Alice.

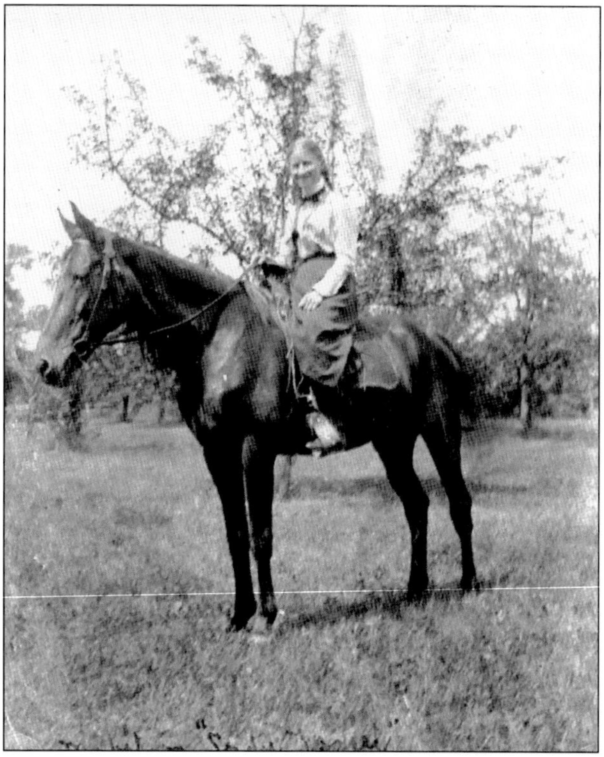

Mabel Van Wagoner is seen riding Lady Tassel. The Van Wagoners raised fine riding horses and took great interest in equestrian affairs. B.B. Van Wagoner was even issued a patent for a checkrein.

Three generations of the Van Wagoners are seen here. They are, from left to right, Addison, John, and B.B.

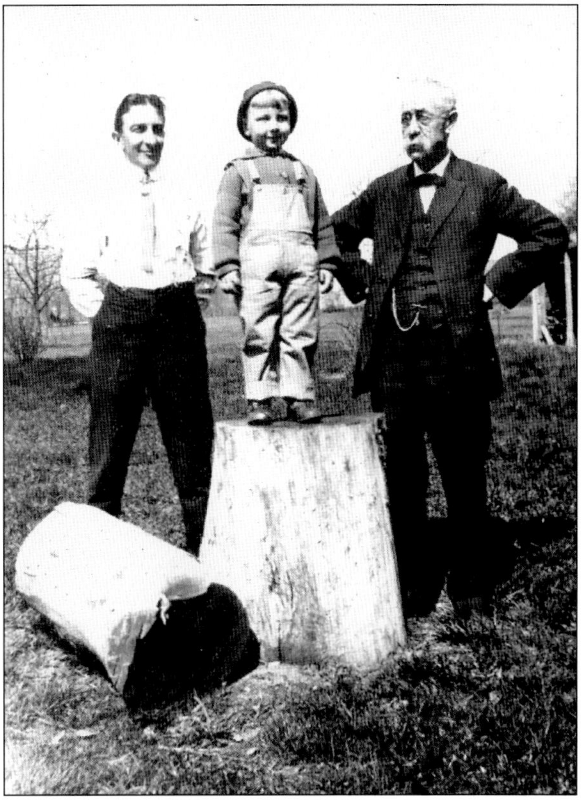

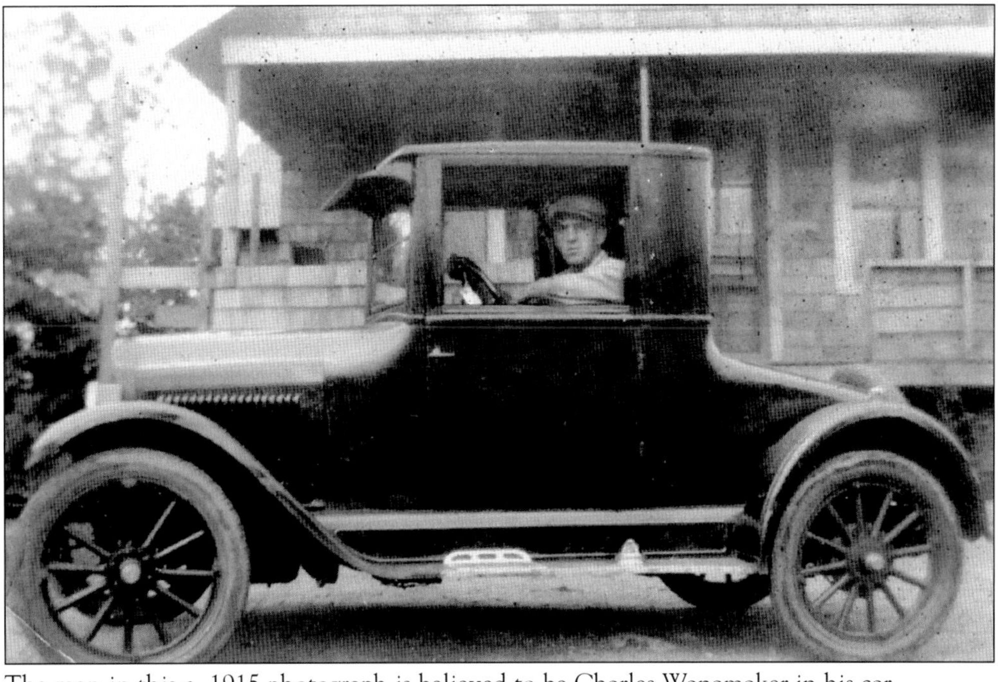

The man in this c. 1915 photograph is believed to be Charles Wanamaker in his car.

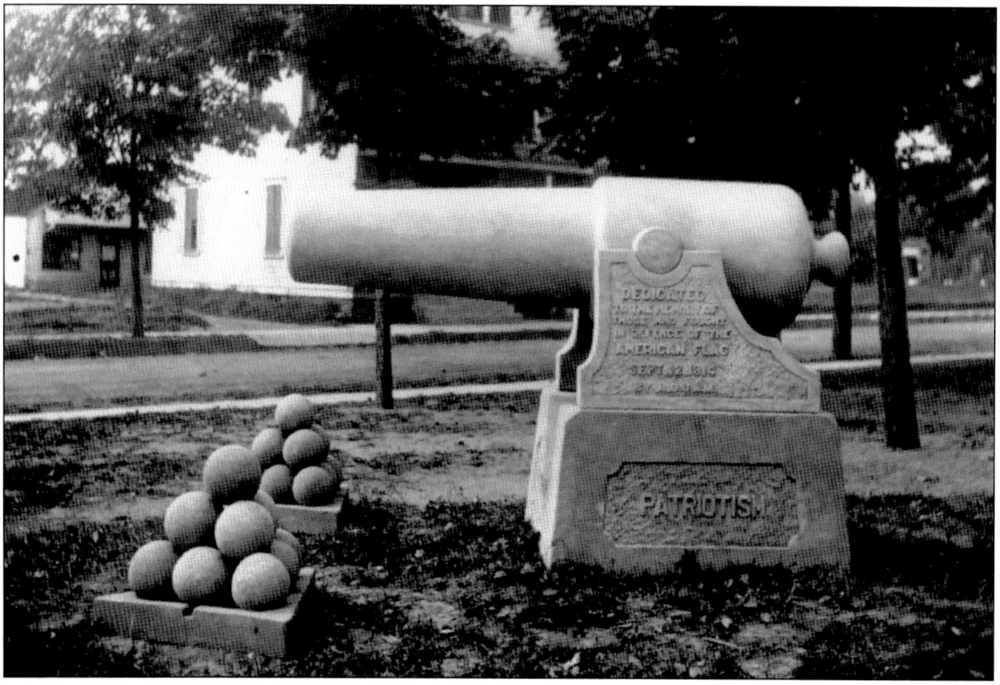

Seen is the famous cement cannon of Waldwick. It was built by Charles Cordes (a railroad baggage handler) and was presented by the Junior Order of U.S. Associated Mechanics to the Waldwick School. It was dedicated "to the memory of those who fought in defense of the American flag." The only one of its kind, it was handmade of Portland cement and weighed over 2,300 pounds.

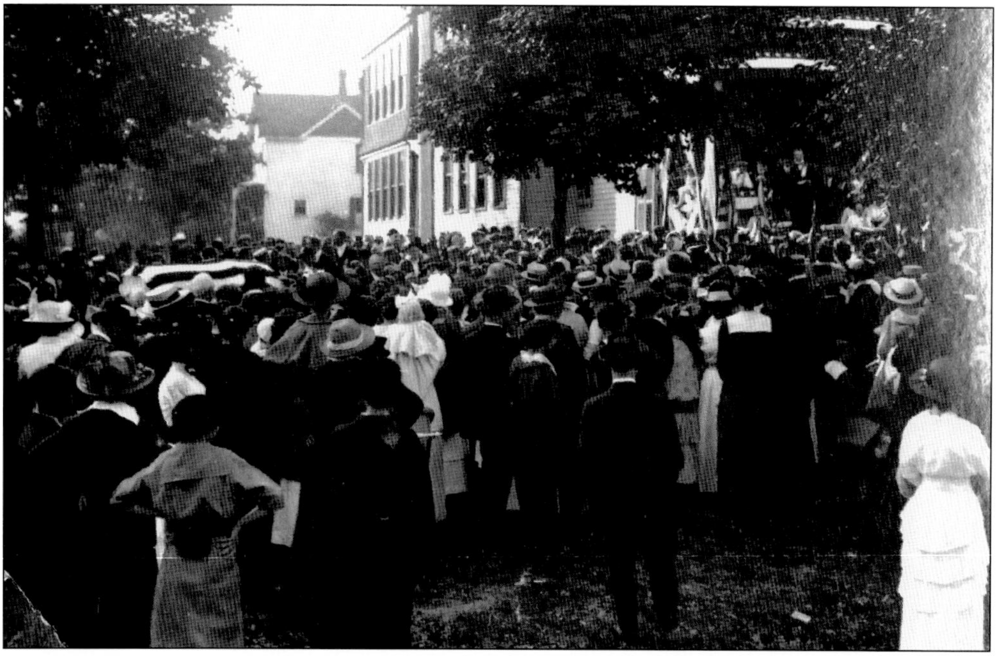

The dedication of the Cordes cannon took place in front of the Waldwick School on September 12, 1914.

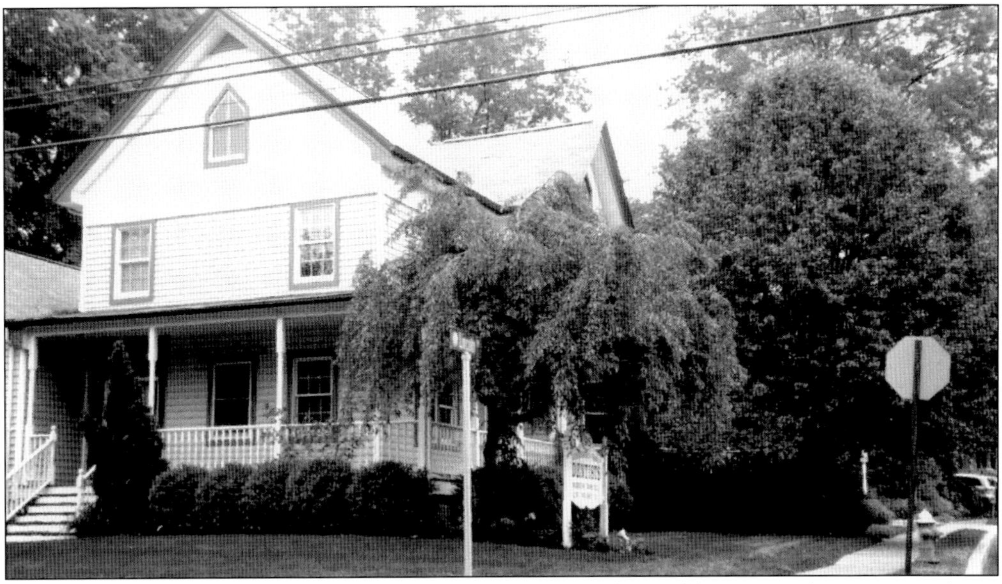

The Harvey Springstead house, at Lincoln Place and Franklin Turnpike, is seen here. Springstead moved into Waldwick in 1890 with his wife and two boys and purchased this home for $225 from Matthew and Ann White. He was a well-known Erie locomotive engineer, having worked for the railroad since 1873. He used to park his locomotive on the wye, located just north of his home next to Franklin Turnpike. He was also active in local politics and served as councilman, treasurer, and special tax collector for Orvil Township.

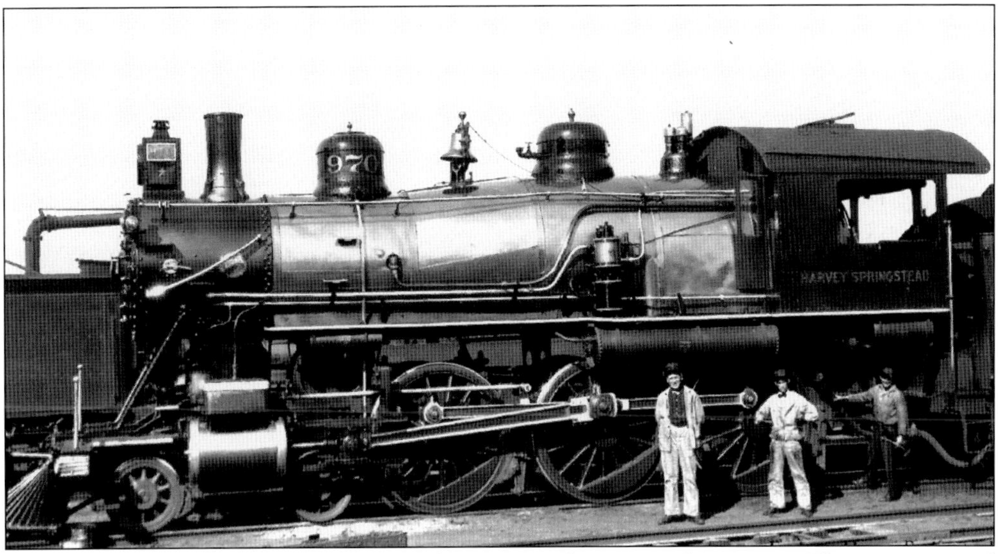

Harvey Springstead (left) is seen with a locomotive fireman and inspector. They are pictured in front of his well-known engine No. 970. A popular story about Springstead detailed the races between his engine and the North Jersey Rapid Transit trolley that ran from Paterson to Suffern through Waldwick. With the tracks running parallel from Waldwick to Suffern, bets were placed between the competing passengers. Springstead was a 40-year veteran of the rails, receiving the top honor from the Erie Railroad by being inducted into the Order of the Red Spot in 1912. His name was painted in gold leaf on his engine. He was also well known for getting 3,000 passengers through a snowstorm in 1917.

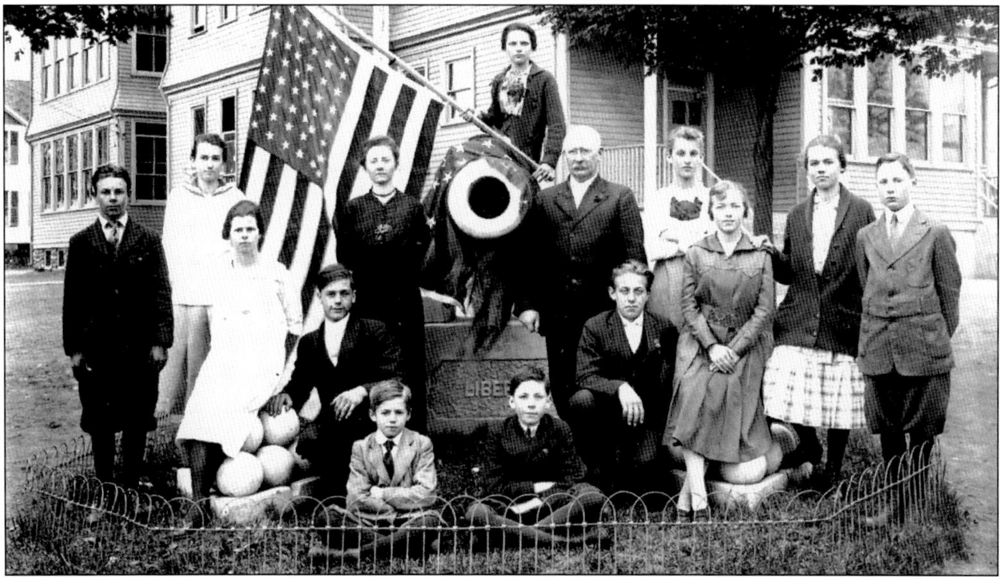

The Waldwick School Class of 1917 is patriotically pictured in front of the cannon. From left to right are Adrian Hopper, Anna McDowell, Katherine Wilking, James Monroe, Julia A. Traphagen, Olive Shuart (on the cannon), S.E. Barnes (the principal), John Powley, Hilda Kalt, Olive Perry, Kathleen McDowell, and Kenneth Wynne. Sitting on the grass are Lester Powley (left) and Donald McKeown.

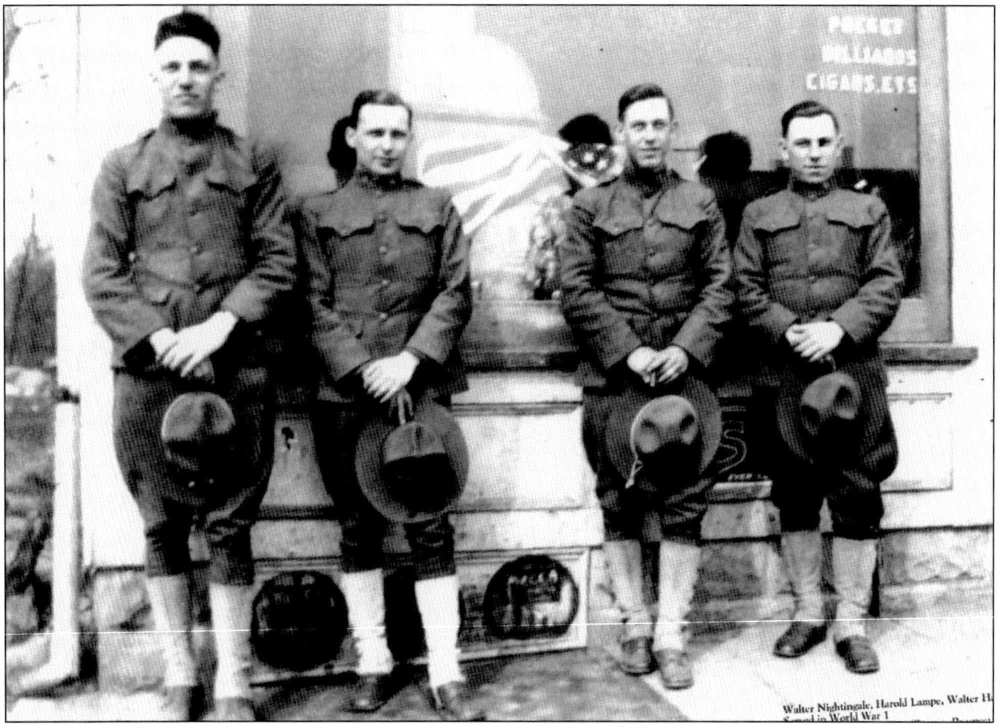

Four doughboys are pictured in front of Salfia's Barber Shop on West Prospect Street. From left to right are Walter Nightingale, Harold Lampe, Walter Hammond, and Alfred P. Wagner.

Enrico (Harry) LaPorta, of the 69th Infantry, is shown in his World War I uniform in France c. 1918. He was a founding member of the local American Legion post.

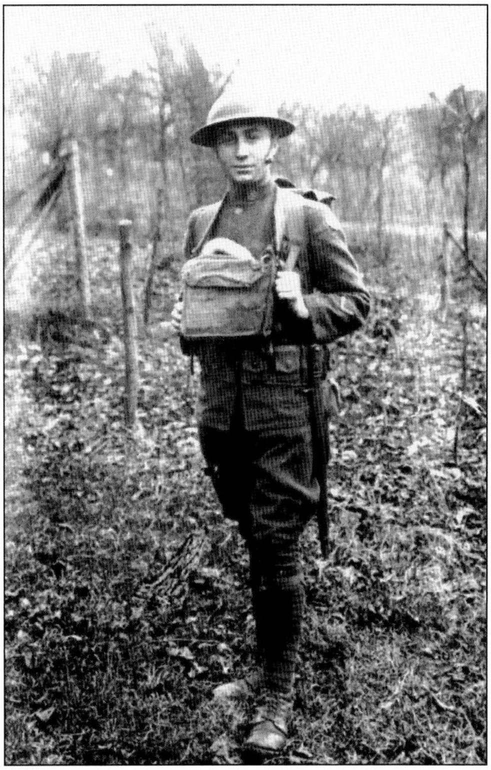

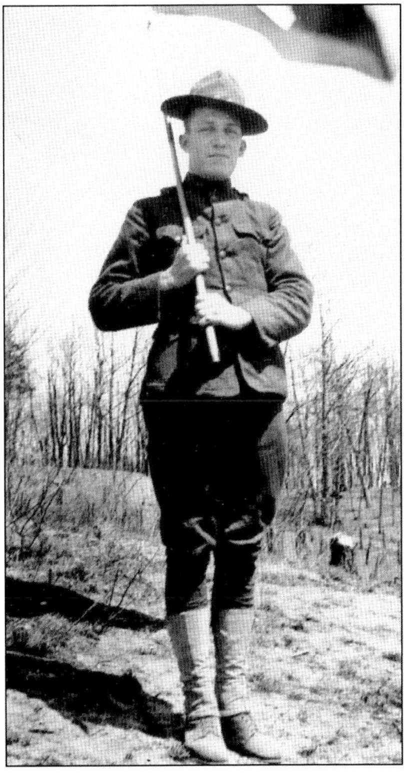

Walter Nightengale (pictured in France) was a member of the 78th Division, 303 Signal Corp. Battlion. He lost his life on November 1, 1918, in France. Along with Walter Nightengale, four other Waldwick residents lost their lives in World War I. William Demarest died on September 30, 1918; John L. Dow died on November 1, 1918; Walter Hammond died on September 28, 1918; and Guglielmo Zazzetti died on September 29, 1918.

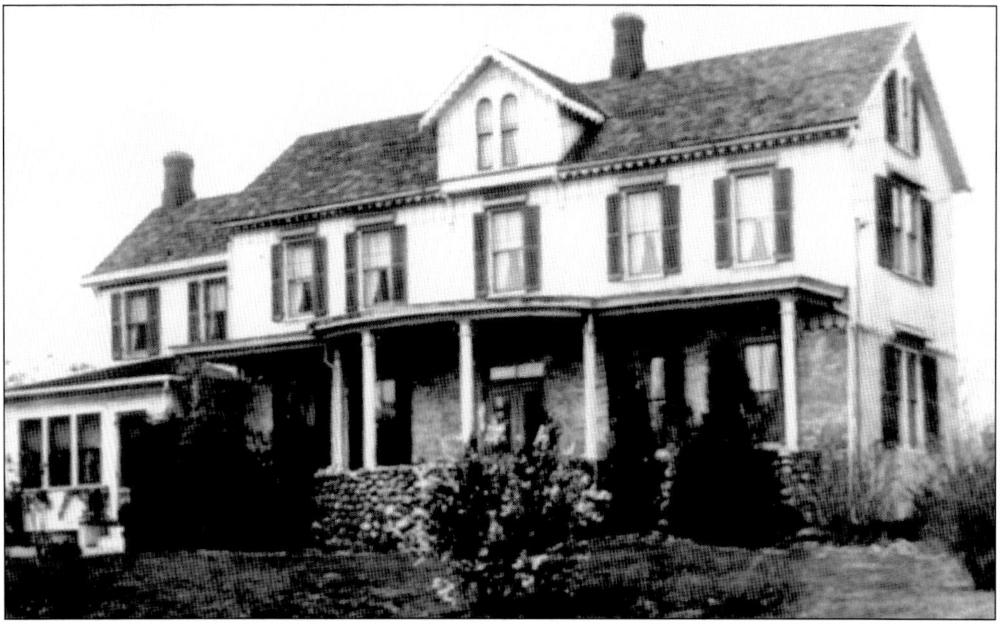

The Miller-Green-Ritter-Henderson house, at the northwest corner of Crescent Avenue and Wyckoff Avenue, is seen in this 1921 photograph. It was built before the 1860s and was owned by the Millers prior to the Civil War. Maj. Edward Green later bought the house. Green was a Civil War veteran who participated in the capture of assassin John Wilkes Booth in April 1865 as member of the 16th New York Cavalry. It later became Henderson's candy store.

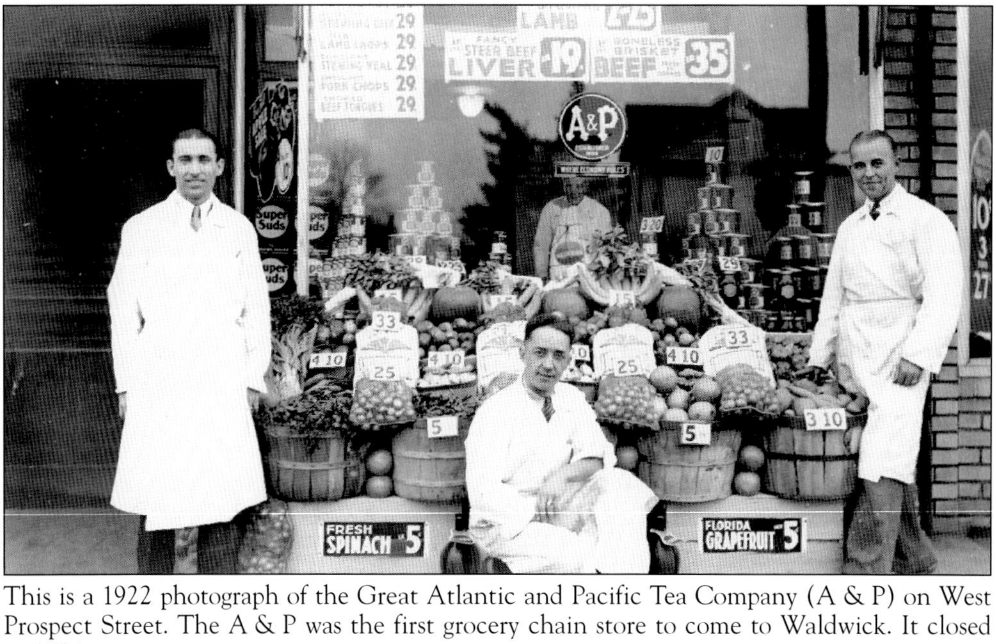

This is a 1922 photograph of the Great Atlantic and Pacific Tea Company (A & P) on West Prospect Street. The A & P was the first grocery chain store to come to Waldwick. It closed in 1934.

Four

Birth of a Borough

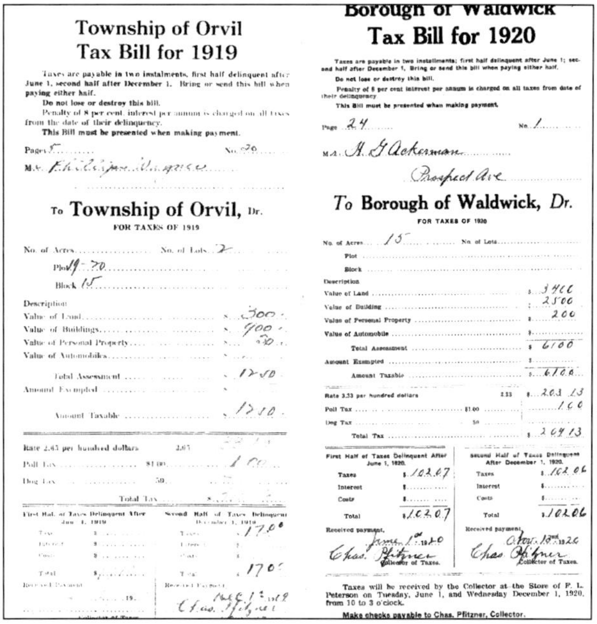

Township of Orvil
Tax Bill for 1919

Taxes are payable in two instalments, first half delinquent after June 1, second half after December 1. Bring or send this bill when paying either half.

Do not lose or destroy this bill.

Penalty of 8 per cent. interest per annum is charged on all taxes from the date of their delinquency.

This Bill must be presented when making payment.

Page 5 No. 70

M

To **Township of Orvil,** Dr.

FOR TAXES OF 1919

No. of Acres No. of Lots 2

Plot 19-70

Block 15

Description

Value of Land	$ 300.
Value of Buildings	$ 900.
Value of Personal Property	$ 50.
Value of Automobiles	$
Total Assessment	$ 1250
Amount Exempted	$
Amount Taxable	$ 1250.
Rate 2.63 per hundred dollars 2.63	
Poll Tax $1.00	1.00
Dog Tax .50	
Total Tax	$

First Half of Taxes Delinquent After June 1, 1919		Second Half of Taxes Delinquent December 1, 1919	
Taxes	$	Taxes	$ 17.00
Interest	$	Interest	$
Costs	$	Costs	$
Total	$	Total	$ 17.0[illegible]

Received Payment 19 Collector of Taxes

Received Payment

Borough of Waldwick
Tax Bill for 1920

Taxes are payable in two installments; first half delinquent after June 1; second half after December 1. Bring or send this bill when paying either half.

Do not lose or destroy this bill.

Penalty of 8 per cent interest per annum is charged on all taxes from date of their delinquency.

This Bill must be presented when making payment.

Page 24 No. 1

M H. G. Ackerman

Prospect Ave

To **Borough of Waldwick,** *Dr.*

FOR TAXES OF 1920

No. of Acres 15 No. of Lots

Plot

Block

Description

Value of Land	$ 3400
Value of Building	$ 2500
Value of Personal Property	$ 200
Value of Automobile	$
Total Assessment	$ 6100
Amount Exempted	$
Amount Taxable	$ 6100
Rate 3.33 per hundred dollars 3.33	$ 203.13
Poll Tax $1.00	1.00
Dog Tax .50	
Total Tax	$ 204.13

First Half of Taxes Delinquent After June 1, 1920.		Second Half of Taxes Delinquent After December 1, 1920.	
Taxes	$ 102.07	Taxes	$ 102.06
Interest	$	Interest	$
Costs	$	Costs	$
Total	$ 102.07	Total	$ 102.06

Received payment, June 1st 1920 Chas. Pfitzner Collector of Taxes.

Received payment, Nov. 13th 1920 Chas. Pfitzner Collector of Taxes.

Taxes will be received by the Collector at the Store of P. L. Peterson on Tuesday, June 1, and Wednesday December 1, 1920, from 10 to 3 o'clock.

Make checks payable to Chas. Pfitzner, Collector.

The borough of Waldwick was created in the frenzy of "boro-itis" that swept New Jersey during the late 1800s and early 1900s. Although there were several reasons for abandoning the township form of government, the primary reason related to the control of the local schools. This image shows two tax bills—one for the old Orvil Township and the other for Waldwick. The borough elected its first governing body on October 7, 1919. Elected to the new borough council were Garret L. Hewson, James Monroe, John O. Van Blarcom, Henry G. Ackerman, Ellsworth R. Bush, and William R. Evans Jr. The first mayor was John W. Quackenbush.

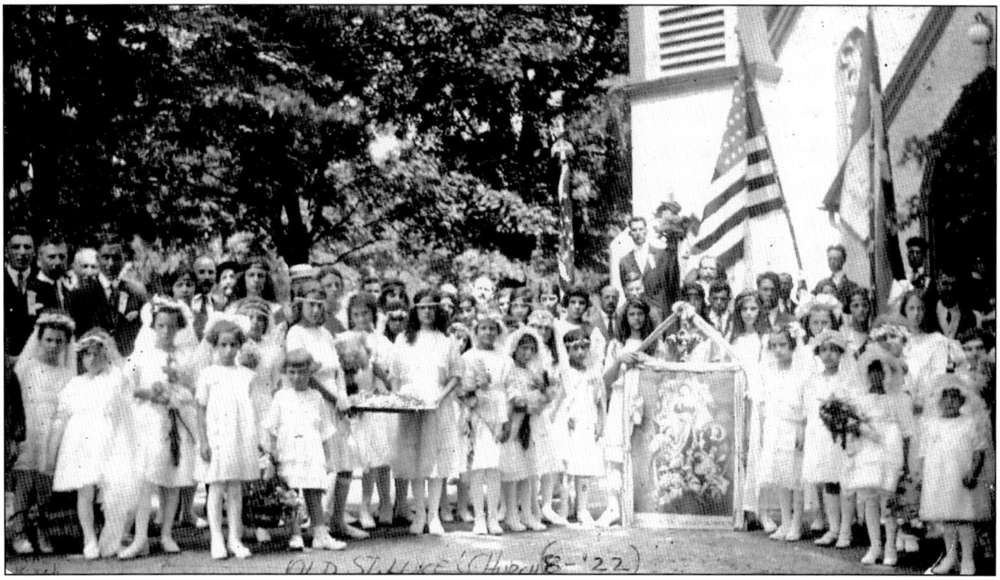

Young girls at St. Luke's Church prepare for the Societa della Maria del' Assunta (MSA) procession, which wound its way from the church to Zazzetti Street, where the official festivities took place. The parade featured colored lights across Zazzetti Street, as well as fireworks and a concert by the MSA band featuring Prof. James Vincent Dittamo.

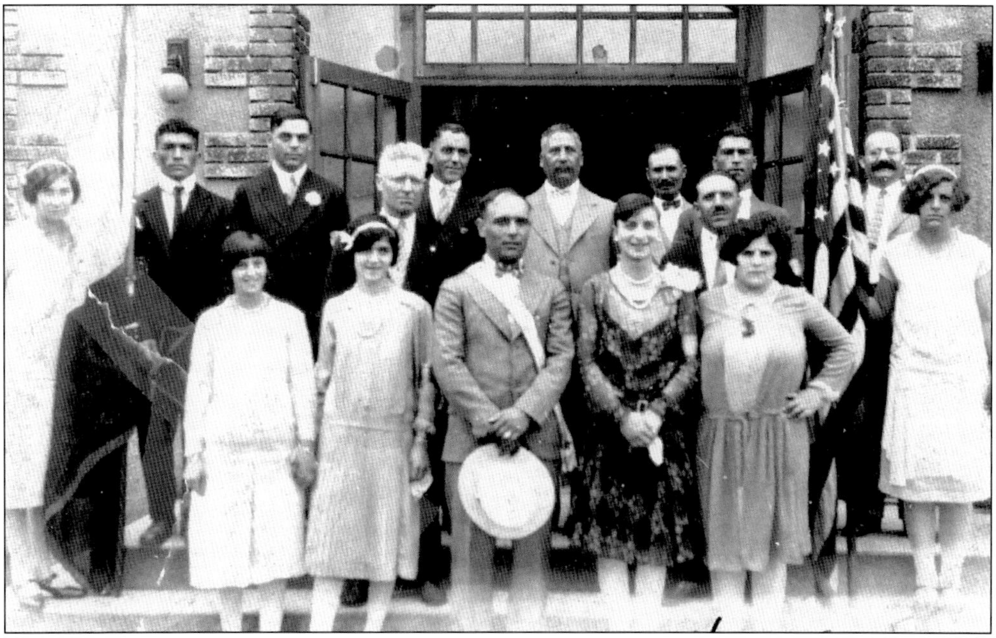

The Italian MSA feast was held in front of Marconi Hall on Zazzetti Street in August 1927. Seen here are, from left to right, the following: (front row) Gennie Biangardi, ? Lupo, Antonio Montenile, ? Salafia, and Adriana Totta; (back row) Josephine Lupo, Sam Olivieri, ? Leodori, Louis Riccardi, Luigi Totta, ? Biangardi, Andrea Agugliaro, Luigi Avaigiano, and two unidentified people. The festival ran from 1922 to 1962, when the Marconi Club closed its doors. The Italian community has its roots in the railroad. Many Italians helped construct an Erie Railroad expansion to include third and fourth rails between 1902 and 1904.

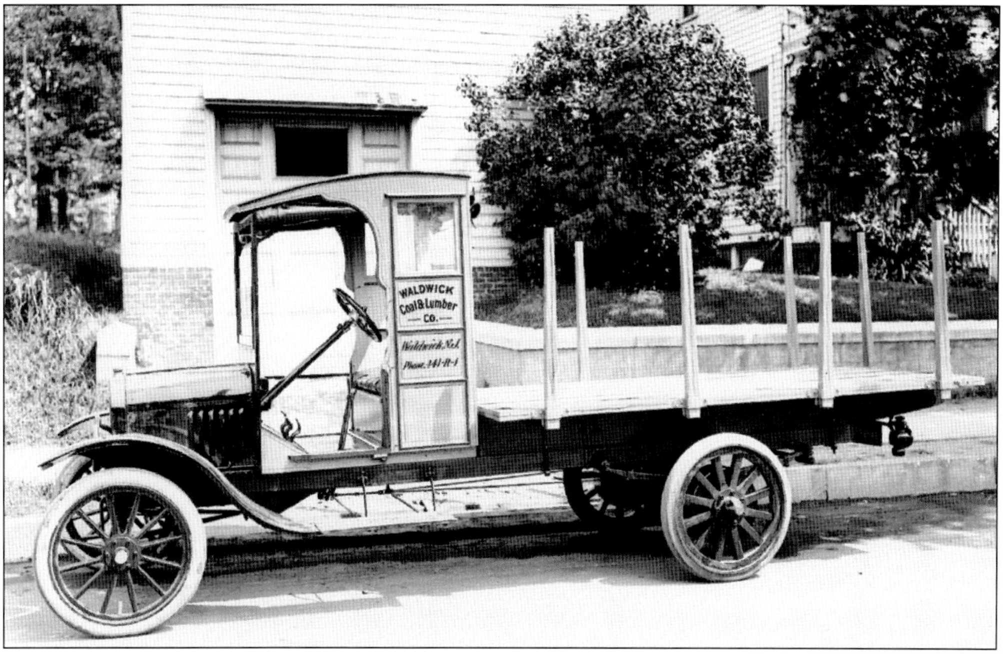

Seen in this *c.* 1910 photograph, taken at the Paterson Vehicle Company's plant in Paterson, is a new Waldwick Coal and Lumber truck.

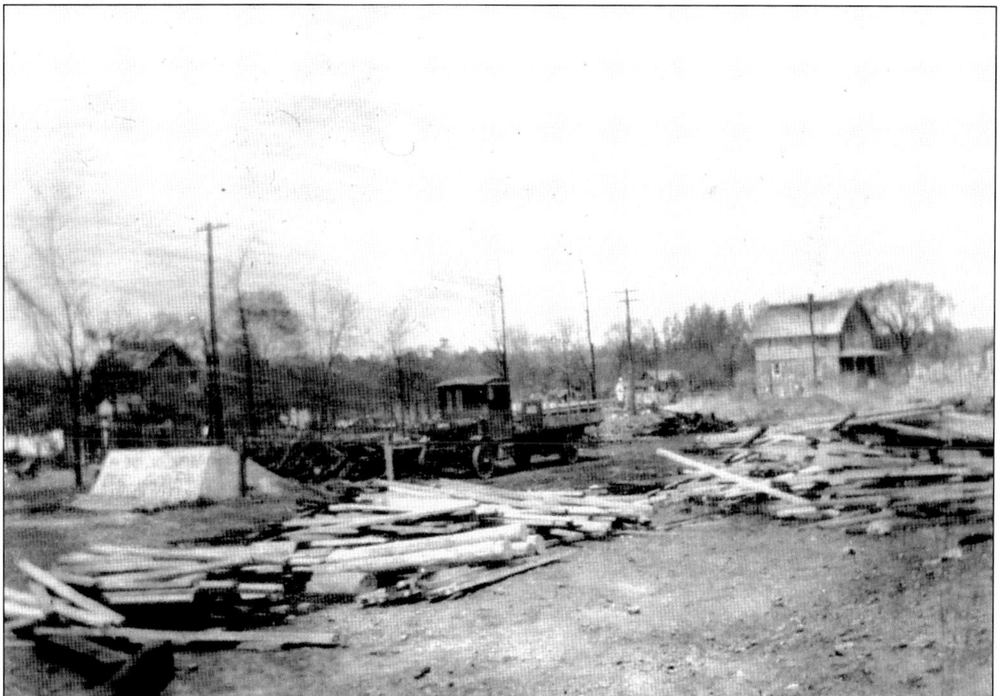

The Waldwick Coal and Lumber Company sustained a devastating fire on May 6, 1923. From a Waldwick Coal and Lumber accounting ledger, it appears that the company was sold soon after the fire.

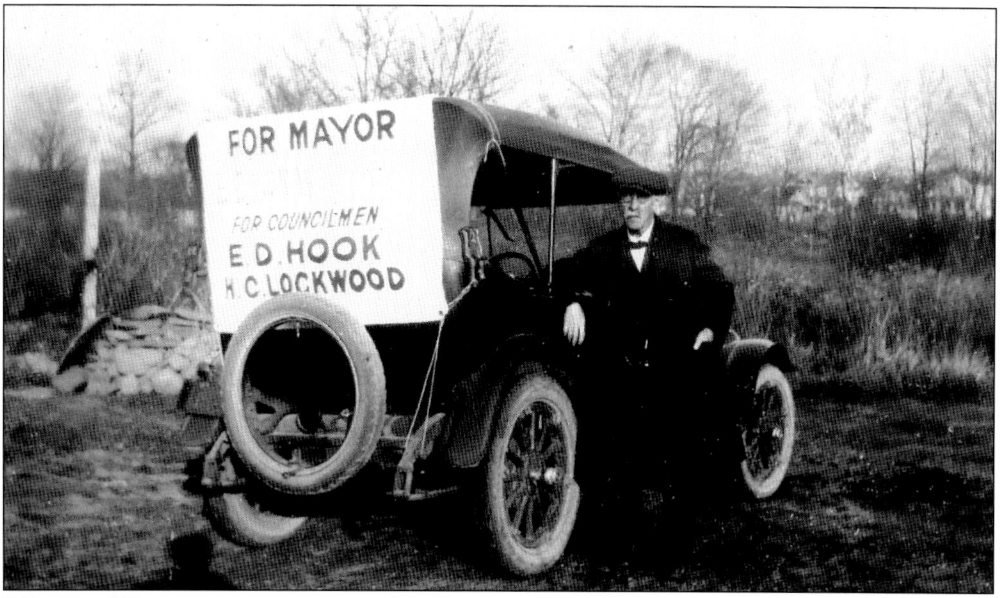

B.B. Van Wagoner is seen next to his new car in 1922, featuring a campaign sign for his successful mayoral run. His running mates were Erskine Hook, the town's first fire chief, and Harry C. Lockwood, who raised eight children and owned a large piece of property at Pennington Street and Hopper Avenue.

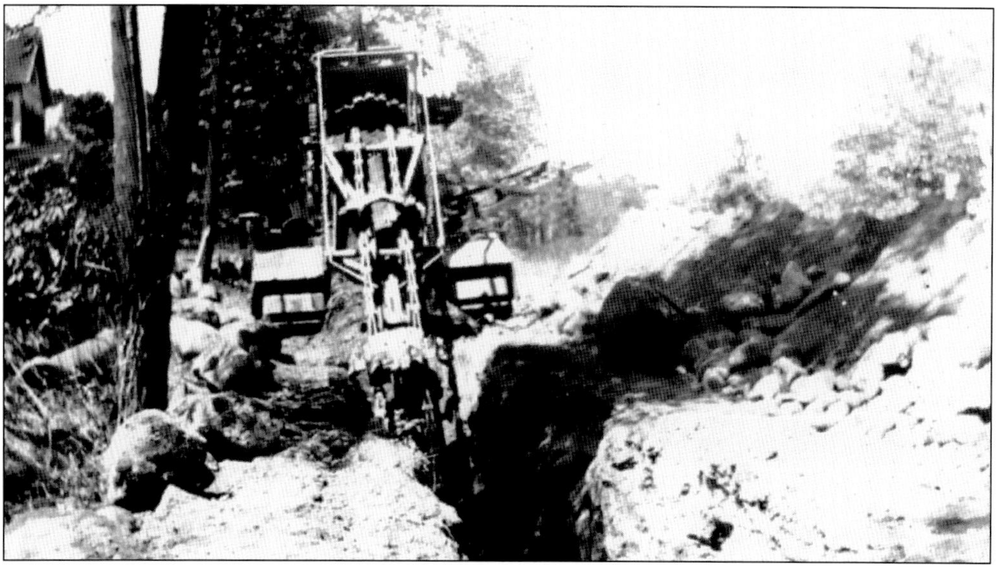

Trenches were dug along Wyckoff Avenue in 1923 in preparation for the installation of the new public water system. The pumping station now located at the Waldwick pool was one of the first in operation when the system was created. The well pump was powered by a water turbine supplied by water flowing from White's Pond. B.B. Van Wagoner and his newly elected fellow councilmen were responsible for getting this project initiated, which included drilling another 600-foot-deep well, located behind the former municipal building. The three politicians were originally on the Democratic ticket and were in favor of creating a water system, even though the Democratic party was not. They switched parties and joined the Republicans and were subsequently elected by the townspeople.

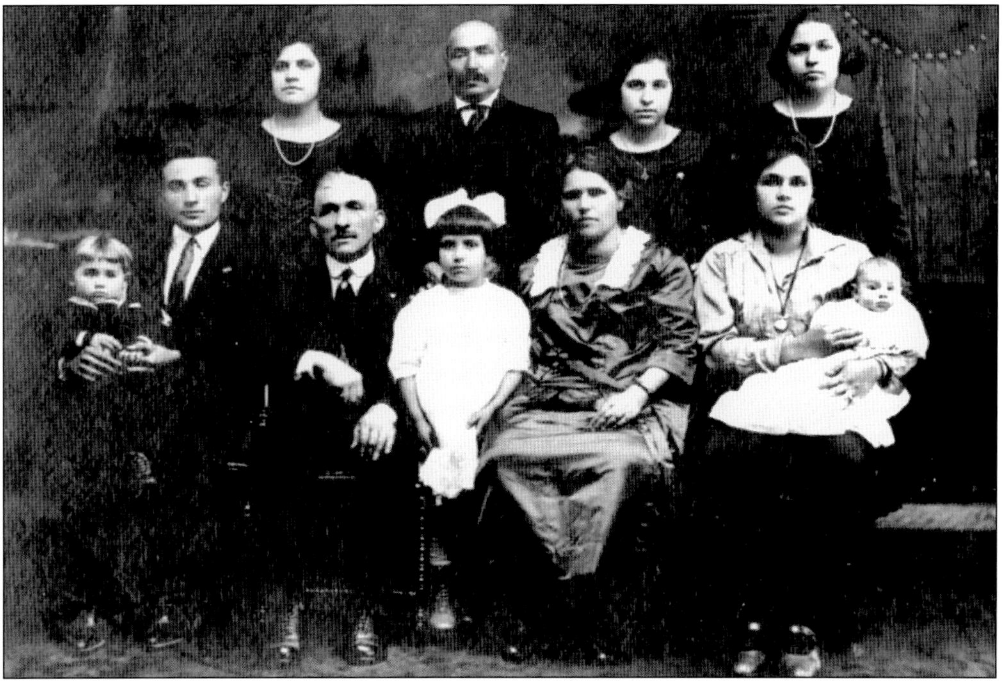

The LaPorta and Picioke families pose for a portrait. Seen here are, from left to right, the following: (front row) Dominic LaPorta, Enrico LaPorta, Steven Picioke, Leana Picioke, Josephina Picioke, Carmella LaPorta, and Beatrice LaPorta; (back row) Anne Picioke, Pasquale Lippilo, Stephanie Picioke, and Patricia Picioke. The LaPorta family moved to Waldwick in the early 1920s and eventually purchased a home on Frederick Street.

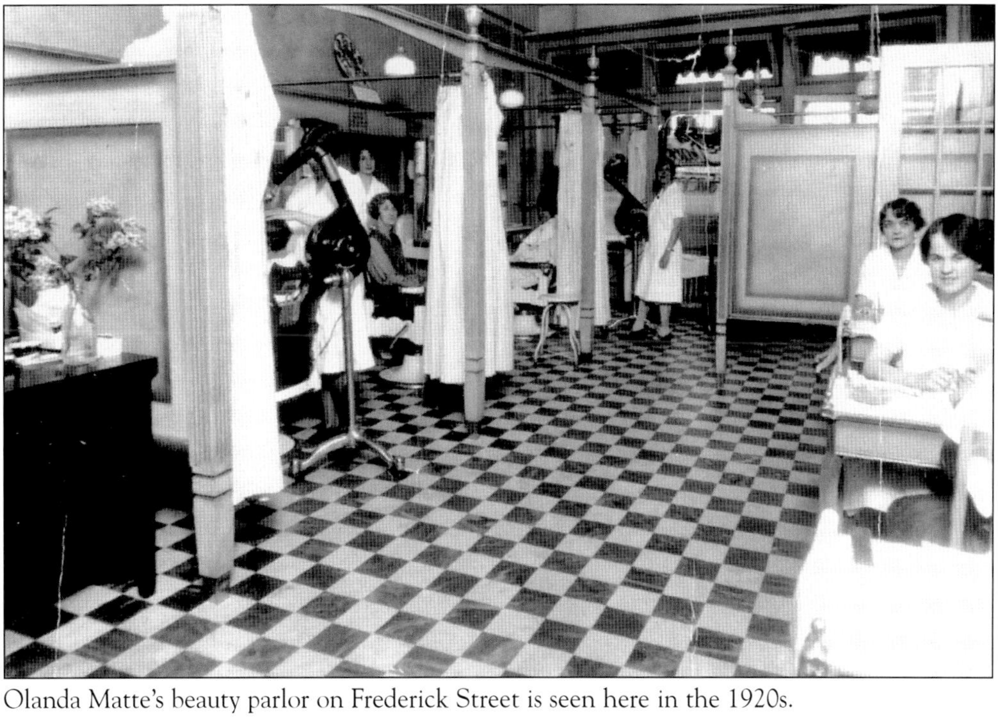

Olanda Matte's beauty parlor on Frederick Street is seen here in the 1920s.

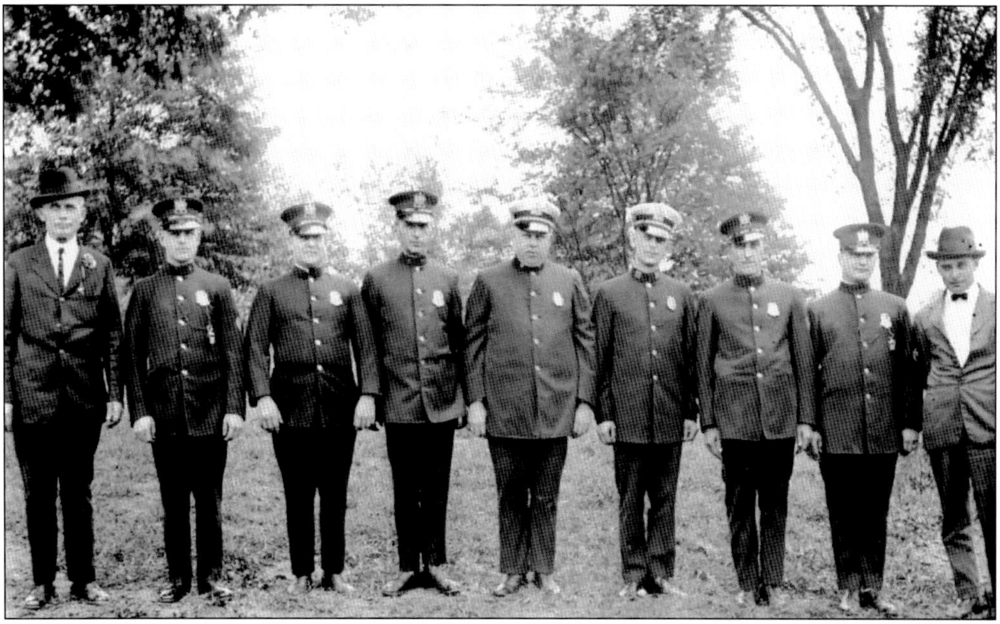

The original police department consisted of nine marshals, shown in this 1924 photograph. From left to right are C.W. Hull, E.R. Litchult, W. Meisner, F.C. Holly, D.J. Mackerly, L.E. Thomas, W. Hunt, E.R. Phitzner, and E. Gill.

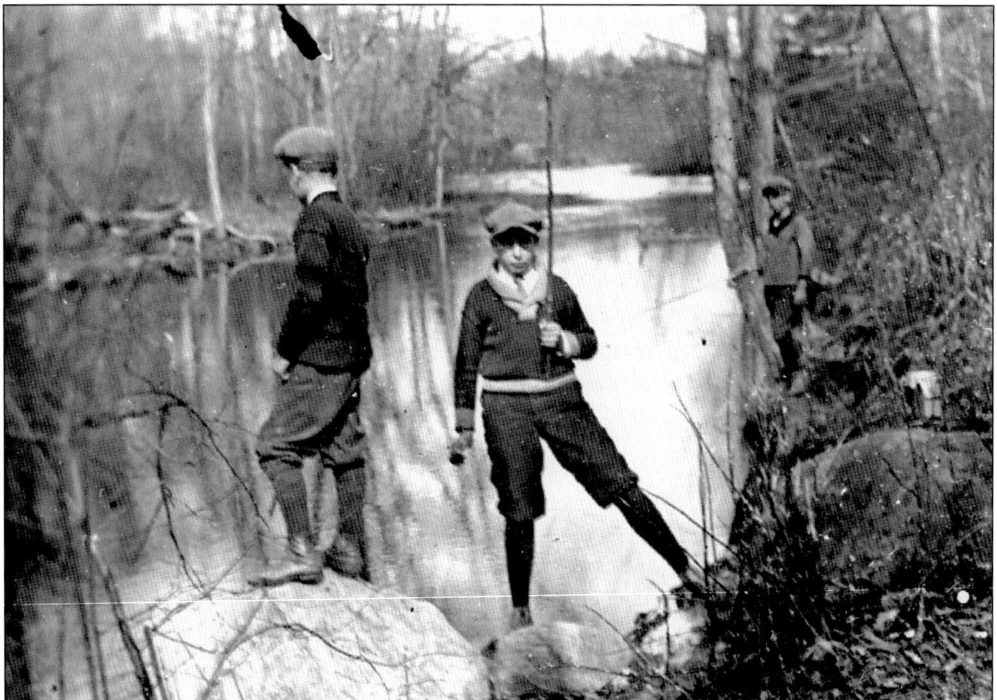

The VanderEl boys are seen fishing on the Ho-Ho-Kus Brook above White's Pond.

Martin VanderEl was an immigrant from Holland. He was an early resident of John Dow Avenue, moving into the Koopman House. He was a prolific amateur photographer and had a large greenhouse. He worked on a Bergen County road crew, and with his wife raised 11 children. Several of their children became Waldwick schoolteachers.

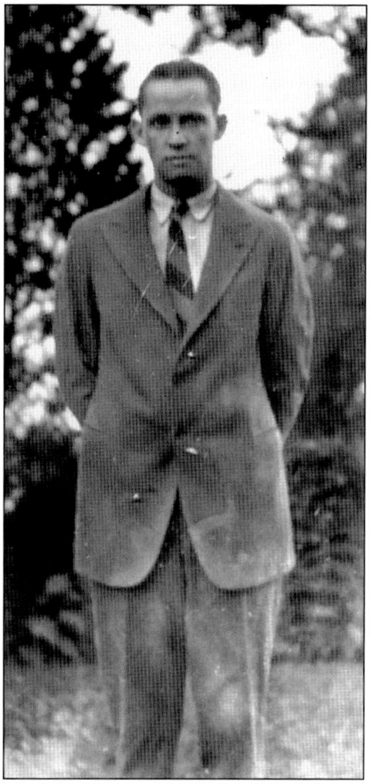

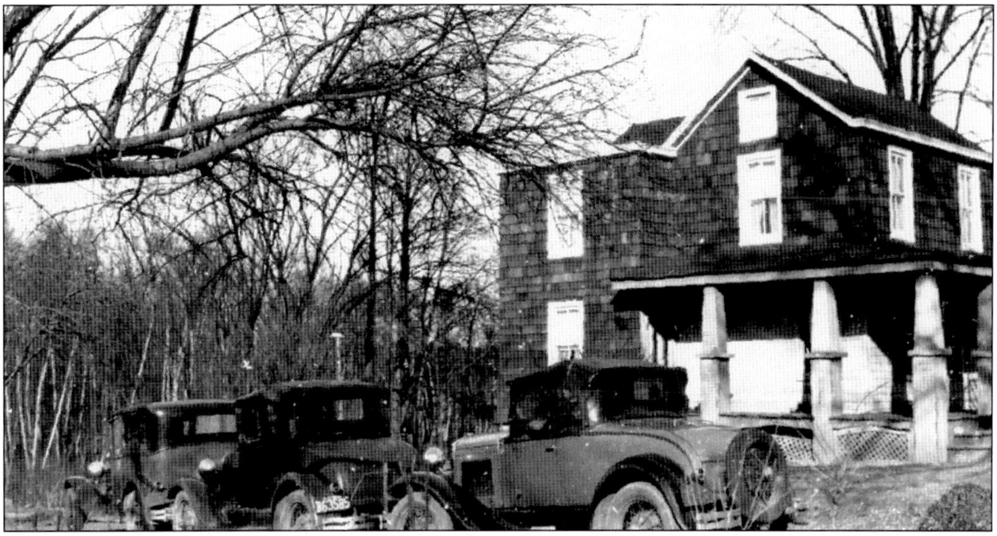

Seen is the Koopman-VanderEl house on John Dow Avenue in the 1920s.

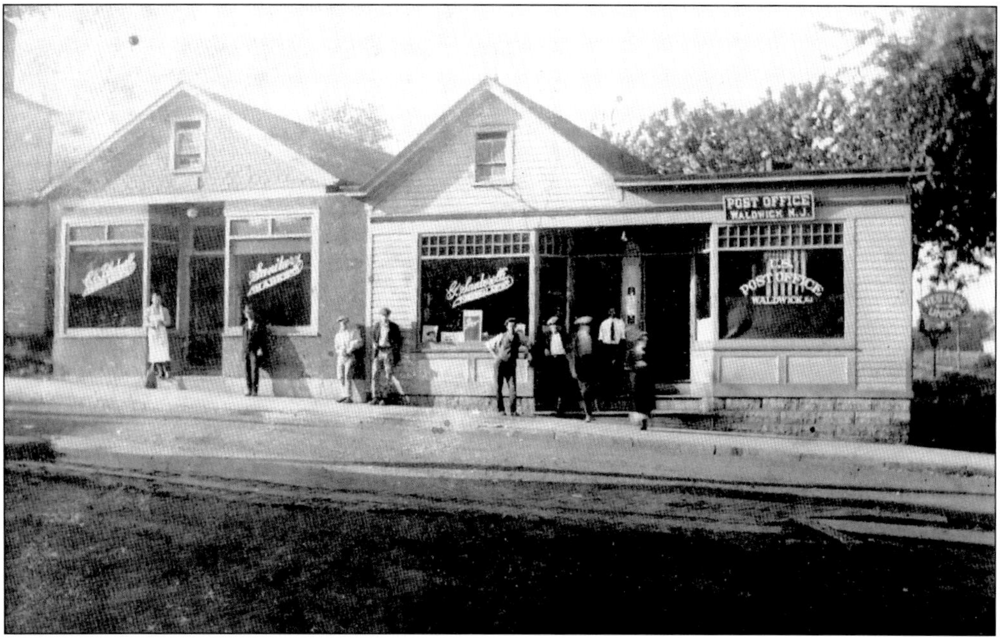

Small stores line the south side of West Prospect Street in the early 1920s. Seen here are, from left to right, the C. Blackwell Sanitary Market, the G. Santoreli Barbershop, and the post office.

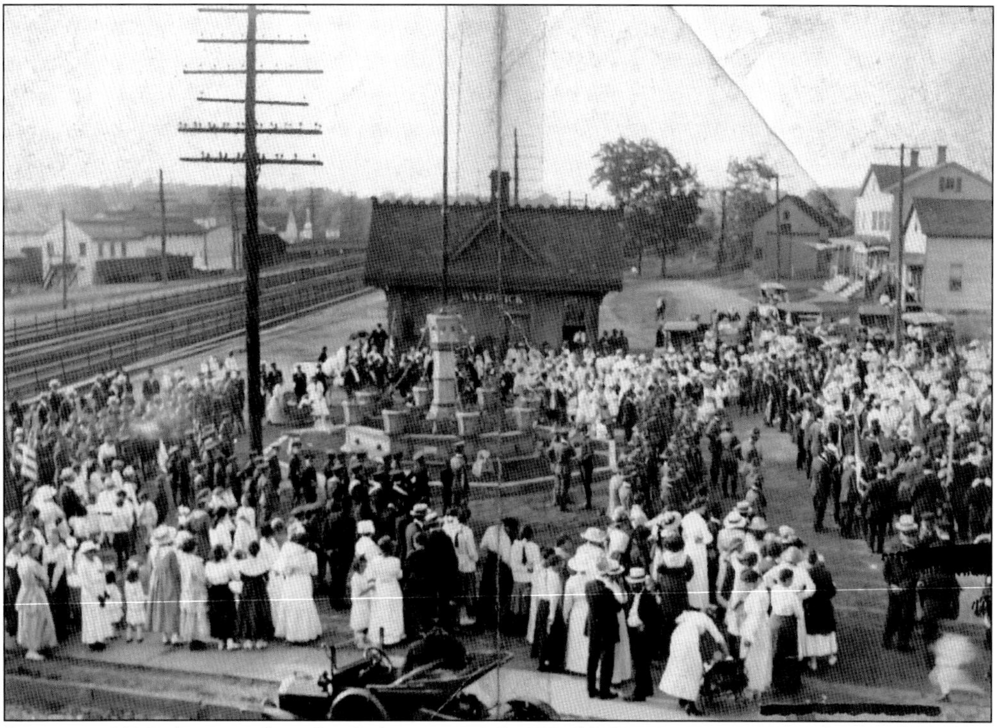

Seen in a 1925 photograph is the dedication of the World War I monument at the train station.

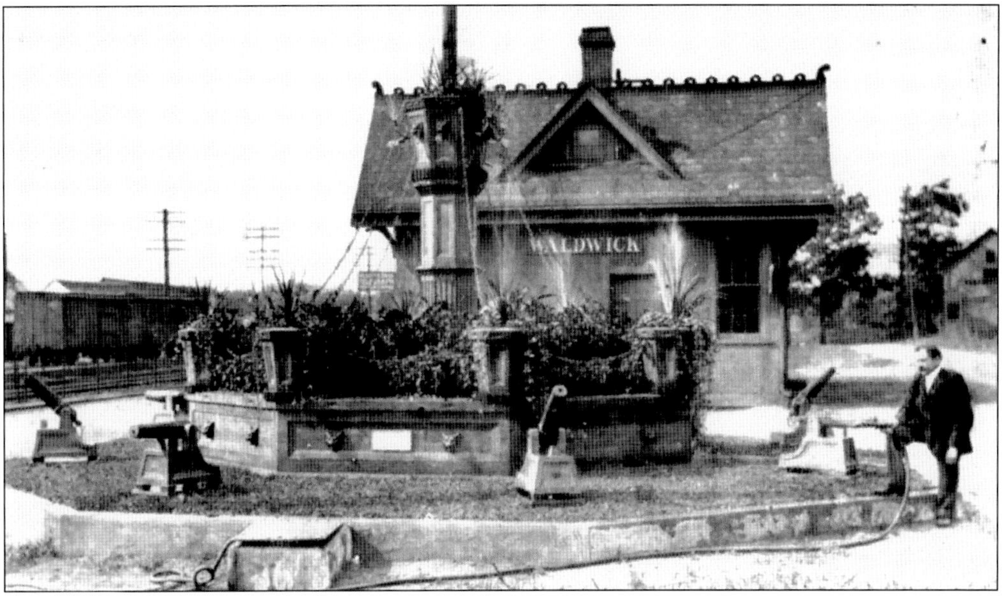

G. Santoreli waters the decorative plants at the World War I monument.

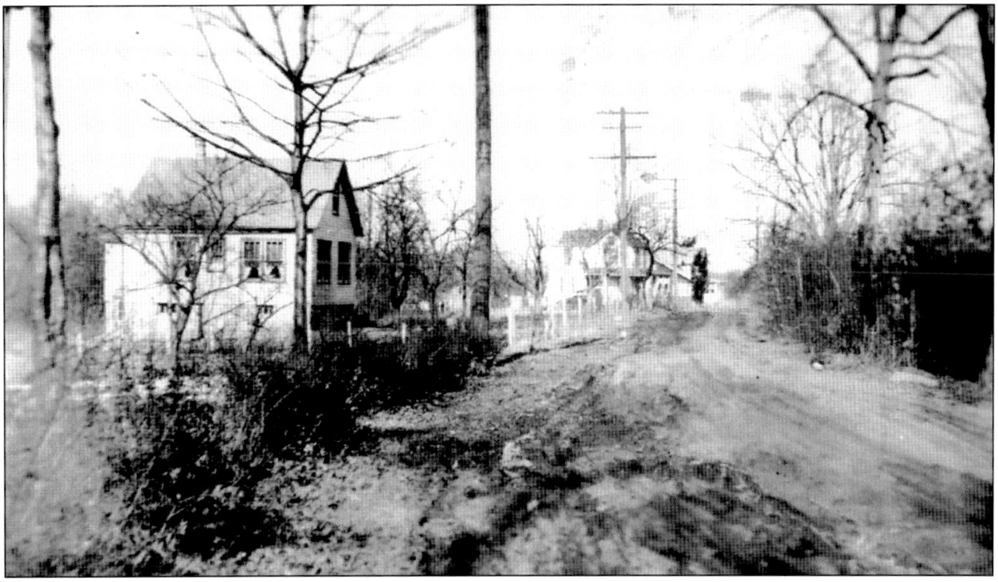

This view was taken near the intersection of John Dow Avenue and Crescent Avenue in the 1920s.

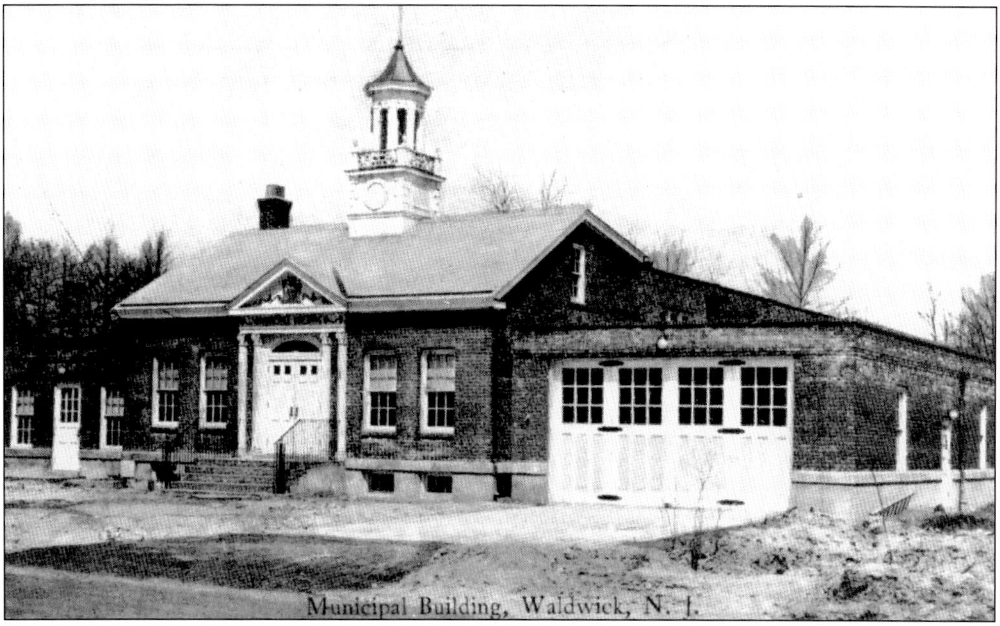

The municipal building, on East Prospect Street, is seen soon after completion in 1927.

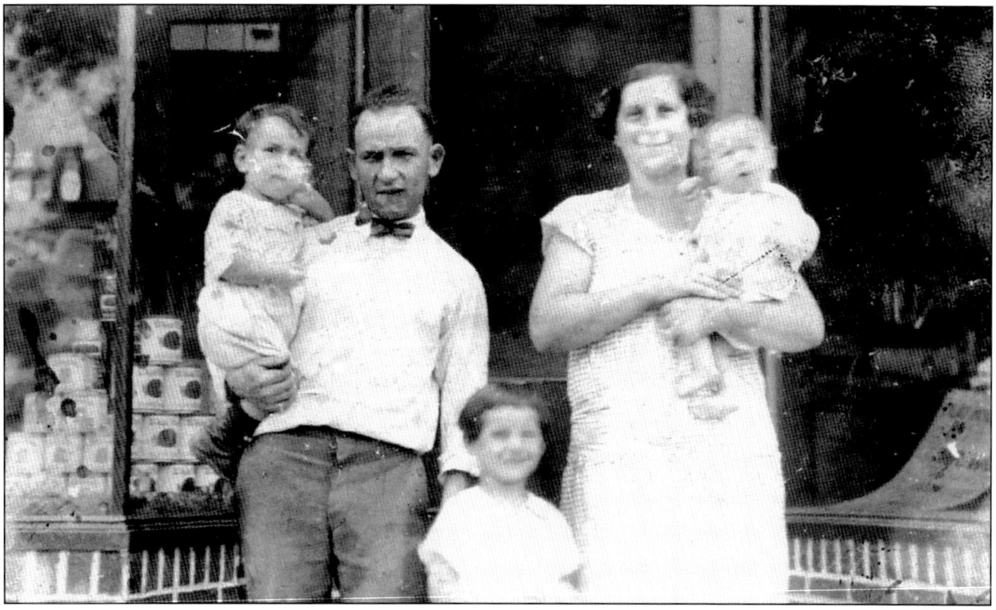

The Amster family poses in front of their new grocery store in the Amster building in 1927. From left to right are Daniel, Saul, Ethel, and Sadie (holding Ruth). They originally had their business in the Dieckman building down the block. Daniel became a local lawyer and served on the borough council. Ruth started her own local newspaper, the *Bergen Herald,* in the late 1940s. It ran until 1972. The Prospect Tavern is still run by the Amster family today.

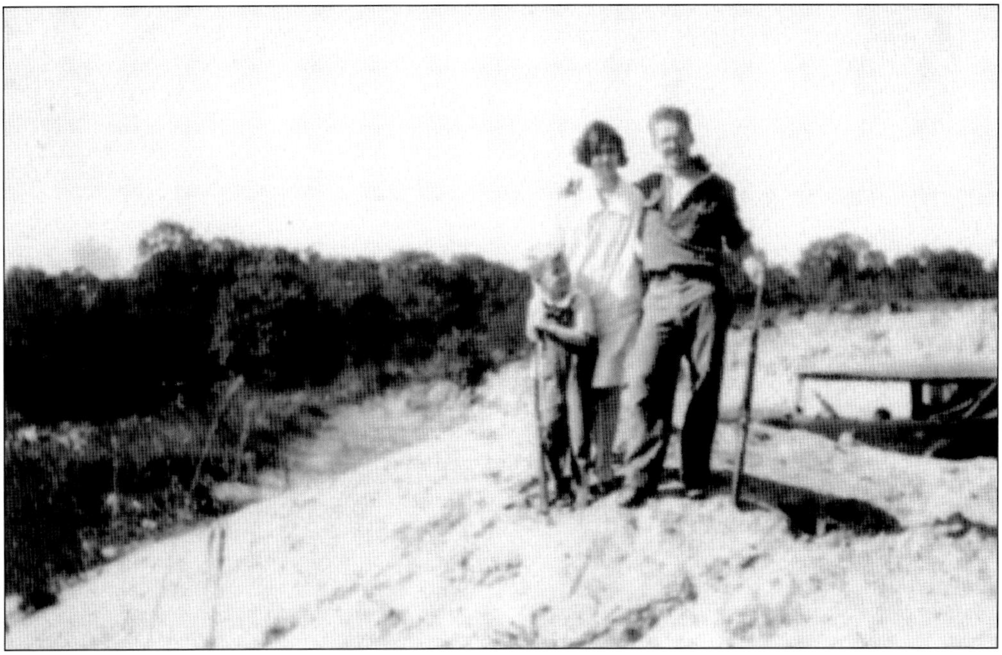

Sandpits were found along Wyckoff Avenue at the old Smith farm. Members of the Koeplinger family, who lived nearby, are seen target shooting during October 1928. They are John, Anna, and son Bobby. Later, during World War II, this location was used as an antiaircraft battery known as Camp Smith. It eventually became the high school baseball field. The Waldwick High School itself has a politically correct version of this photograph—minus the guns—in a permanent historical display near the lobby.

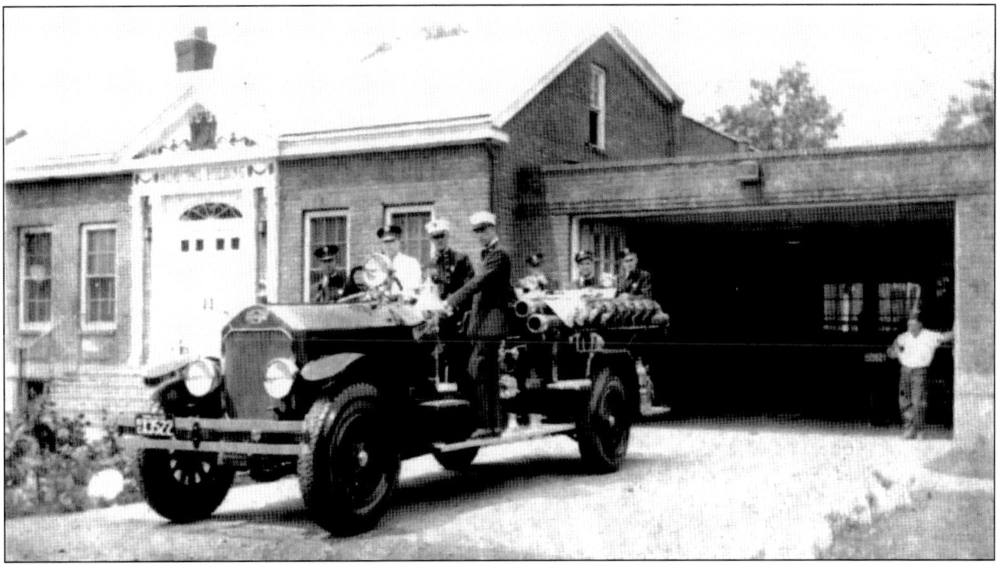

The new American LaFrance fire engine was purchased in September 1928 for $13,200. The town had also bought a GMC pumper in February 1925. Several major fires likely led to the purchase of these motorized pieces of apparatus (all previous equipment was horse-drawn), including the fire at the Captain Frost mansion (on Crescent Avenue), which burned on January 13, 1927.

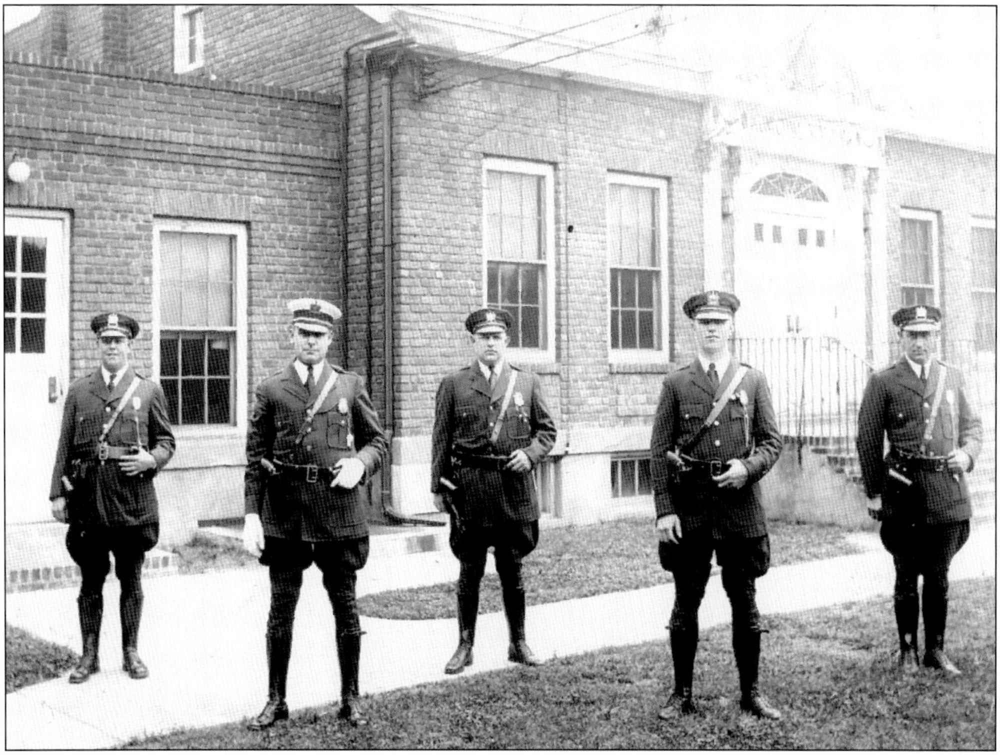

The town marshals are seen in this 1929 photograph. They are, from left to right, Jack Demarest, Eddie Gill (the chief), Melvin Perry, Neil Vriesma, and Blauvelt Ackerman.

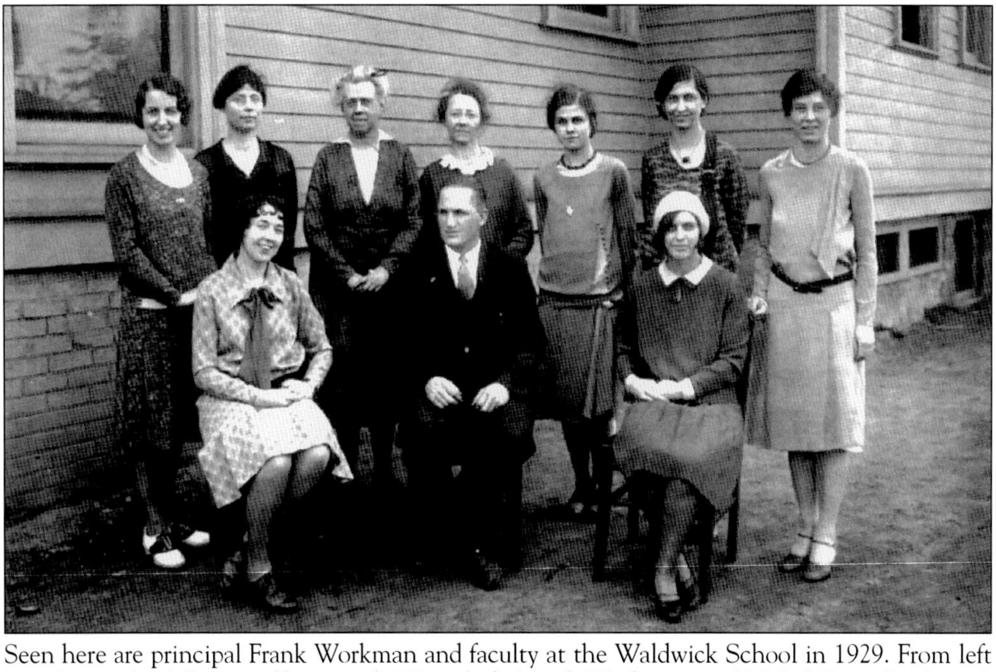

Seen here are principal Frank Workman and faculty at the Waldwick School in 1929. From left to right are the following: (front row) ? Hinschuh, Frank Workman, and Mabel King; (back row) ? Hopper, Jennie Osborn, ? Blaney, Julia A. Traphagen, Laura Hinaman, ? Workman, and ? May.

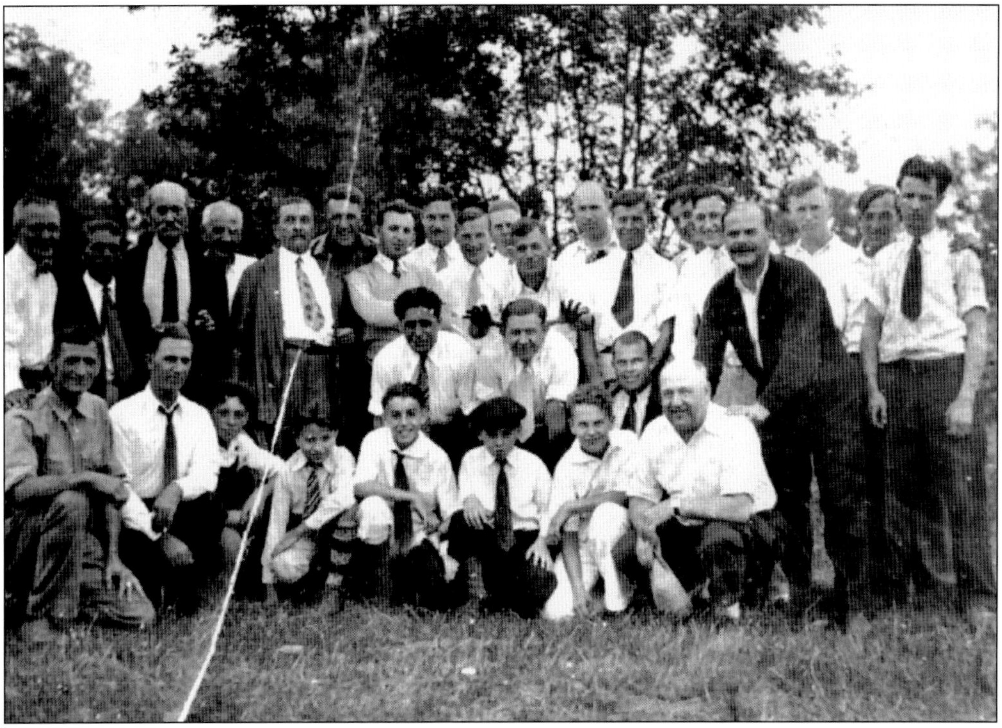

A gun club was located near Wilda Lane in the 1930s. Seen here are, from left to right, the following: (front row) Paul Ritter, two unidentified people, William Webie's son, Jimmy Zaconne's son, two unidentified people, and Phil Werling; (middle row) Jimmy Zaconne, Jim Noonberg, and unidentified; (back row) William Webie, unidentified, Emil Hoffman, John Lemline, "Uncle" Dittrich, Marini Rheingold, two unidentified people, Jim Ritter, unidentified, Henry Van Hull, unidentified, Irv Cole, unidentified, Paul Ritter, Father John, Pete Closterman, Phil Ritter, and Ernie Werling.

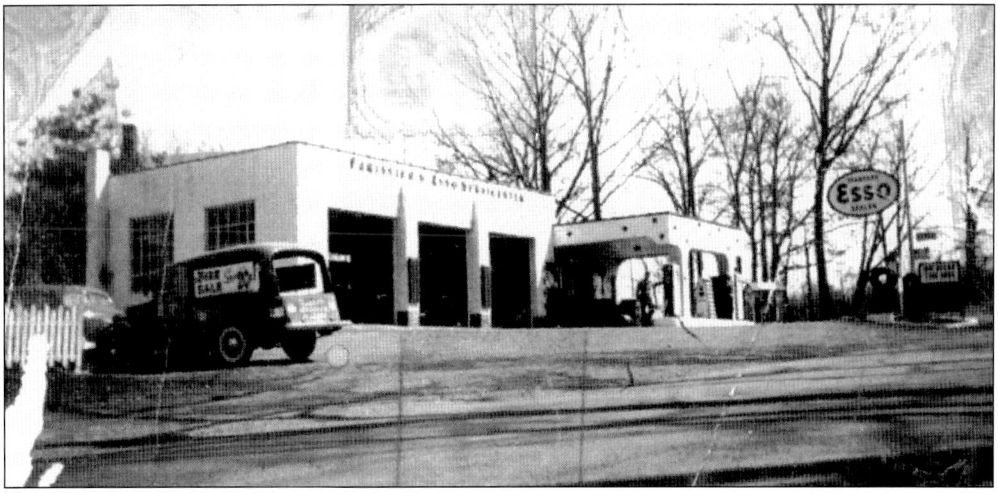

Seen is the Farissier Esso station, at Crescent Avenue and John Dow Avenue. Maurice Farissier and his wife moved to Waldwick in 1926. He did mechanical work out of a rented garage until he had his house moved back and this station built in 1930. His son took over the business, later selling it to Ralph Ten Eyck Sr. in 1974. Ralph Ten Eyck Jr. runs the station today.

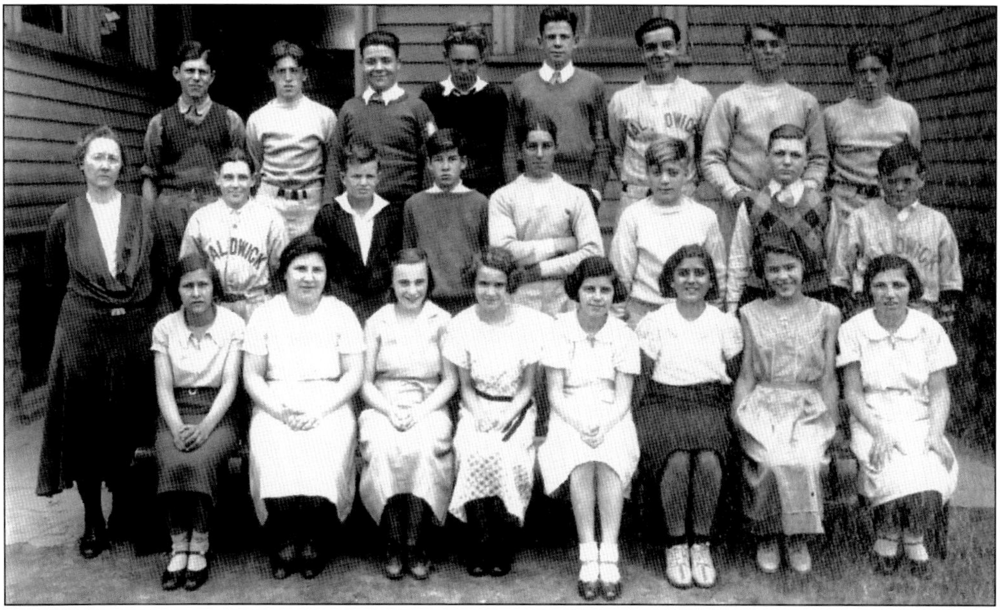

Julia A. Traphagen's Class of 1933 is seen at the Waldwick School. In the back row, second from the left, is Dale Holley. His twin brother, Frank, is the sixth from the left in that row. While in class one day, Frank Holley put a garden snake in a pencil box next to the window. The snake's head would poke out of the box and look around to the delight of the children. When Traphagen approached the box, the snake quickly withdrew. Both Dale and Frank were avid baseball players.

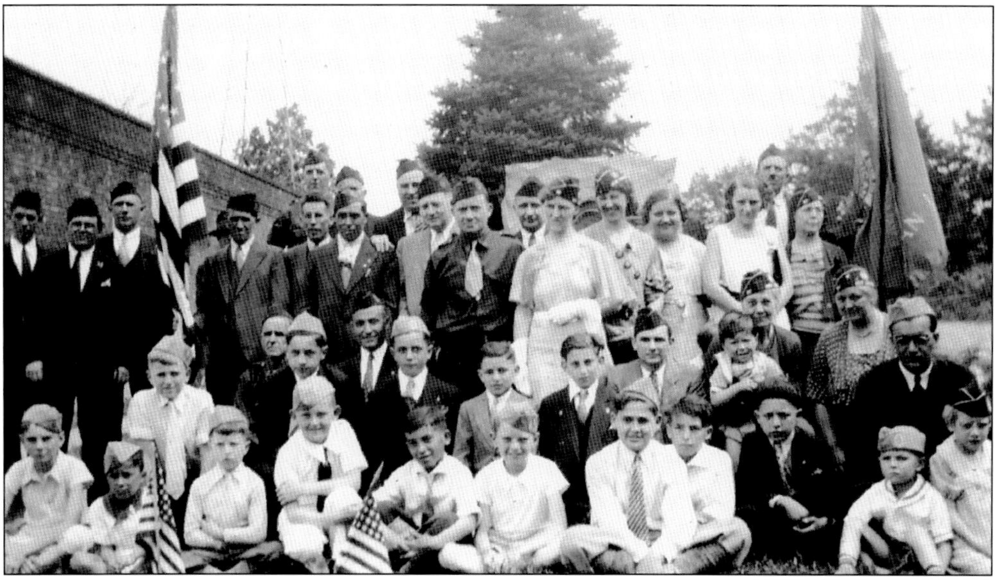

Pictured in front of the municipal building's Victory Memorial on Memorial Day 1935 are, from left to right, the following: (front row) Joe Dockray, William Hewson, Raymond DeYoung, ? May, unidentified, Dominic LaPorta, two unidentified people, and ? Jean; (back row) two unidentified people, John Pick, three unidentified people, Ray DeYoung, unidentified, Phil Wagner, Lyndon Peterson, James McGovern, Harold Lampe, Rita DeYoung, Hazel Lampe, ? McGovern, ? Dockay, and Grace Mott. All of the others are unidentified.

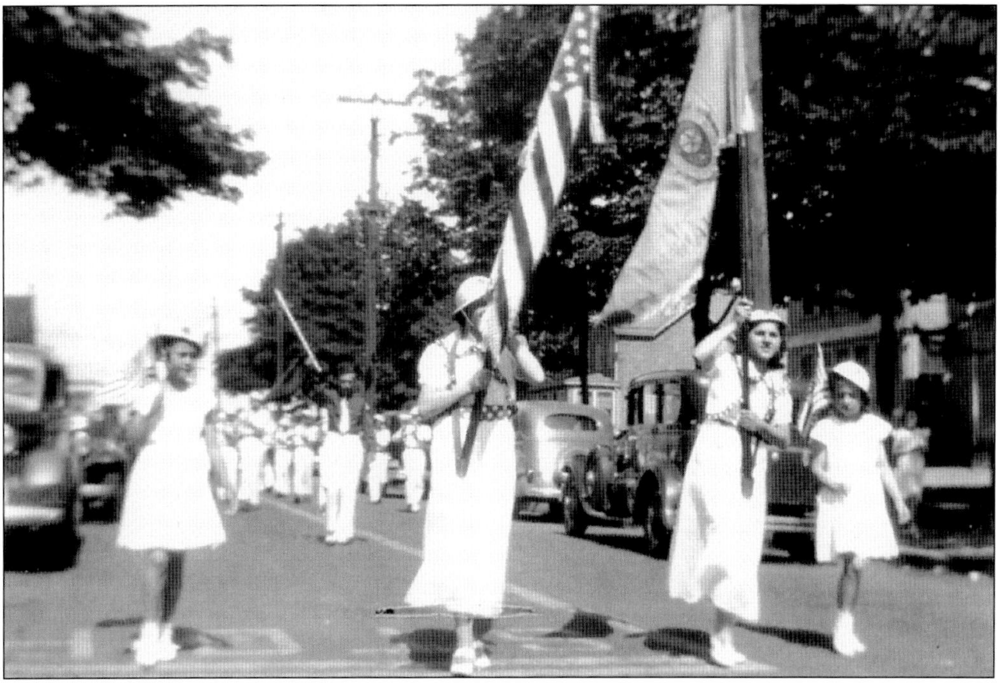

The American Legion's Ladies Auxiliary appeared in the 1935 Memorial Day parade. Leading the group are Doris Wagner and her friend Nellie.

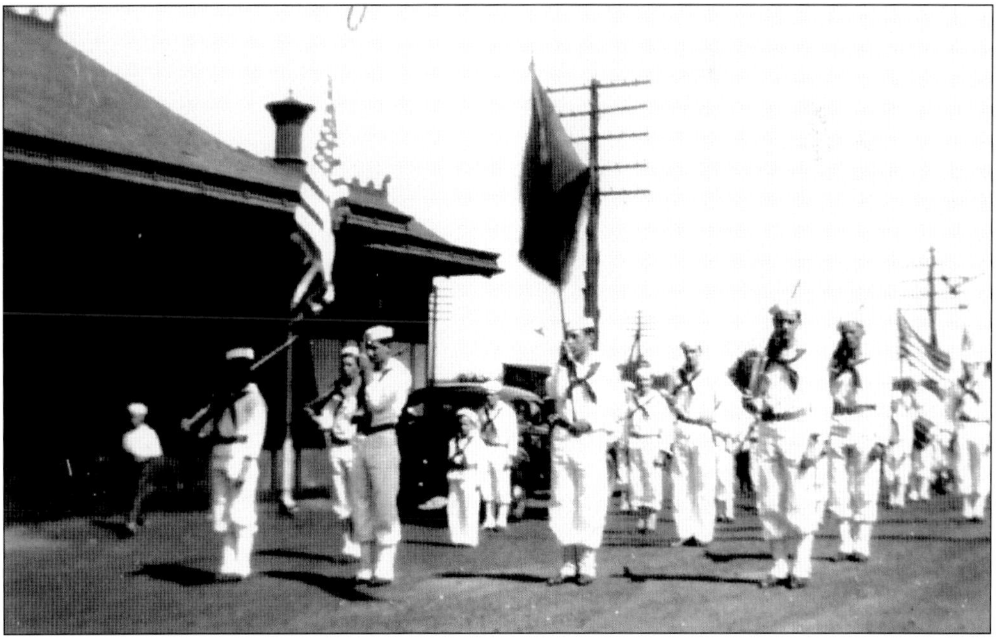

A local fife and drum corps, the Cadets, is seen in the 1936 Memorial Day parade. This photograph was taken on Hewson Avenue next to the railroad station.

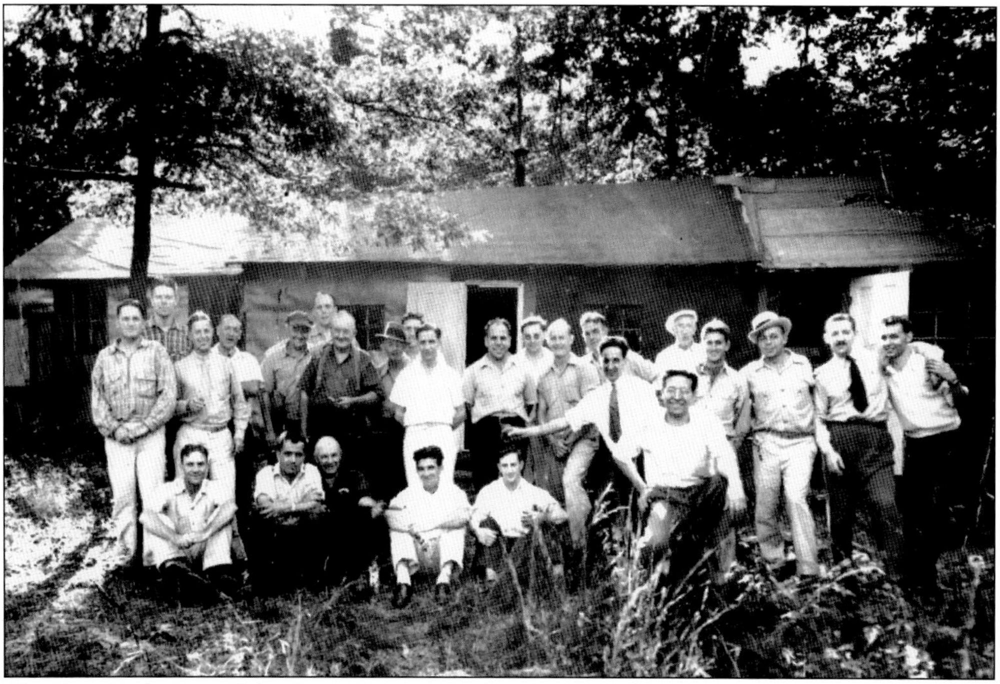

The Deer Park Gun Club of upstate New York was acquired by several local sportsmen in the 1920s. Included in this mid-1930s photograph are Frank Workman, Hank Spies, Bill Cutler, Roy Columbo, Joe Frier, Mel Perry, and Julio Costello.

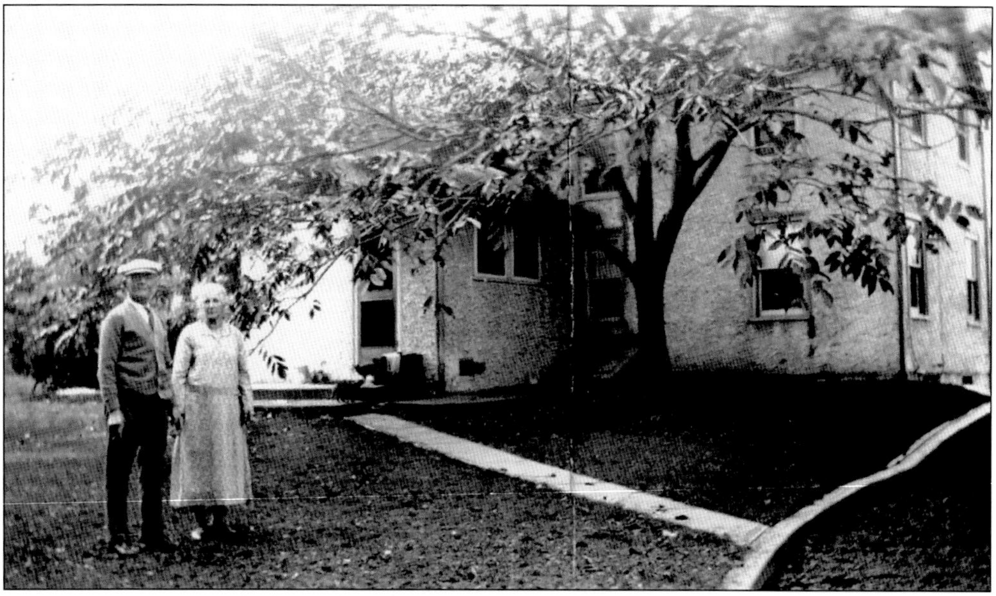

In this 1930s view, Nicholas and Margaret Van Hull are standing in their backyard at 29 John Dow Avenue. They immigrated from Holland in the 1880s and had two boys, John and Henry.

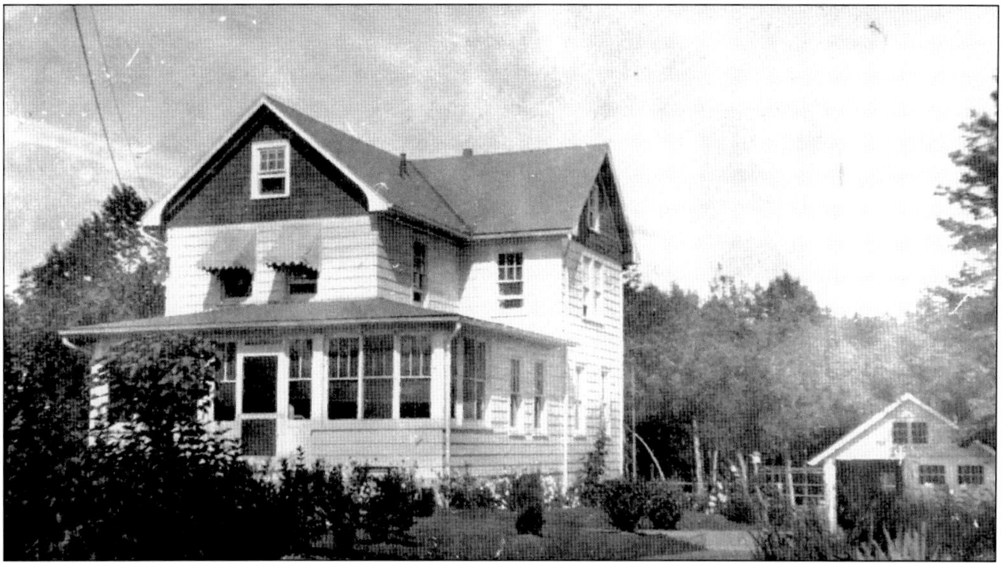

The Henry Van Hull house, at 30 John Dow Avenue, is seen here. Henry was a councilman in the 1930s. He and his wife had two children, Madeline and Katherine. Madeline and her husband, Harold, built their own home at 34 John Dow Avenue.

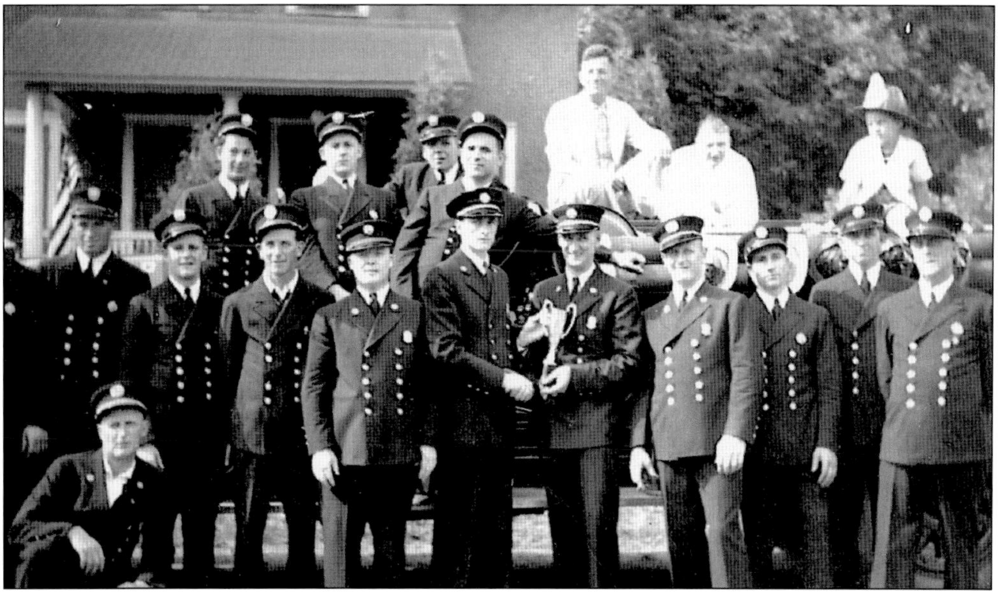

Councilman Henry Hull is seen sitting atop a fire department engine in this 1930s photograph.

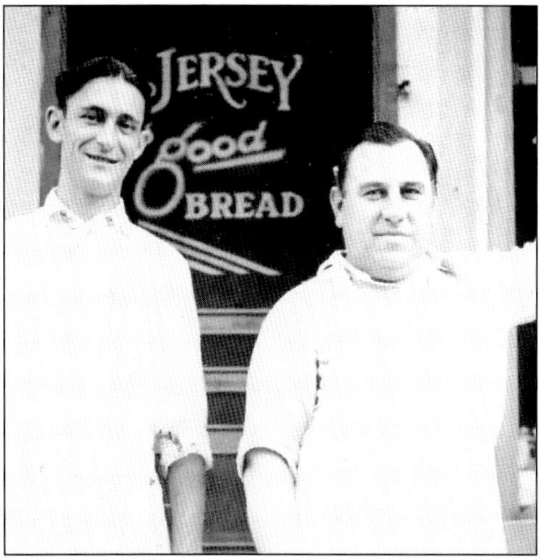

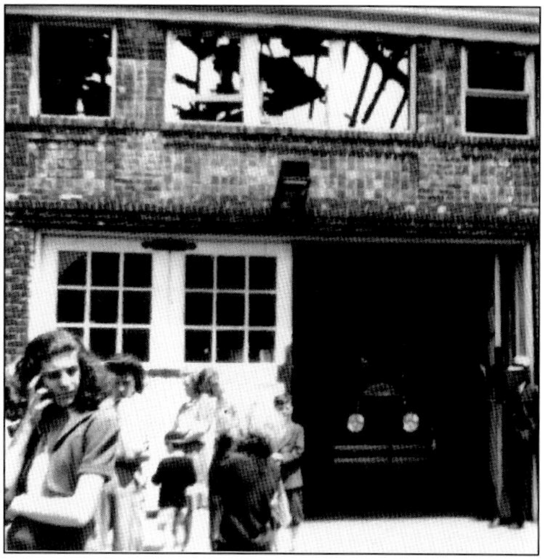

Left: Tony Riccardi (left) and Phil Wagner are seen standing in front of Wagner's Waldwick Market on West Prospect Street in this 1930s photograph. Wagner operated the store from 1924 to 1942. *Right:* The municipal building expanded to include a full second floor a few years after its initial construction. This photograph by Joseph Johler shows the aftermath of a fire on the second floor of the firehouse in the 1930s.

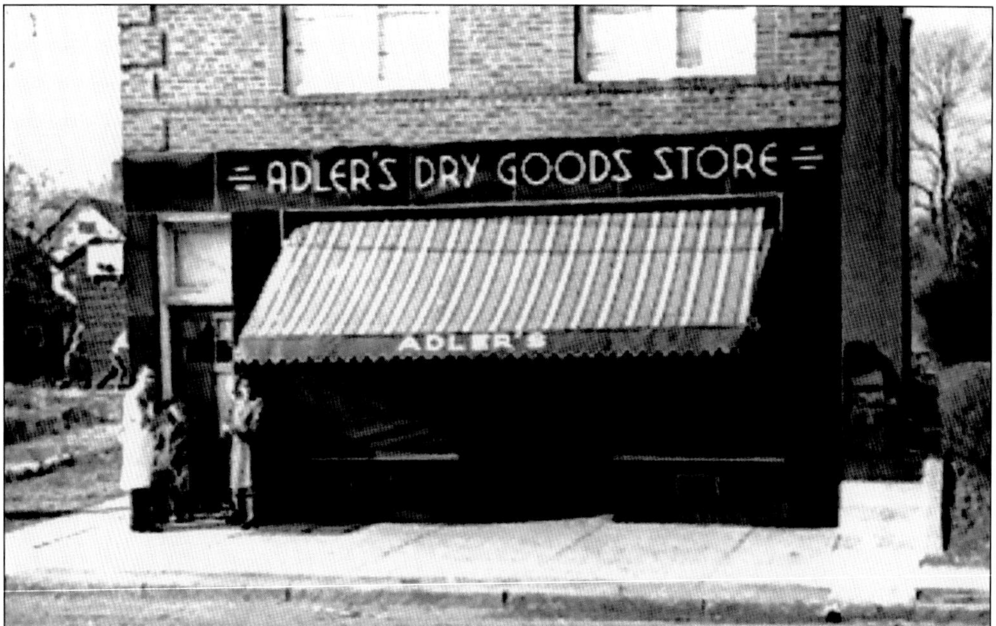

Aaron Adler and daughter Ruth pose in front of Adler's store on West Prospect Street. His first location was at Dieckman's store in 1928. This new store was built in 1939 at 13 West Prospect Street.

Andrew Agugliaro (left) and John Riccardi sit on their 1939 Harley-Davidson motorcycles at Riccardi's parents' house on Zazzetti Street.

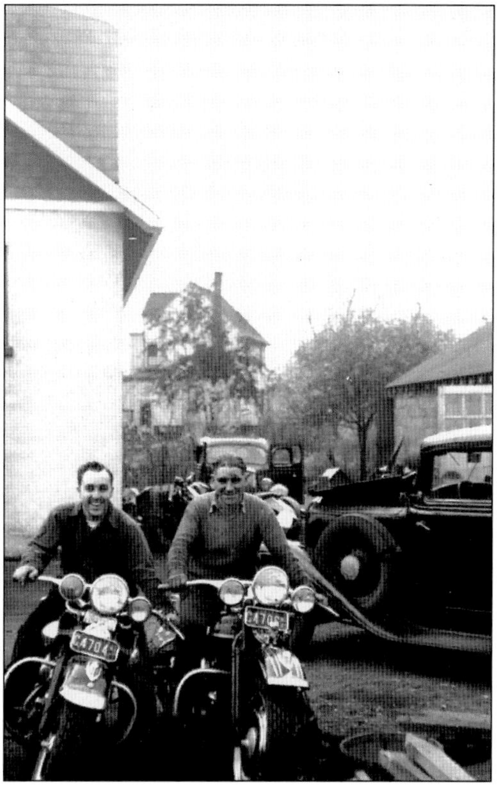

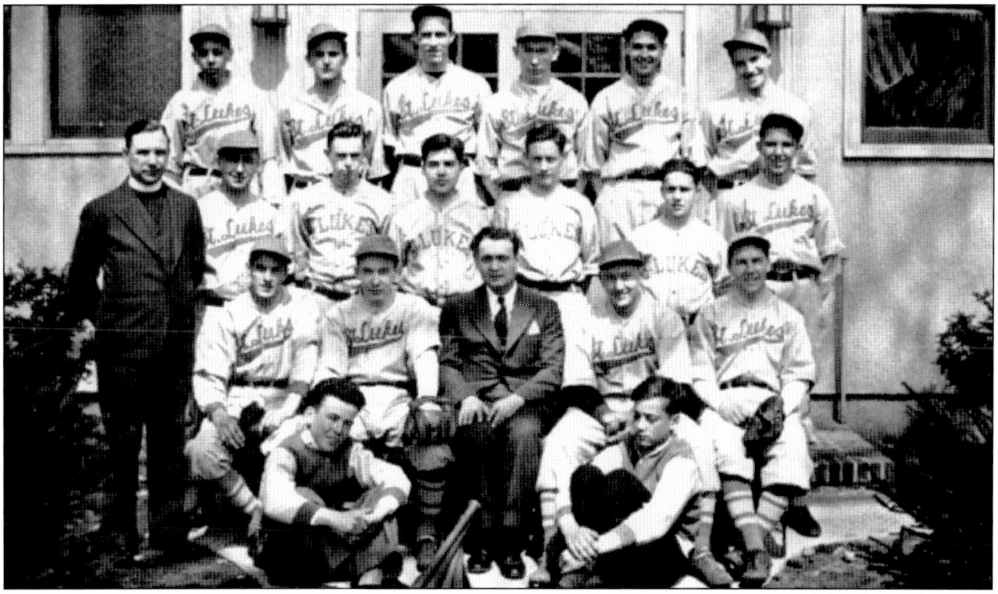

The 1939 St. Luke's baseball team had many members from Waldwick. Pitcher Dominic LaPorta remembered many of his classmates traveling by trolley to school from the surrounding towns before 1929. The trolley used to run right behind his garage on Frederick Street and passed just behind St. Luke's School.

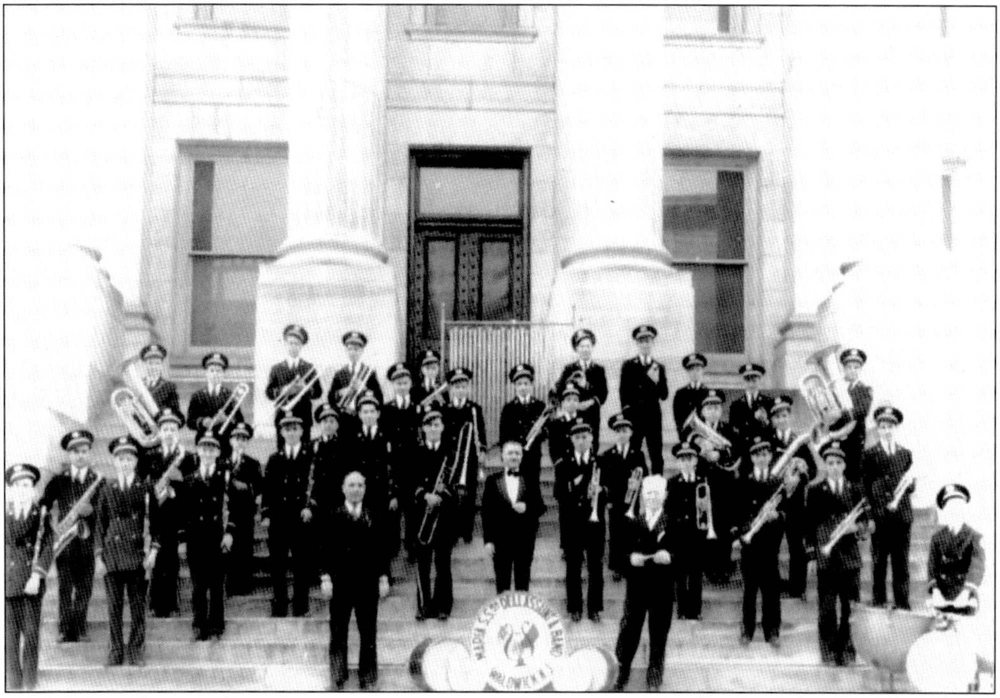

Pictured on the courthouse steps in Paterson, Prof. James Dittamo's MSA band was well known for playing at many area events, including the Italian festival held every August in Waldwick.

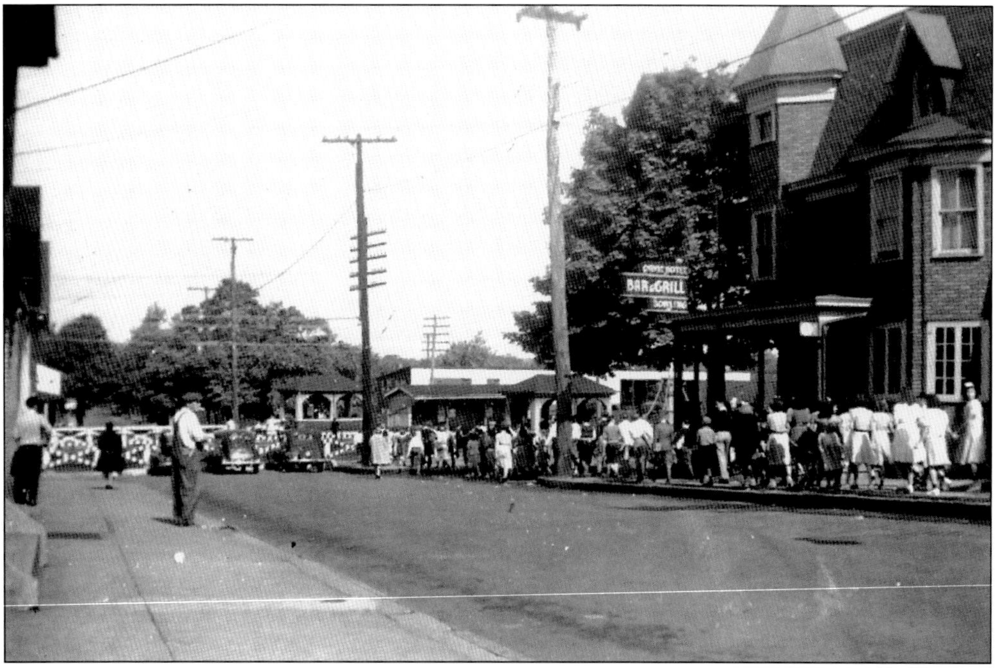

Students parade down Prospect Street from the old Waldwick School on Franklin Turnpike to the new Prospect Street School at Hopper Avenue. This event took place on June 3, 1940. The dedication of the school itself took place on June 5, 1940.

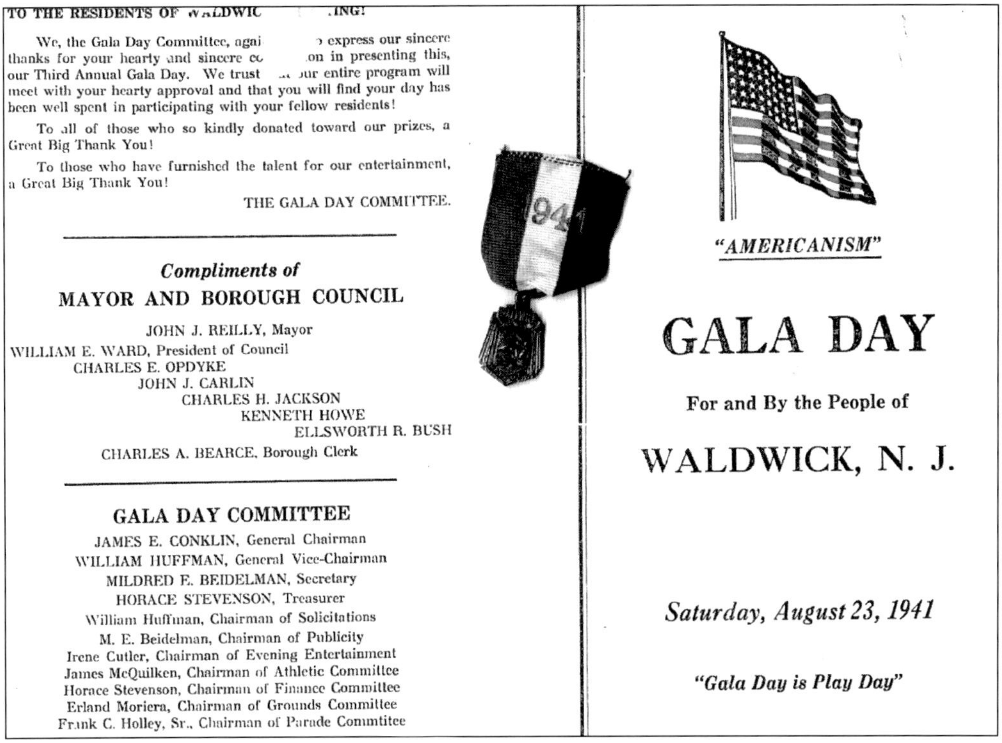

TO THE RESIDENTS OF W...LDWIC ...ING!

We, the Gala Day Committee, agai... ...express our sincere thanks for your hearty and sincere co... ...on in presenting this, our Third Annual Gala Day. We trust ... our entire program will meet with your hearty approval and that you will find your day has been well spent in participating with your fellow residents!

To all of those who so kindly donated toward our prizes, a Great Big Thank You!

To those who have furnished the talent for our entertainment, a Great Big Thank You!

THE GALA DAY COMMITTEE.

Compliments of

MAYOR AND BOROUGH COUNCIL

JOHN J. REILLY, Mayor
WILLIAM E. WARD, President of Council
CHARLES E. OPDYKE
JOHN J. CARLIN
CHARLES H. JACKSON
KENNETH HOWE
ELLSWORTH R. BUSH
CHARLES A. BEARCE, Borough Clerk

GALA DAY COMMITTEE

JAMES E. CONKLIN, General Chairman
WILLIAM HUFFMAN, General Vice-Chairman
MILDRED E. BEIDELMAN, Secretary
HORACE STEVENSON, Treasurer
William Huffman, Chairman of Solicitations
M. E. Beidelman, Chairman of Publicity
Irene Cutler, Chairman of Evening Entertainment
James McQuilken, Chairman of Athletic Committee
Horace Stevenson, Chairman of Finance Committee
Erland Moriera, Chairman of Grounds Committee
Frank C. Holley, Sr., Chairman of Parade Commtitee

1941

"AMERICANISM"

GALA DAY

For and By the People of

WALDWICK, N. J.

Saturday, August 23, 1941

"Gala Day is Play Day"

This program from the Waldwick Gala Days tells of the summer swim competitions and festivities held each summer from 1939 through the end of World War II. This ribbon was given as a prize in a swimming competition.

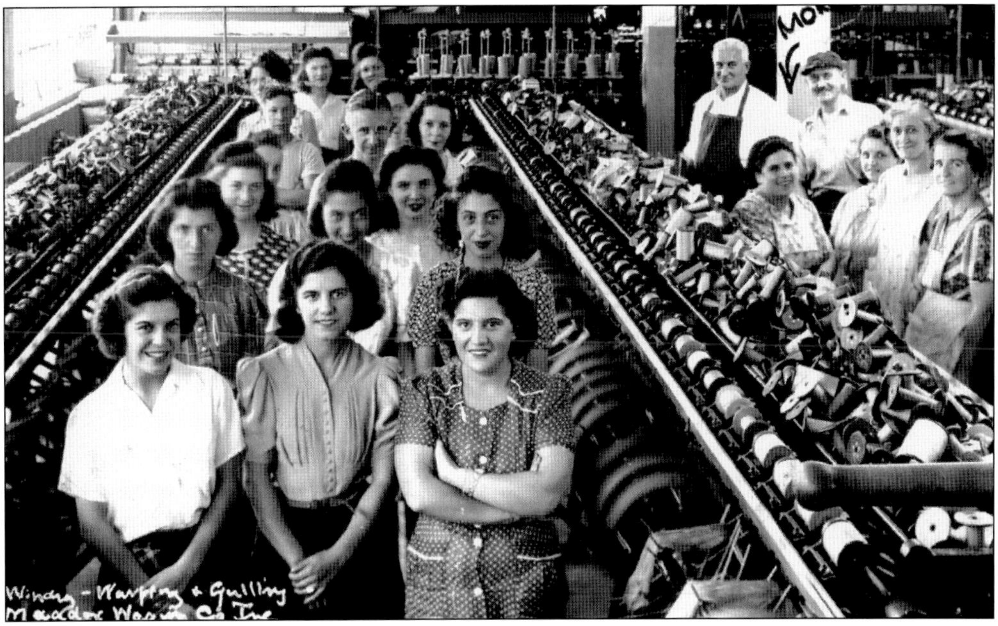

The Meadox Weaving Company was located in the old Post Silk Mill building at 60 West Prospect Street, as seen in this June 10, 1941 photograph. Meadox was several textile-related companies at this location after Post discontinued operations.

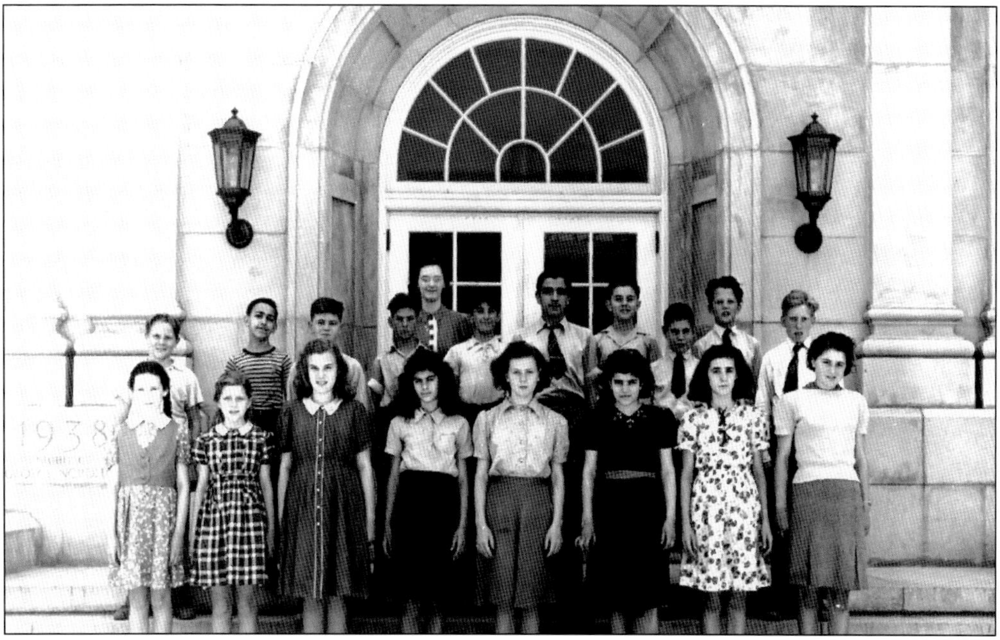

This is one of the first classes to occupy the Prospect Street School in 1941. Teacher Dorothy Dockray and her seventh-grade students stand on the steps of the new school. Although the new school originally had 10 classrooms, many additional classrooms had to be added due to the rapid growth in the student population.

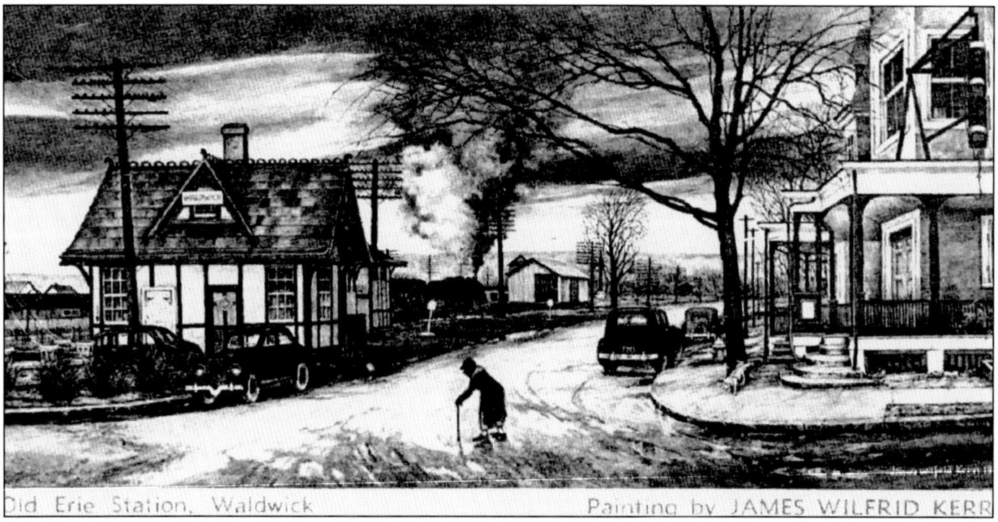

In a painting done by local artist James Kerr in 1943, Fannie Ryer crosses Hewson Avenue. Ryer grew up in Waldwick and was the daughter of slaves. She worked for the Bamper family, living in a small house on the property where the present-day Stop & Shop is located. In 1953, the town threw a 100th birthday party for her.

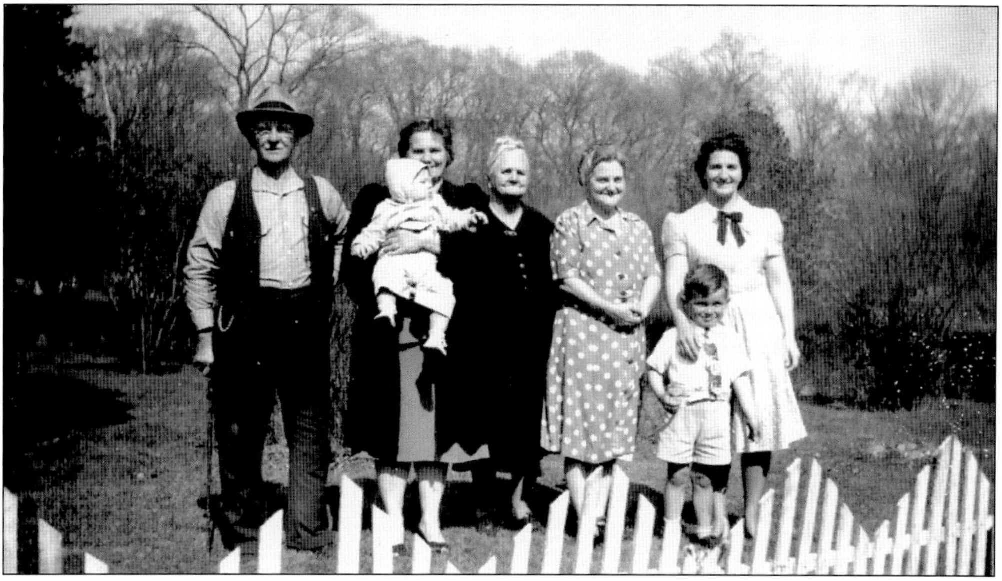

Members of the Morgan family pose in 1953. From left to right are George; Ruth Moore (née Morgan), holding her son; Mary, George's wife; Georgiana; Stella; and Ronny Moore.

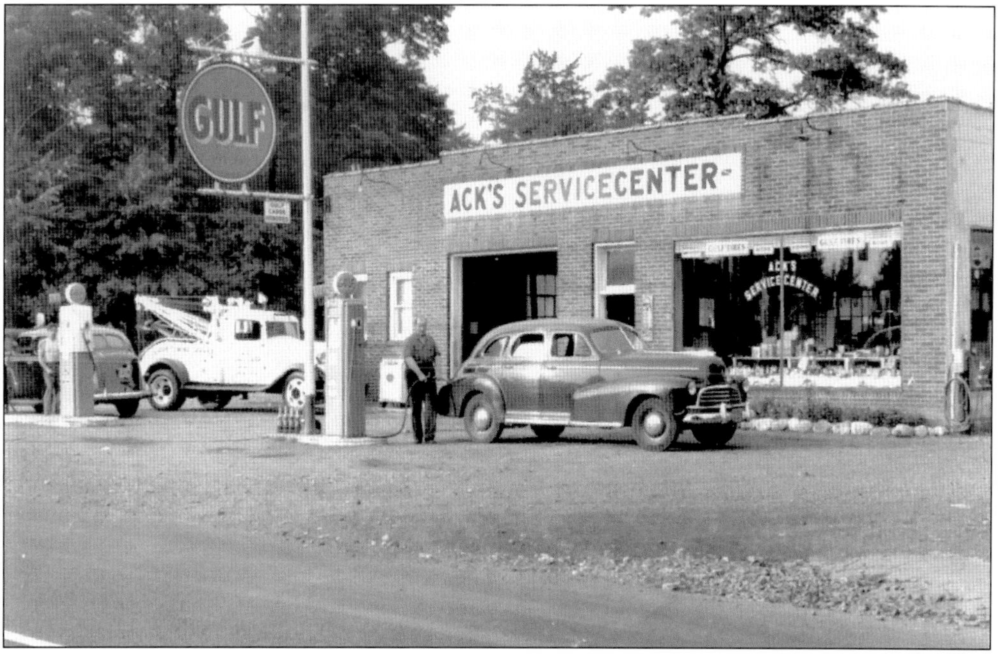

Ack's Service Center is seen in the mid-1940s, with owner Benjamin Morgan pumping Gulf gasoline. The station was built in the 1920s by Blauvelt Ackerman and Mel Perry as an Esso station on the southeast corner of East Prospect and Franklin Turnpike.

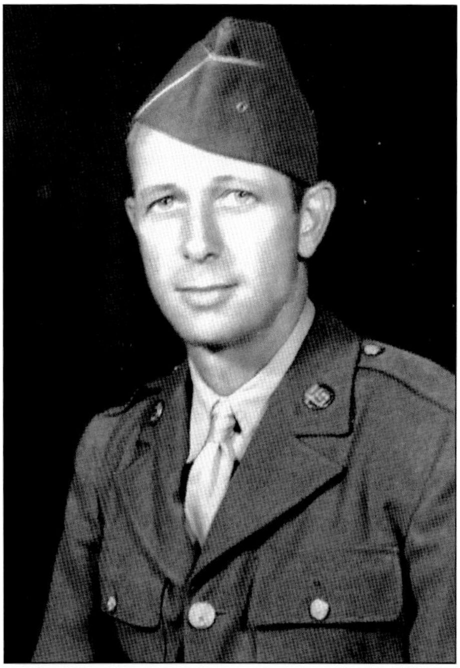

"Sonny" Harry Lockwood went off to fight in World War II and gave his life at a river crossing in Germany on April 20, 1945.

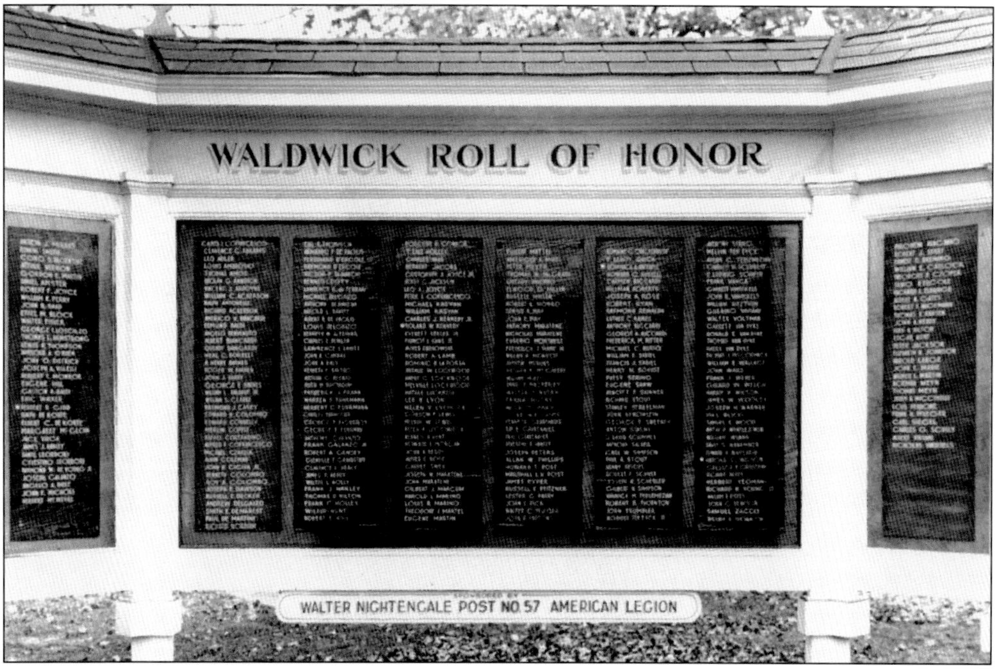

Several other men from Waldwick gave their lives for their country not only in World War II, but also in Korea and Vietnam. They are as follows: (World War II) Henry P. Wilson, Henry F. Schaefer, Roland W. Kennedy, Herbert D. Gibb, Dominick A. Raffaele, John Bender, Lee B. Lyon, Earl R. Thompson, and John A. Cambra; (the Korean War) John E. Phelan, Raymond A. Vernon, Bernard A. Chopek, Raymond A. Estes, and Robert O. Masterson; (Vietnam) Robert E. Viggiano. This honor roll was located on the northwest corner of Franklin Turnpike and West Prospect Street to recognize all World War II veterans.

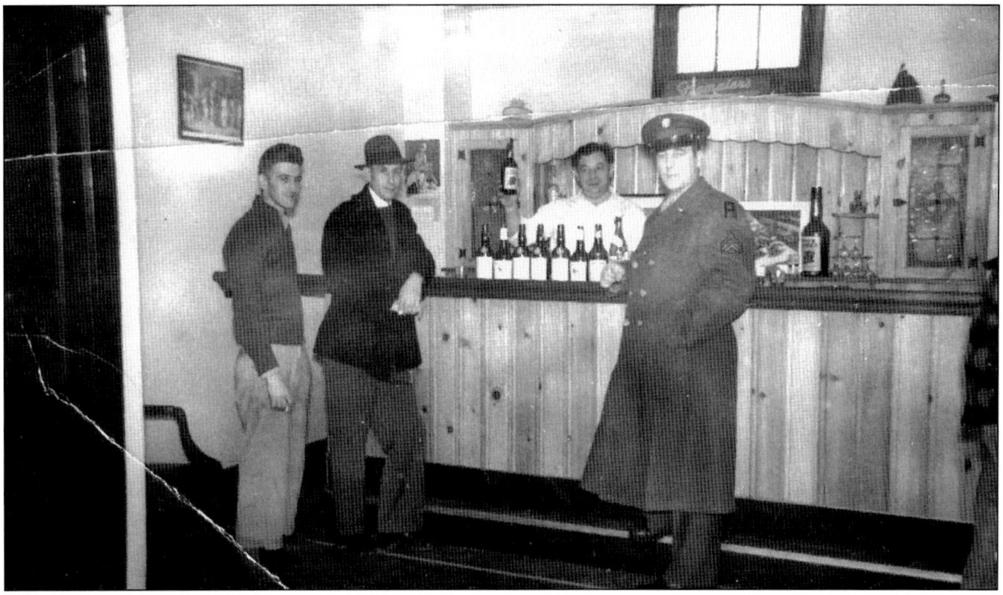

Seen is the interior of the Waldwick Fire Department's second floor on Prospect Street sometime in the late 1940s or early 1950s. Returning veterans also spent time at the American Legion, located on Franklin Turnpike. The two veterans' organizations alternate the sponsorship of the annual Memorial Day parade.

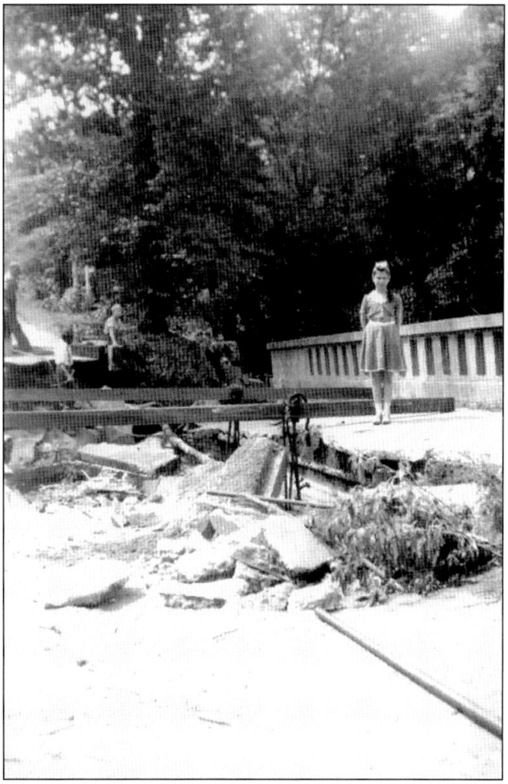

A major flood took place in August 1945. This photograph shows the bridge over the Ho-Ho-Kus Brook on Wyckoff Avenue. Edna Mae Wagner stands on the sidewalk.

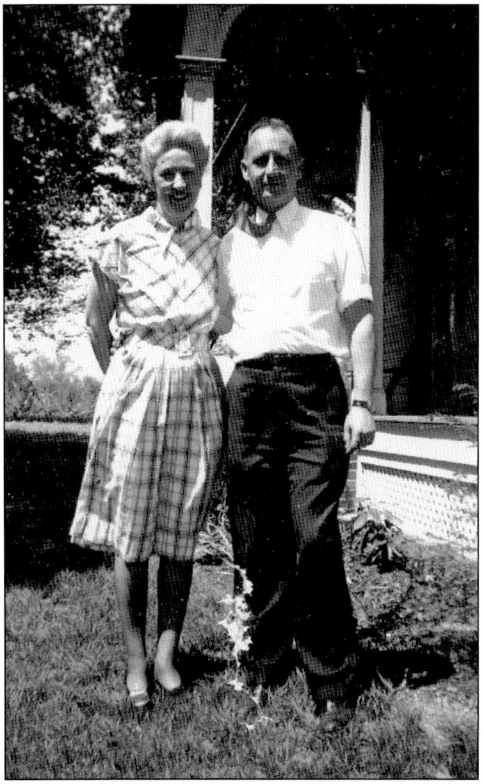

Hazel and Harold Lampe are seen in front of the old Ackerman house on Saddle River Road. This house was razed in 1960.

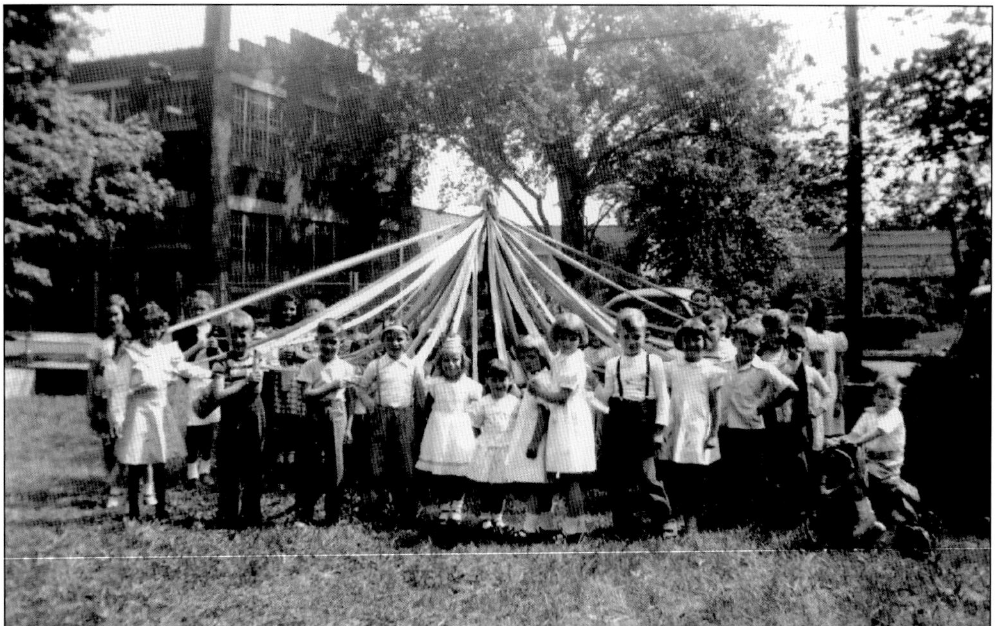

The May Day festival was held at the Reformed church on West Prospect Street. The Post Silk Mill is in the background. These May Day celebrations were held from the 1930s to the 1950s.

Fireman John Riccardi and his future wife, Jean Agugliaro, are seen in this view. Jean was a charter member of the Ladies Auxiliary.

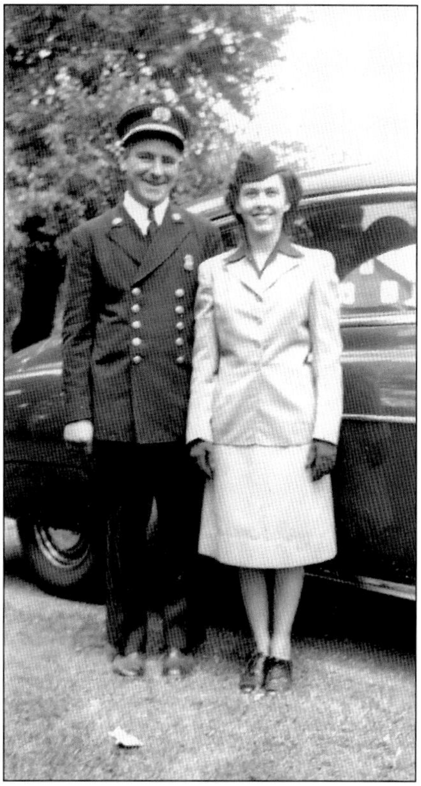

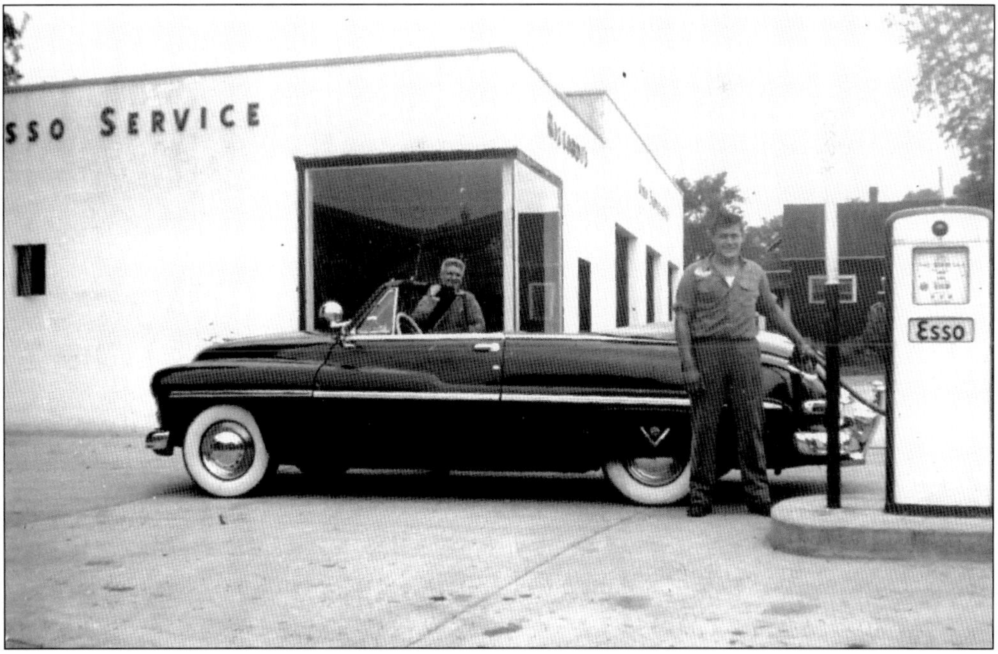

John Riccardi (left) is seen at his brand-new filling station on West Prospect Street and Wanamaker Avenue in 1951. Ralph Olivieri (right) worked with John for many years.

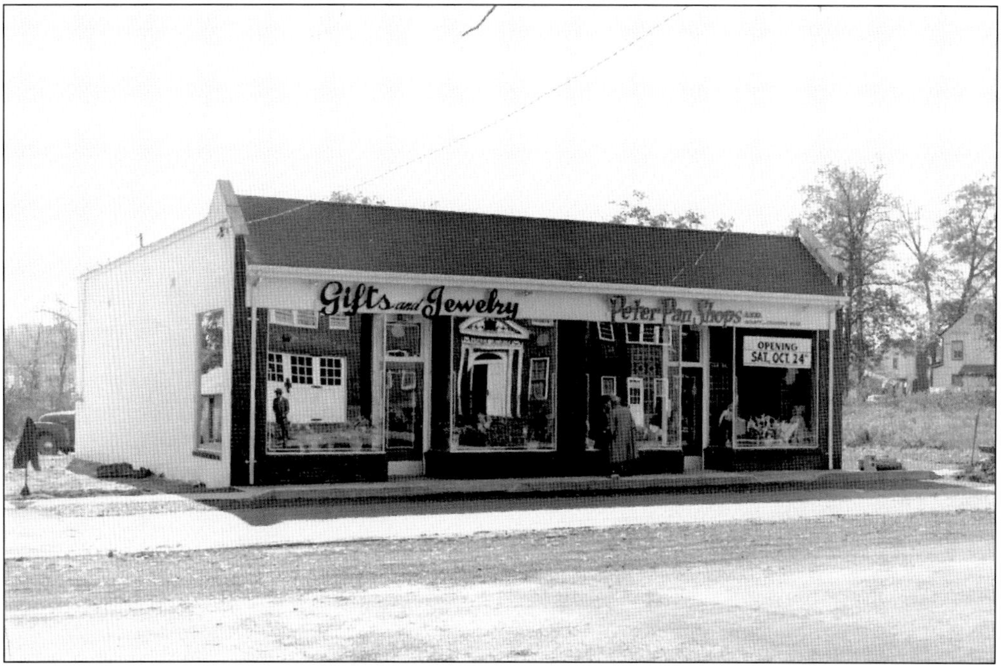

George Zumbano's Plaza jewelry store was built in 1952. Today, it is operated by his son James. Maratene's Liquors eventually moved into the space previously occupied by the Peter Pan Shop.

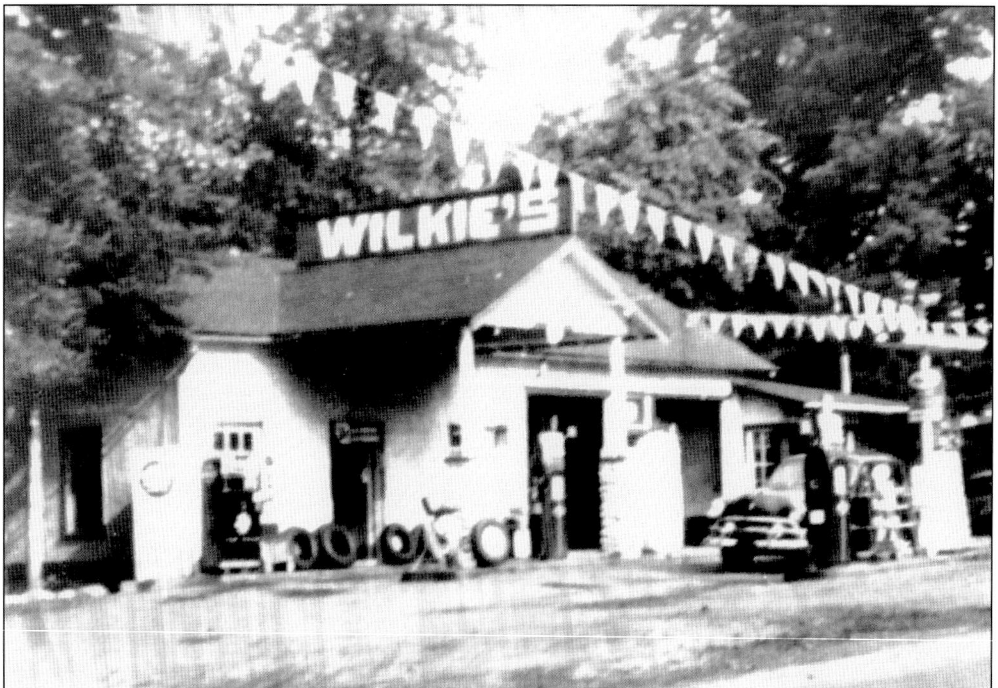

Seen in this 1953 photograph is Wilke's, on Franklin Turnpike at the Allendale border. In 1973, the building became a Huff Muffler chain store, later becoming Adamo's Mobil station.

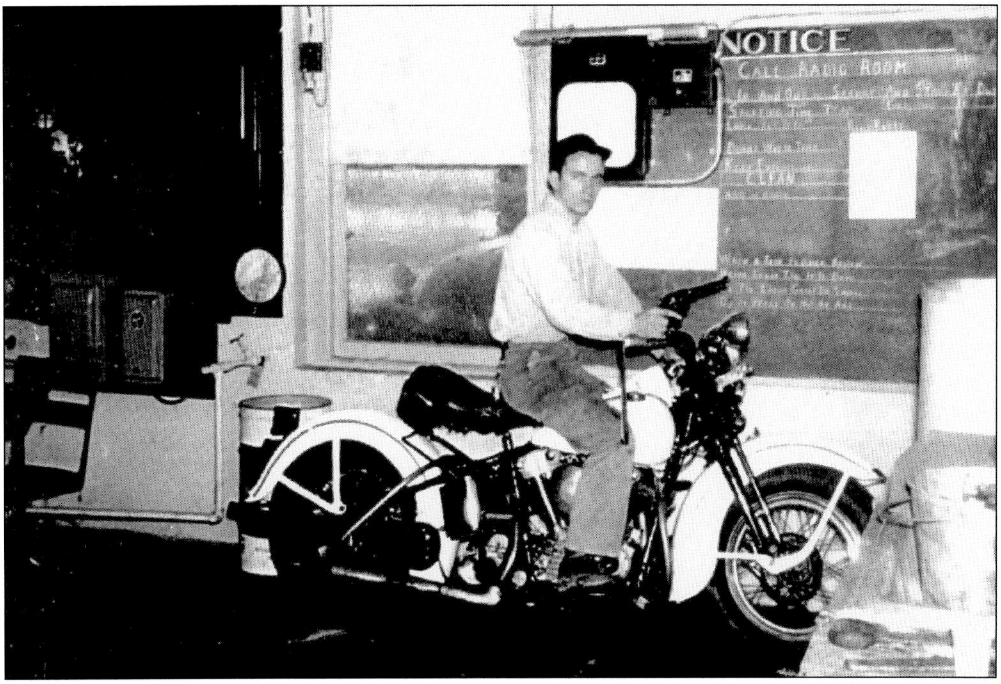

Ralph "Pug" Ten Eyck Sr. is seen at the Waldwick Water Works on his motorcycle in 1953. He served as a special police officer and worked for the department of public works for 40 years.

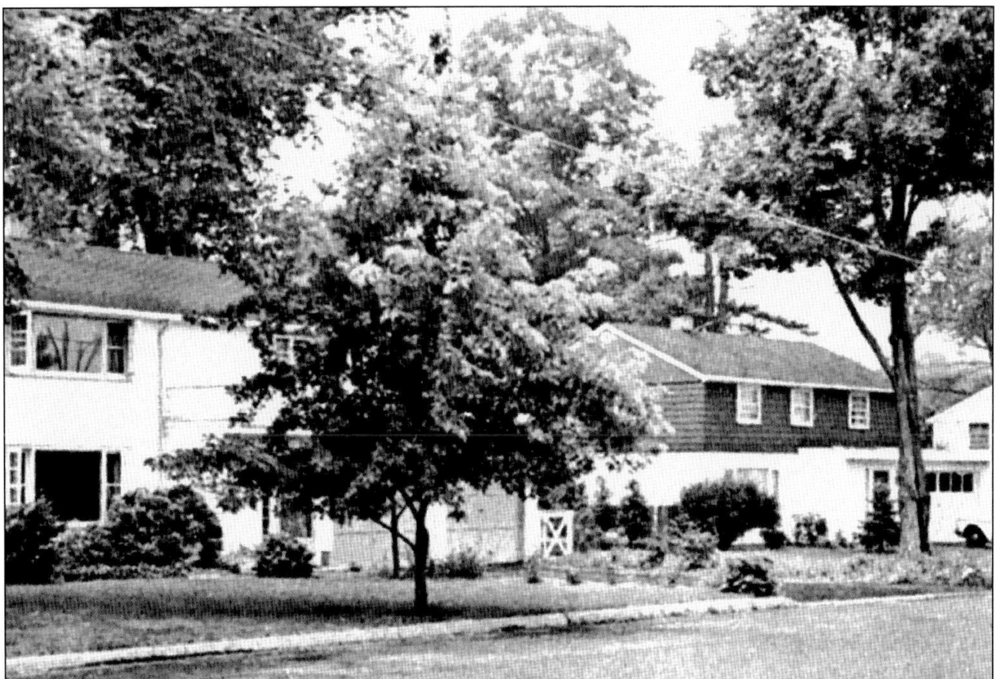

Zamore tract homes spread throughout Waldwick in the late 1940s into the early 1950s. They are very prevalent on the east side of Route 17. They were featured in an article in the *Saturday Evening Post*.

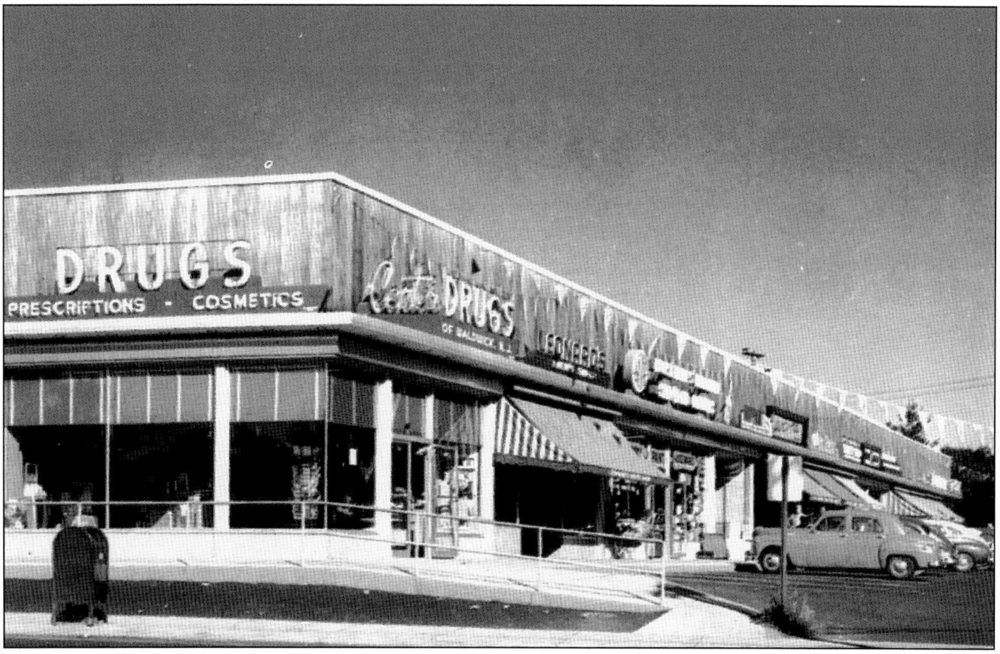

The Golden Block, pictured here, replaced the Bamper house, which fell victim to an arsonist on May 4, 1953. The spectacular blaze even singed a fire engine parked nearby. A few of the original tenants of this shopping center still remain, including the Waldwick Delicatessen and the Cathay Chinese restaurant.

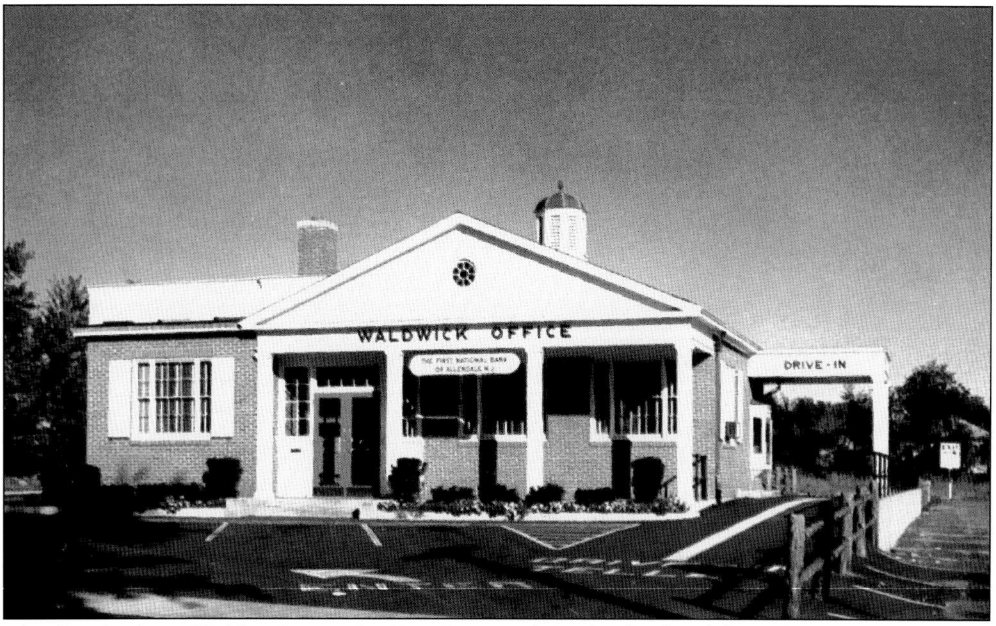

The first bank in Waldwick was the First National Bank of Allendale and was located at the northeast corner of Walter Hammond Place and Wyckoff Avenue. Opening on May 15, 1954, it changed hands several times over the succeeding years and became Citizen's First, National Westminster, and finally Fleet Bank, as it is today.

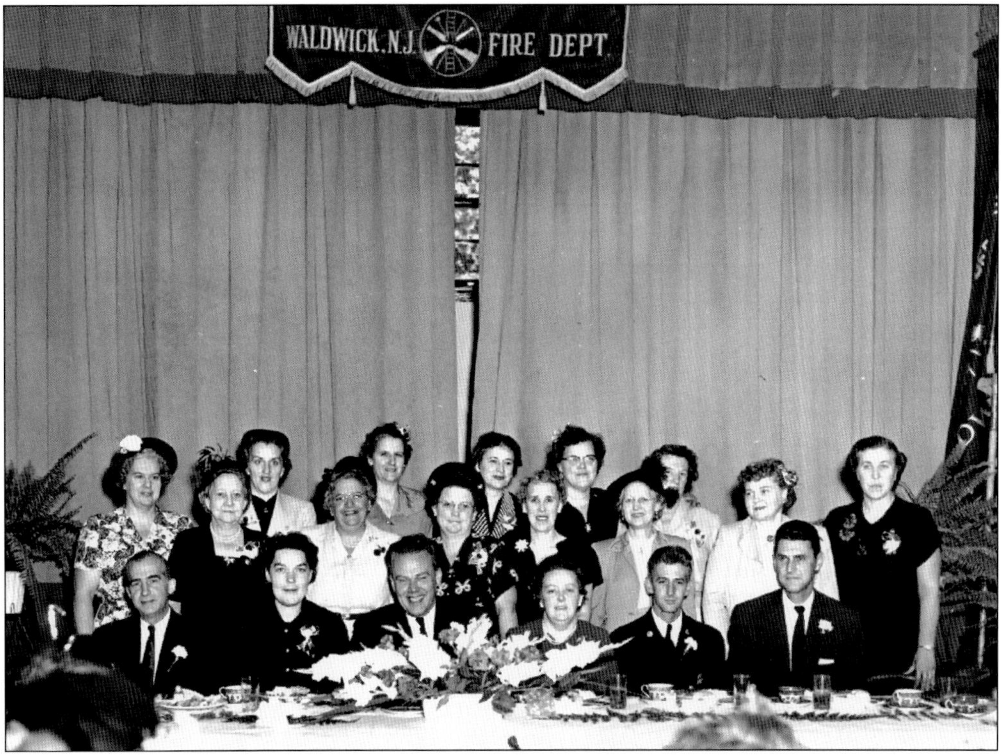

The state convention of the New Jersey State Firemen's Ladies Auxiliary was held in Waldwick in the mid-1950s.

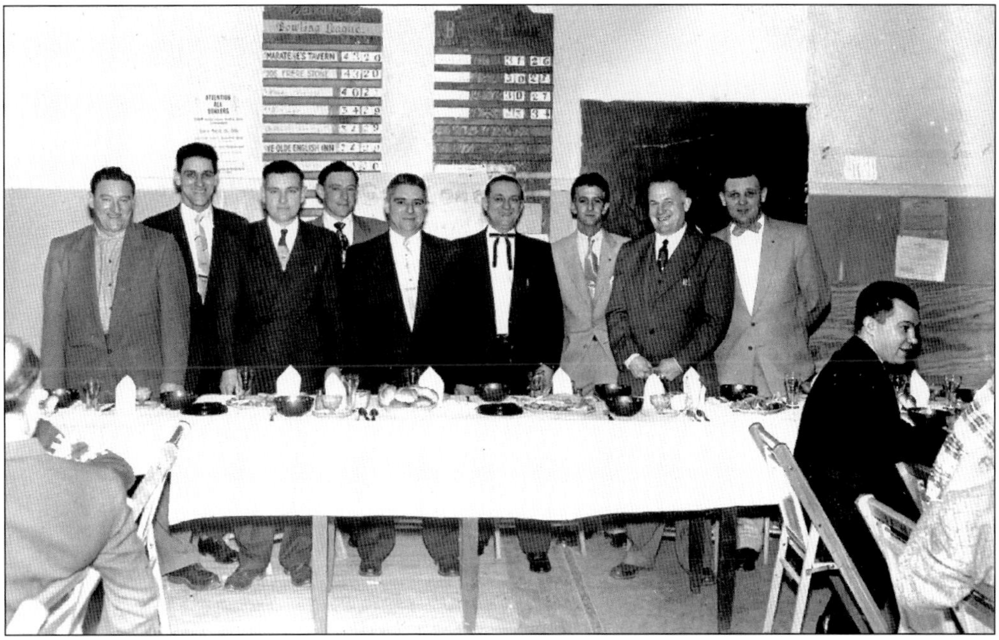
John Riccardi's 100-attendee bachelor party was held in the bowling alley of the old Orvil House, known as the English Inne. Seen here are, from left to right, George, Nick, Carmen, Albert, John, and Tony Riccardi and Roy Columbo, Frank Workman, Bill Schust, and Ed Kuklinski.

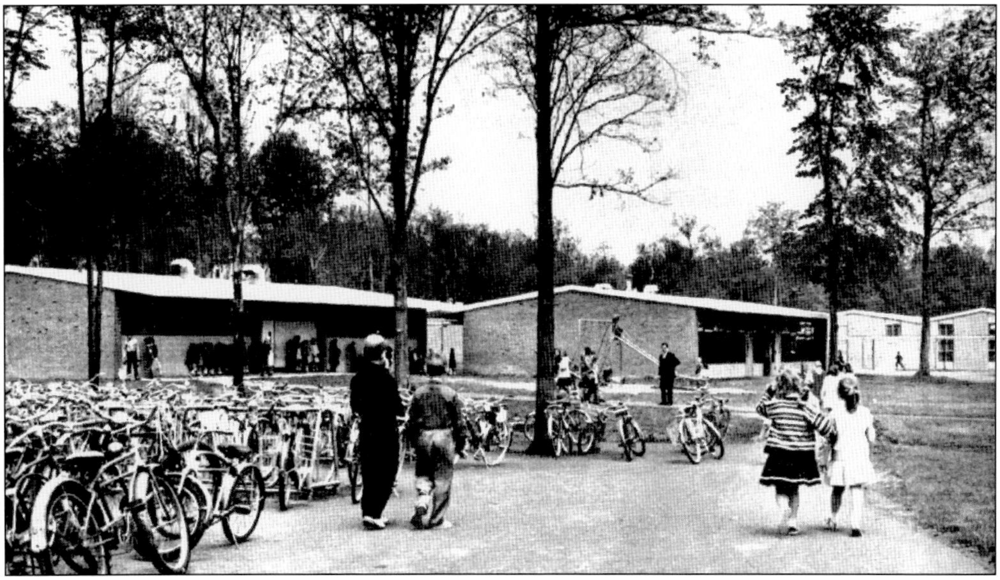

The modern cluster classroom Traphagen School was built in 1956 along Summit Avenue at Ridge Street. At the time it was built, it was believed the only one of its kind in the state. It was named in honor of Julia A. Traphagen, who taught for over 50 years in the Waldwick schools. Principal Michael Elia is seen watching as students arrive for school.

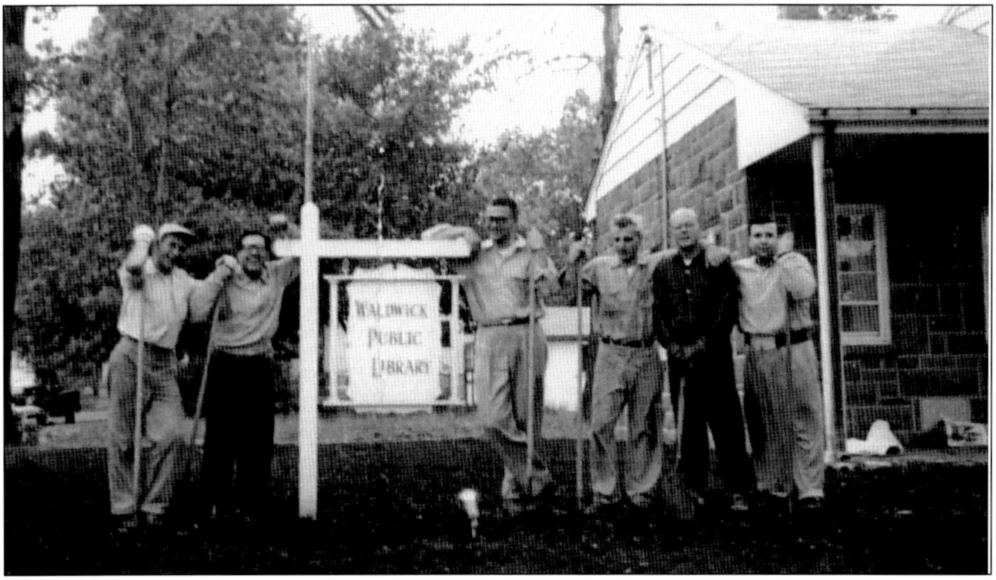

The Waldwick Public Library was an effort of many organizations pooling their efforts to raise the $19,000 necessary to construct the building. The funds included $875 in game-show winnings from *Sense and Nonsense* contestants Eileen Maturniak, Mrs. Clocko, and Arthur Tower. The library was opened on June 26, 1956. Several additions were made to the building in 1965, 1972, 1980, and 2003. The Waldwick Lions Club, founded in 1955, played a critical role in the development of the library. Shown here are, from left to right, unidentified, ? Marconna, Phil Salmon, Neil Borrelli, Edward Bowden, and George Zumbano. The Lions Club has made many donations over the years to local organizations. They built the children's playground at the borough park as well as the health clinic next to the ambulance corps building.

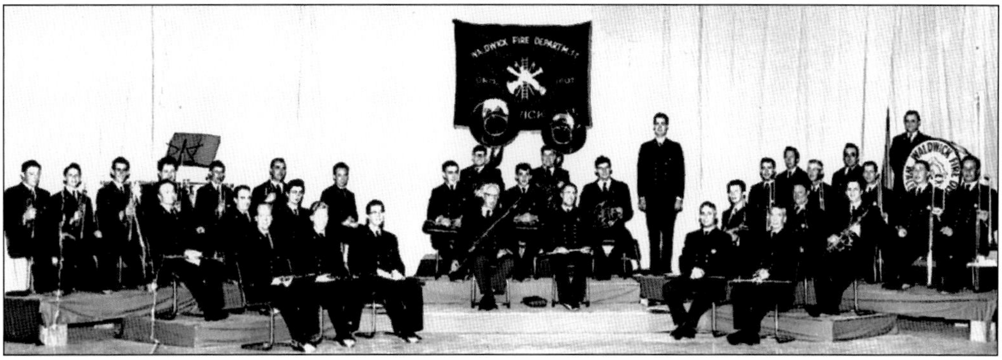

The Waldwick Fire Department Band, formed by Walter Nallin in 1954, is shown in the 1950s. It was made up of musicians from other former bands, including the MSA band. In 1968, Nallin reorganized the band into the Community Band of Waldwick. For many years, they played Friday nights at the Bergen Mall. Ed Moderacki took over the band in 1978.

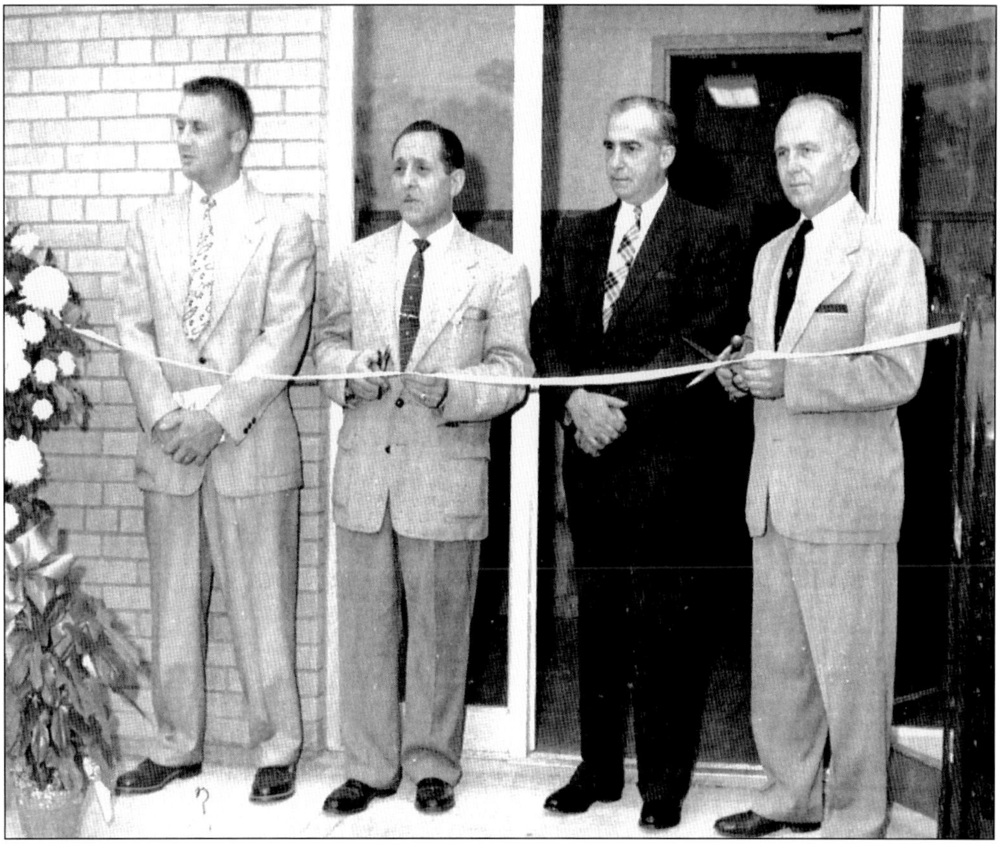

The Waldwick post office moved into its new building on Walter Hammond Place in 1956. Seen here are, from left to right, Charles Shubert (a postman), Anthony Scafuro (the mayor), Nelson Lumley (the former mayor), and Bruno Zorn (the postmaster).

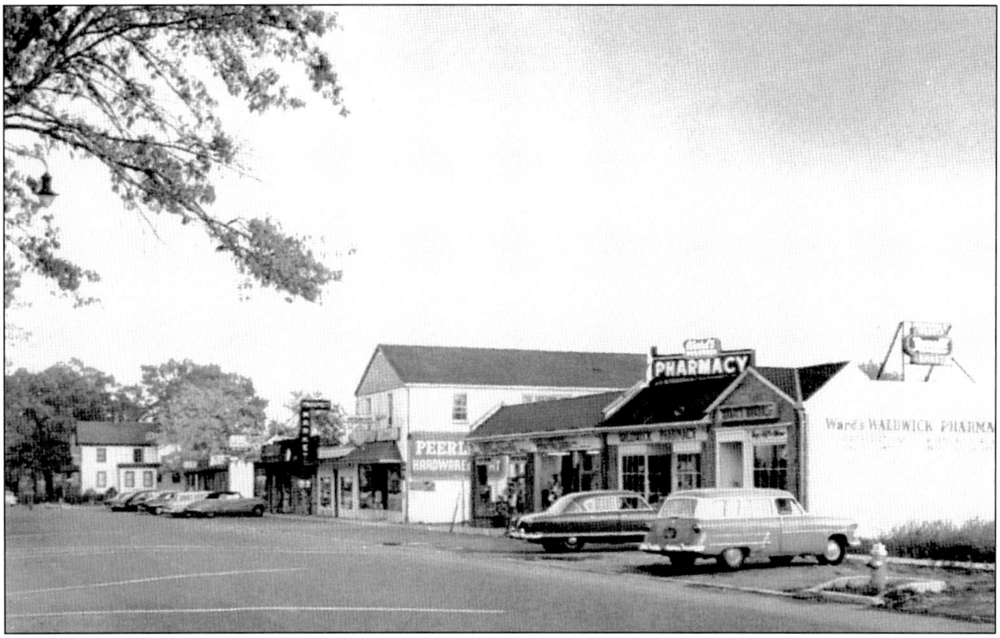

The center of the shopping district moved from West Prospect Street to East Prospect Street in the 1950s. This view includes the Waldwick Pharmacy and a hardware store.

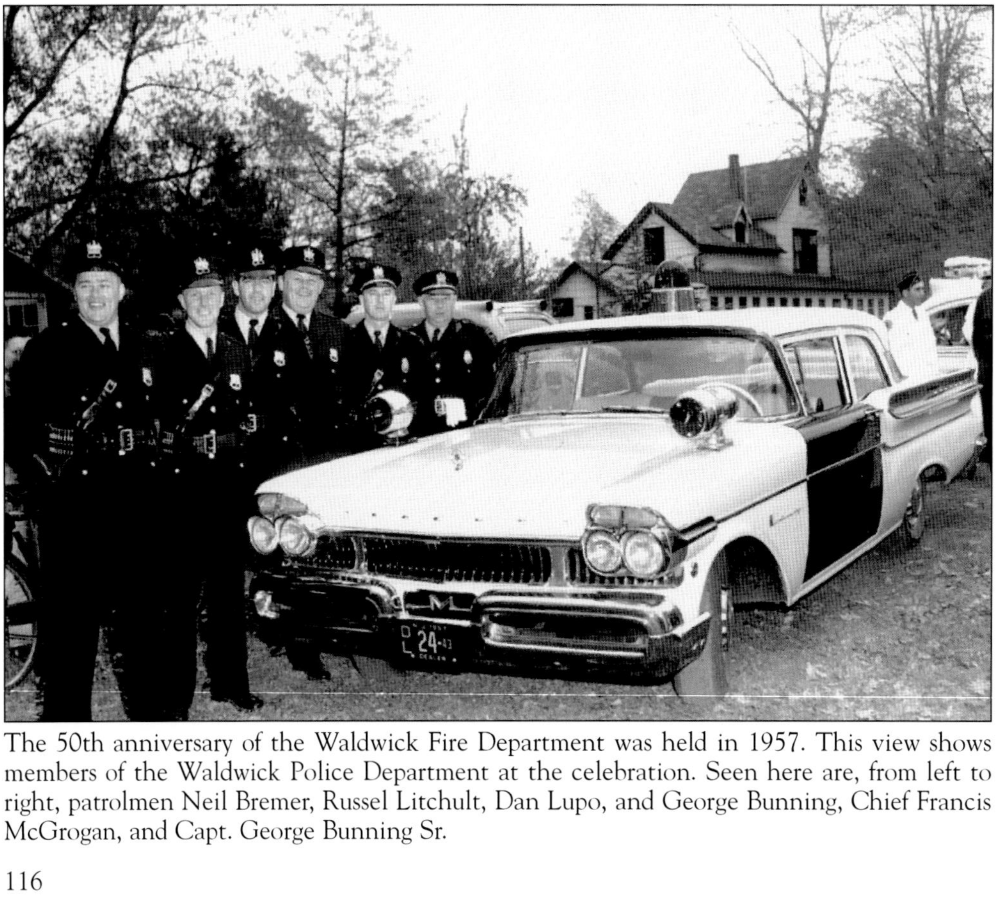

The 50th anniversary of the Waldwick Fire Department was held in 1957. This view shows members of the Waldwick Police Department at the celebration. Seen here are, from left to right, patrolmen Neil Bremer, Russel Litchult, Dan Lupo, and George Bunning, Chief Francis McGrogan, and Capt. George Bunning Sr.

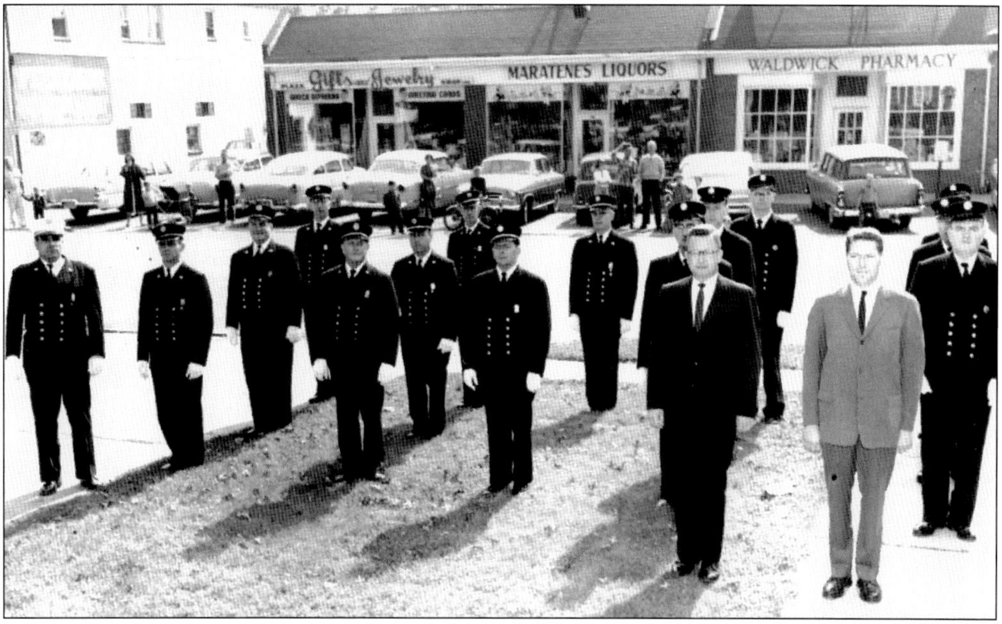

Mayor Charles B. Guernsey is shown with the Waldwick Fire Department in the early 1960s. The chief of the fire department (in the white hat) is Angelo Biele.

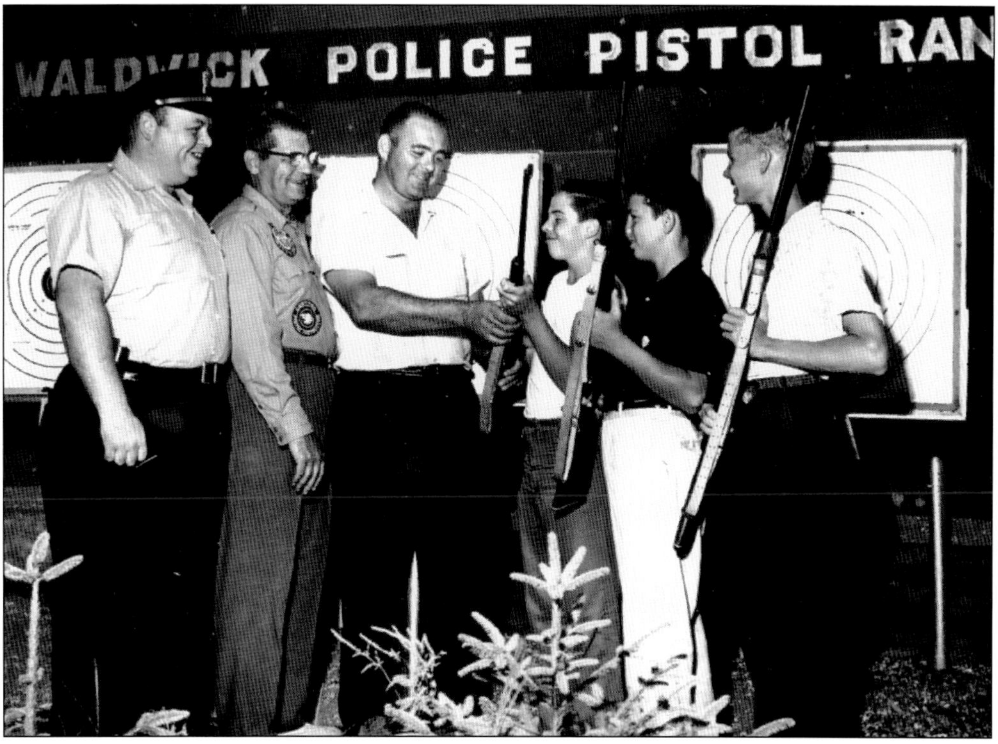

The new Waldwick police pistol range was opened on May 22, 1960. In this photograph, builder Lee Riffe of Crescent Park homes presents rifles donated from his firm to the youth rifle club. From left to right are Sgt. George Bunning Jr., range instructor George Smith, Lee Riffe, Russ Simon, Garry Smith, and Drew Churchson.

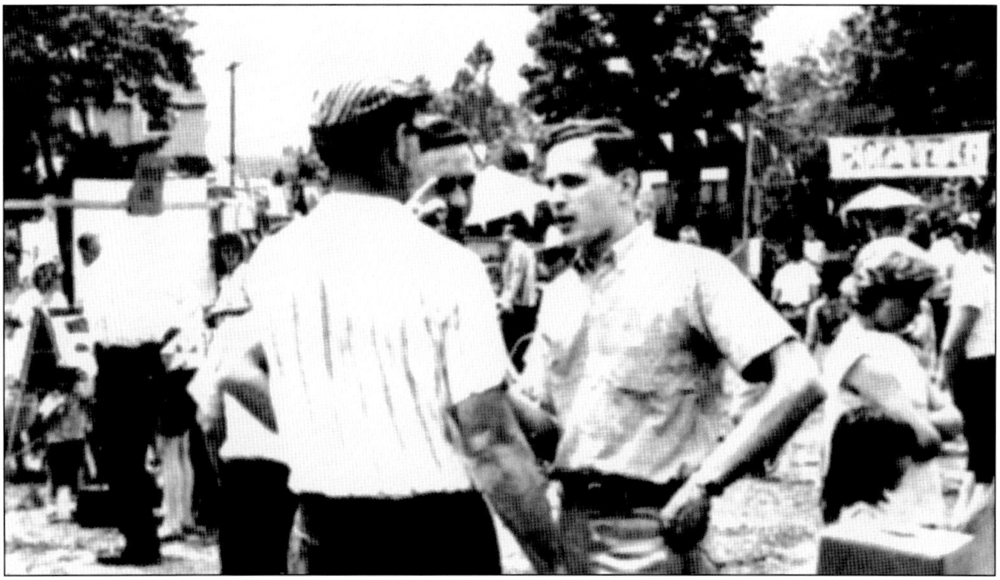

Highlands Community Association (HCA) president Tom Tison (right) is shown talking to residents at their annual fair in the 1960s. The park itself was a gift donated by developer Zamore to the community. The HCA encompasses residences west of Route 17.

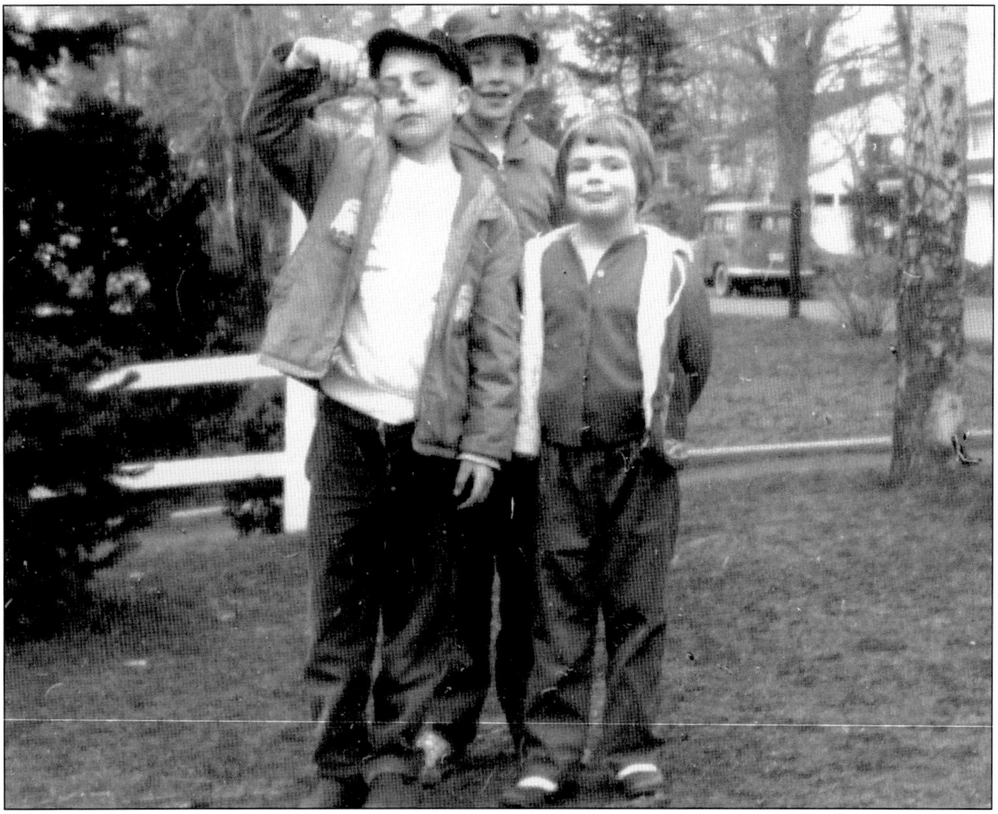

Michael Brunkhorst is seen with his twin brother, Mark, and sister Bea. Michael is holding the first fish Mark caught in the Saddle River.

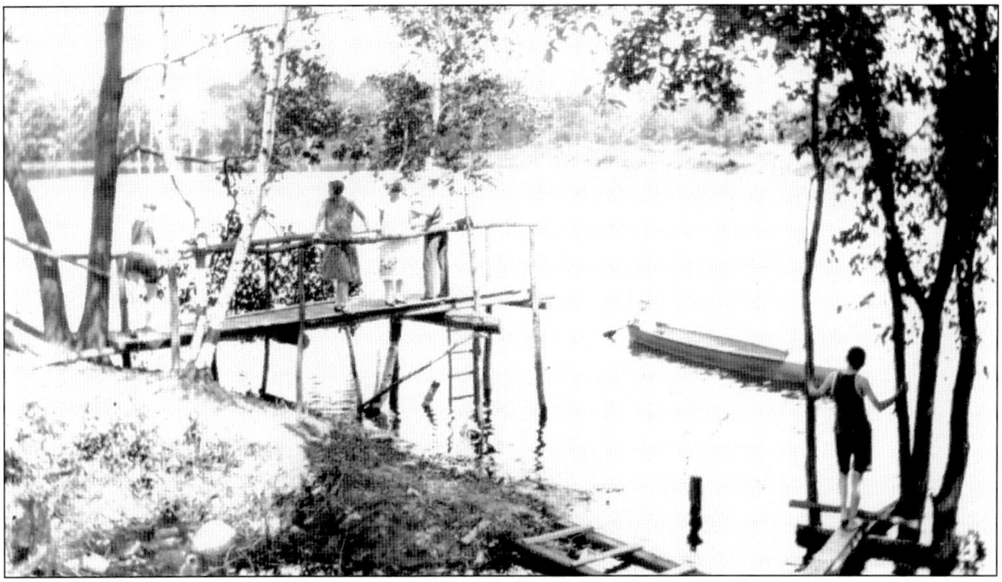

Swimmers enjoy White's Pond in the 1920s. Town residents received the benefit of a municipal pool, a Works Progress Administration project completed in 1936. For the first several years, it was filled annually by the Waldwick Fire Department directly from White's Pond. It was sometimes said that there were more fish than swimmers in the pool.

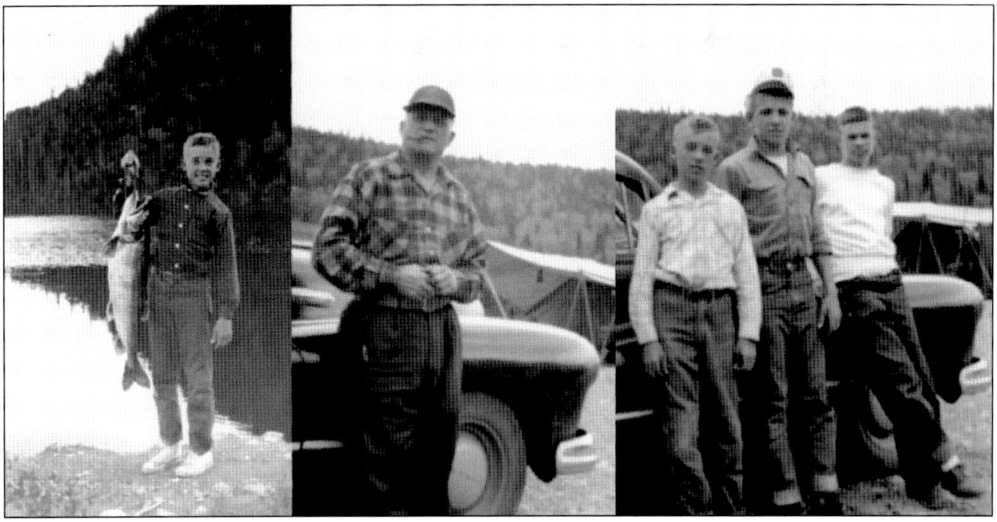

During his 33 years of tenure in the Waldwick school system, Frank Workman (in the center image) was also an avid outdoorsman. Each summer, he shared a fishing trip to Canada with two or three local boys and created unforgettable experiences for them. These three pictures were taken in 1957 at Chibougamau Lake. Holding up a fish on the far left is Jim Antoine. The right image shows, from left to right, Jim Antoine, George Martin, and Bob Hunt.

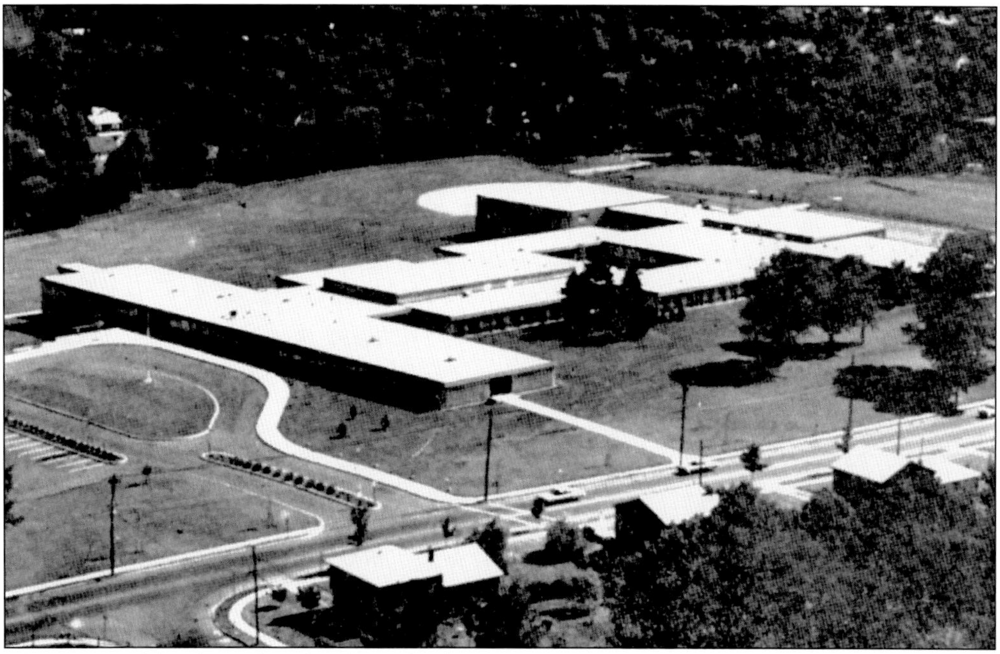

The new Waldwick High School was built in 1963. Superintendent John J. Finnessy and his wife, Clare Finnessy, along with Edna Mills and Lenore Coomber, worked throughout the summer of 1963 to prepare the main office, the guidance counseling office, and the library.

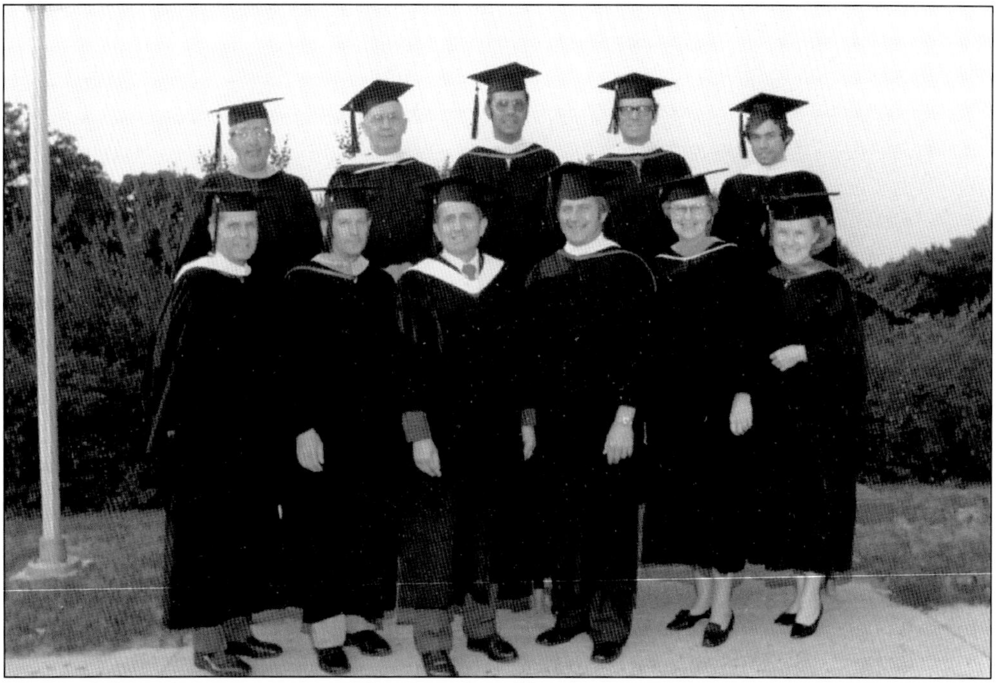

Some of the administration and faculty of Waldwick High School are seen in this early-1970s photograph.

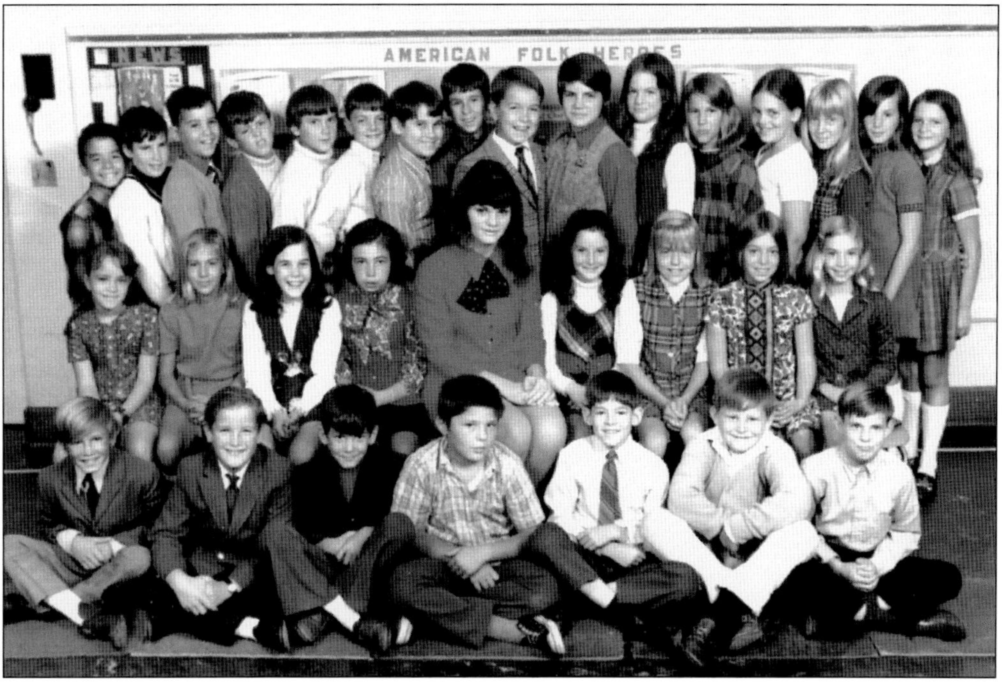

Class photographs were a staple of many Waldwick students. Shown here is author Glenn Corbett (back row, ninth from the left) in Miss Lawless's fourth-grade class at Traphagen School in 1970.

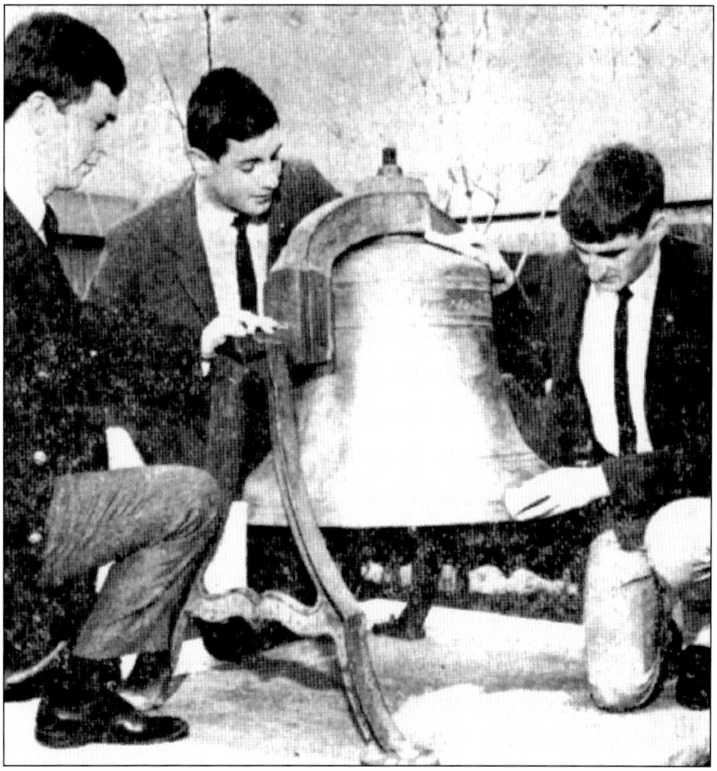

John Surak (left), local teacher and avid historian, served as the advisor to the Key Club at the Waldwick High School. The club was successful in having the bell from the old Waldwick School on Franklin Turnpike installed at the high school on November 18, 1966. Shown with Surak are Jack Carter (center) and Steven Brash (right).

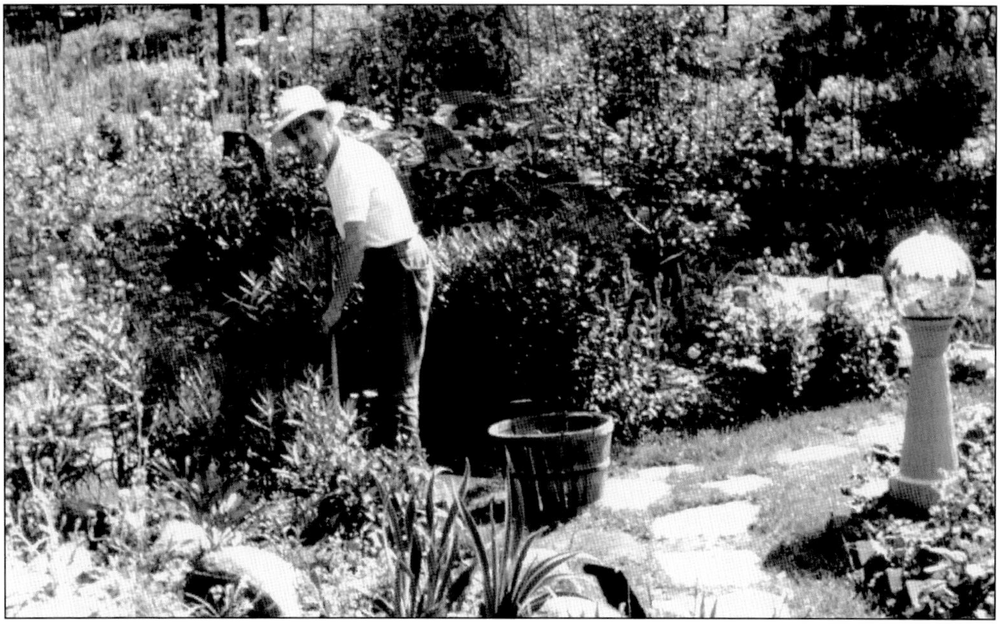

Luigi Totta is shown working in his ornate Frog Hollow garden. Frog Hollow is that area of Waldwick just north of Bohnert Place, now occupied by the Public Service Electric and Gas Company electric distribution plant. Andrea Mistretta, a famous local artist, is the granddaughter of Luigi Totta.

Program of Dedication
CRESCENT SCHOOL
Waldwick, New Jersey

December 1, 1968
3:00 P.M.

Star Spangled Banner . . . . Mrs. Karen Lagos, Music Instructor
(Audience please sing)

Flag Salute . . . . Mrs. Irving Lasner, President
Parent-Teacher Association

Invocation . . . . Reverend J. Earl Starkey, Pastor
United Methodist Church

Choral Selection, "This Is My Country" . . . . Grade IV Students
Mrs. Lagos, Director

Welcome and Introduction of
Board of Education and Guests . . . . Mr. Harold C. Greenberg, President
Board of Education

Greetings . . . . Mr. Emmett B. Johnson, Mayor
Waldwick, New Jersey

Remarks . . . . Dr. Anne S. Hoppock, Director of Elementary Education
New Jersey State Department of Education

Prayer of Dedication . . . . Rt. Reverend Monsignor William J. Duffy,
Pastor, Saint Luke's Church

Presentation of Building . . . . Mr. John Robert Gilchrist, Architect

Acceptance of Building . . . . Mr. Harold C. Greenberg, President
Board of Education
. . . . Dr. Edward F. Donahue, Superintendent
Waldwick Schools
. . . . Mr. Warren R. Jensen, Principal
Crescent School

Benediction . . . . Reverend R. Jamieson Hallenbeck, Pastor
Community Church of Waldwick

Open House Tours . . . . Crescent School Staff
Student Guides

Please return to auditorium for refreshments provided by
Crescent School Parent-Teacher Association

BOARD OF EDUCATION
Mr. Harold C. Greenberg, President
Mrs. Virginia K. Brown, Vice President — Mr. Richard R. Biros
Mrs. Helen C. Hammond — Mr. Donald J. Kwederis
Mr. Frank T. McKenna — Mr. Gordon E. Graham

Mr. Dan Ramella, Mr. Charles G. Boehm, Business Administrators
Mrs. Ruth Epstein-Honig, Attorney

Dedication

CRESCENT ELEMENTARY SCHOOL

Waldwick, New Jersey

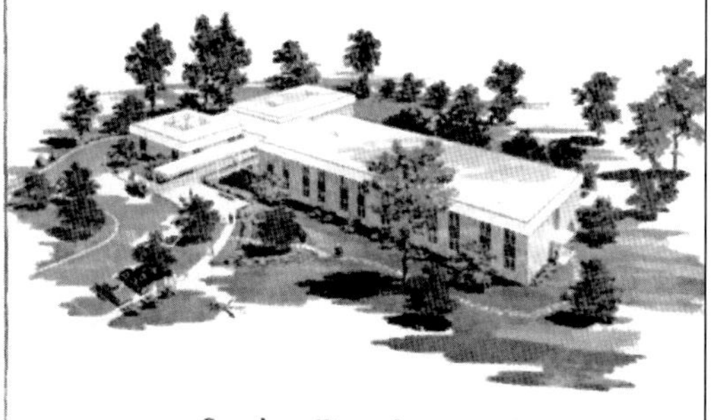

Sunday, December 1, 1968

3:00 P. M.

Waldwick Board of Education

The Crescent School was dedicated on December 1, 1968, to serve the students of the west side of Waldwick. The school system saw explosive growth in the 1950s and the 1960s.

The Lions Club has sponsored an annual July carnival for many years. Brother Lion Bernie O'Connell is shown in his carnival game booth in the early 1970s.

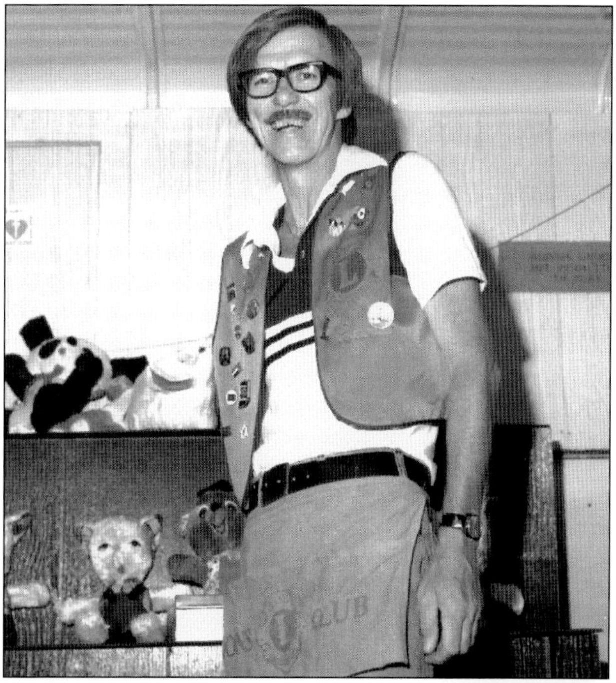

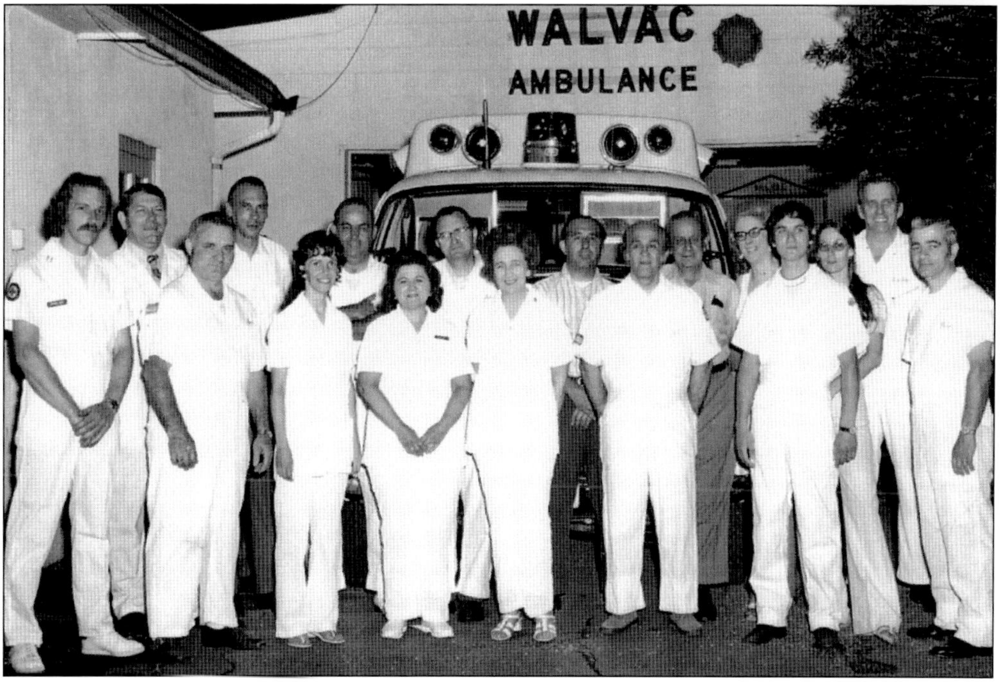

The Waldwick Ambulance Corps was created by the American Legion in 1952, sponsoring the group for many years. In 1978, the ambulance corps moved to their present two-bay building on White's Lane. Shown here in the late 1970s are, from left to right, the following: (front row) Ed Cohen, Bob Morey, Pat Donagen, Carmella Morey, Ceil Grippo, Joe Grippo, and Tony Sabino; (back row) Emmett Johnson, Jim Markstein, Art Barthold, John Girard, Vince Ruta, Vic Tapelki, Joan Ebbereck, Diane Sabino, Charles Ebbereck, and Phil DeNardo.

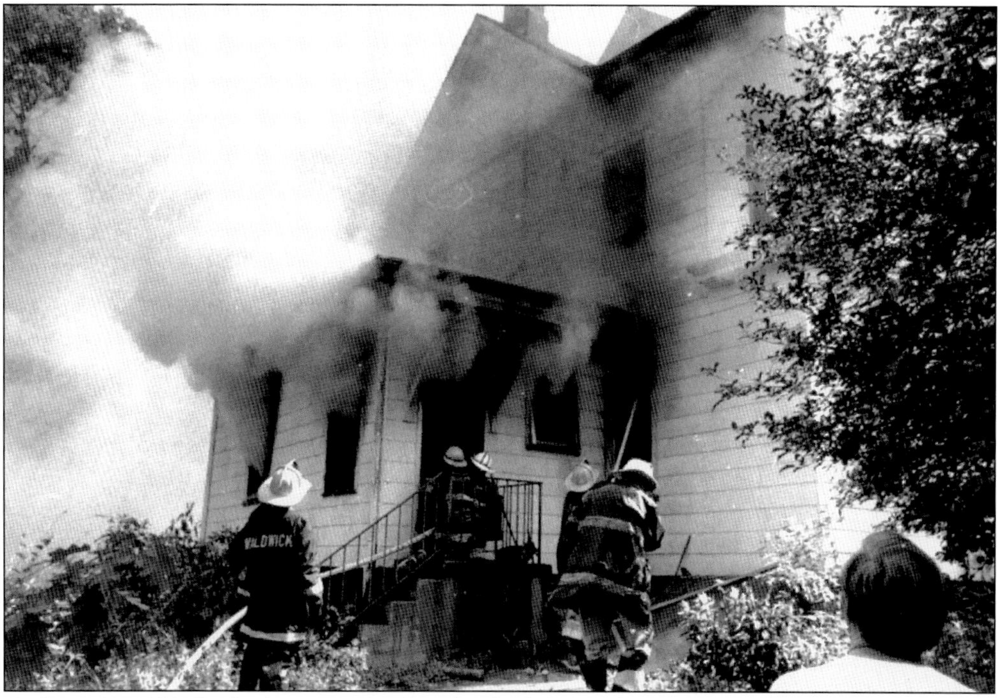

On June 12, 1978, fire broke out in the Quackenbush house (now an animal hospital) on Franklin Turnpike opposite Grove Street. Waldwick firefighters quickly contained the kitchen fire.

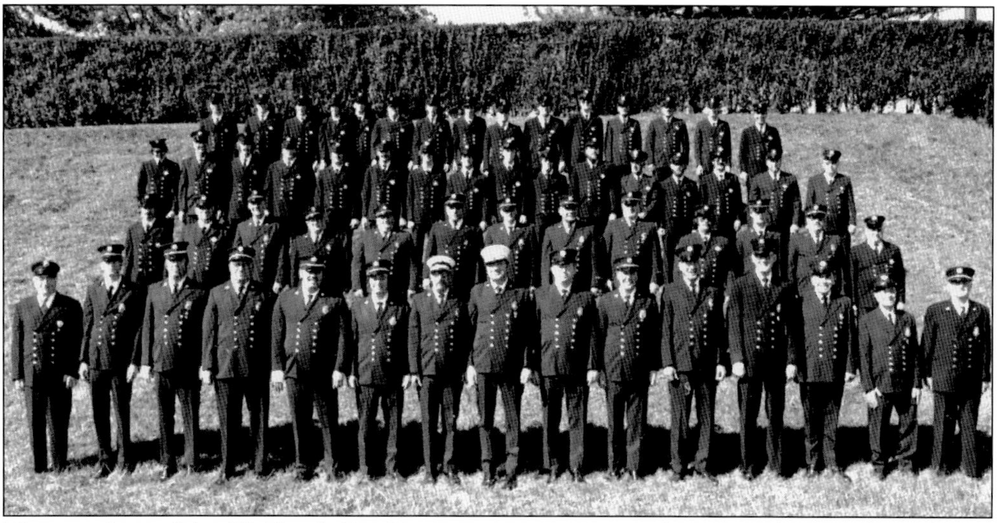

The members of the Waldwick Fire Department are seen in this 1979 photograph. Since its inception in 1907, the department has expanded to two companies and over 80 firefighters. The original municipal building—housing Fire Company No. 1 and the police department—was replaced by a new public safety building in 2002. Fire Company No. 2 at Wyckoff Avenue and White's Lane was first occupied in 1971 to provide protection for the west side of the borough. It is also the site of the borough's September 11 World Trade Center memorial honoring victims of the disaster, including Waldwick resident John Griffin. Incorporated in the memorial is a piece of steel from the World Trade Center.

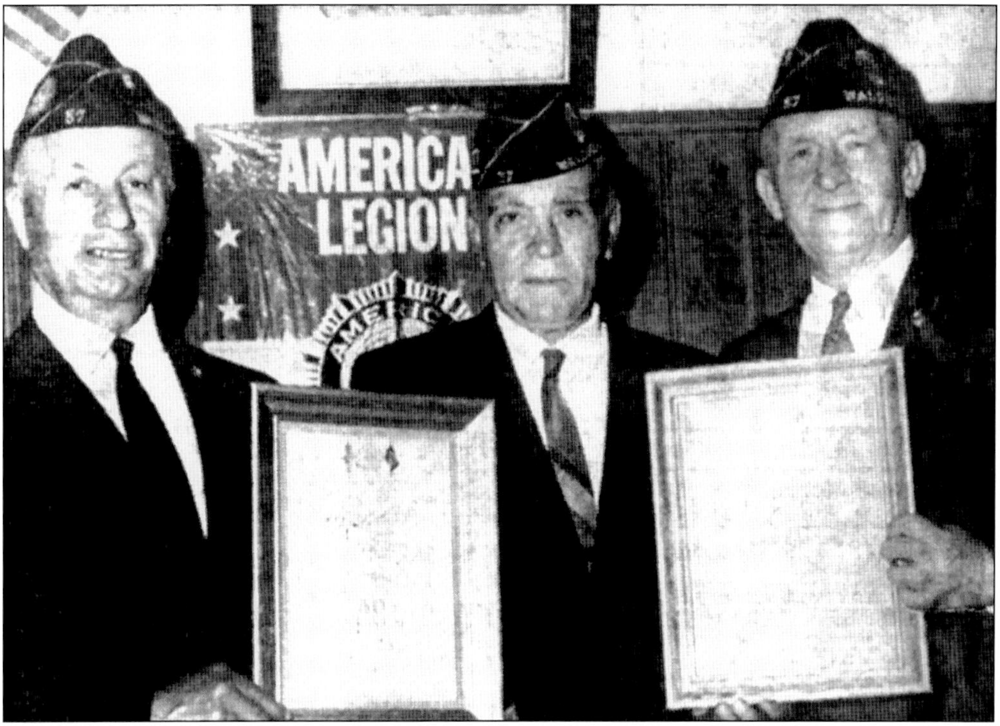

Harold Lampe and Harry LaPorta receive their 50th-year certificates from the American Legion in 1969. The Walter Nightingale Post No. 57 was created in 1927, first meeting in the Waldwick School on Franklin Turnpike. They erected their own building just south of the school on Franklin Turnpike and held their first meeting in November 1934. In the photograph are, from left to right, Harry LaPorta, Louis Parrone, and Harold Lampe.

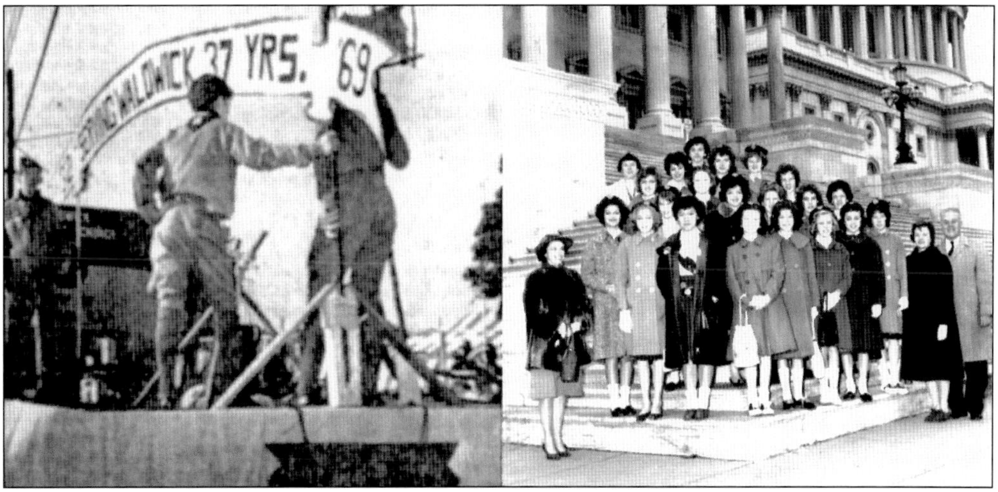

Left: The borough of Waldwick celebrated its 50th anniversary with a parade in 1969. Shown here are Boy Scouts from the then 37-year-old Troop 88. Troop 308 has also been a longstanding Boy Scout troop in Waldwick. *Right:* The Girl Scouts have also long been part of the community. They have had numerous troops over the years, including Troops 737, 812, and 1034. Girl Scouts from Waldwick are shown here visiting the Capitol on February 23, 1962.

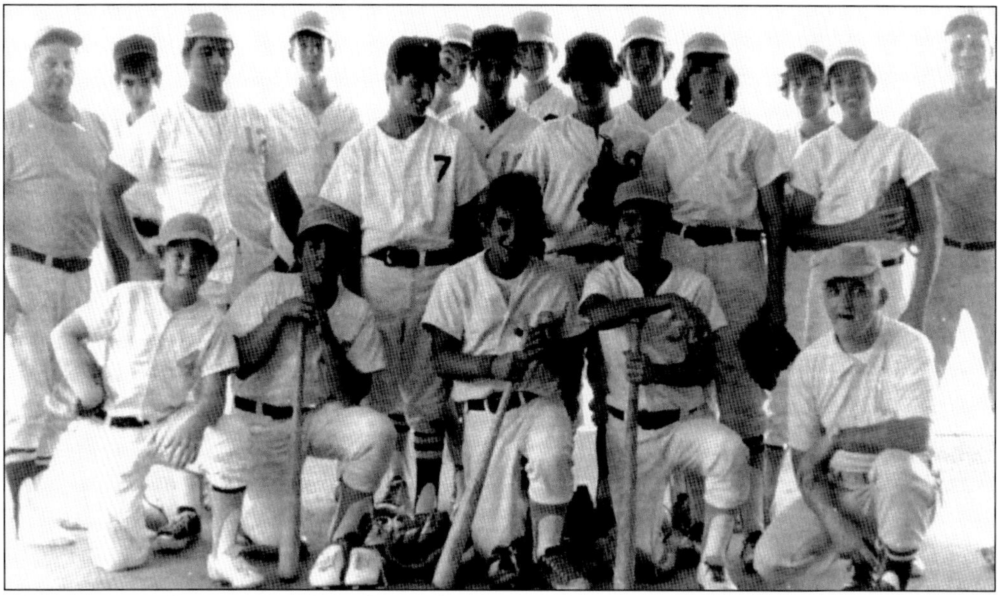

The championship 1972 Waldwick Sandy Koufax all-star baseball team is seen here. Team members are, from left to right, as follows: (front row) Pete Stummer, Jim Marciano, Bill Stegle, Steve Williams, and Phil Wilk; (back row) Dave Anderson Sr. (coach), unidentified, Nick Parisi, Tom Branagh, Jim Friedel, Bob Manzo, Jeff Overdahl, Roger Turley, Artie Platz, Rocky Venn, Punky Williams, and Jessie Overdahl (coach).

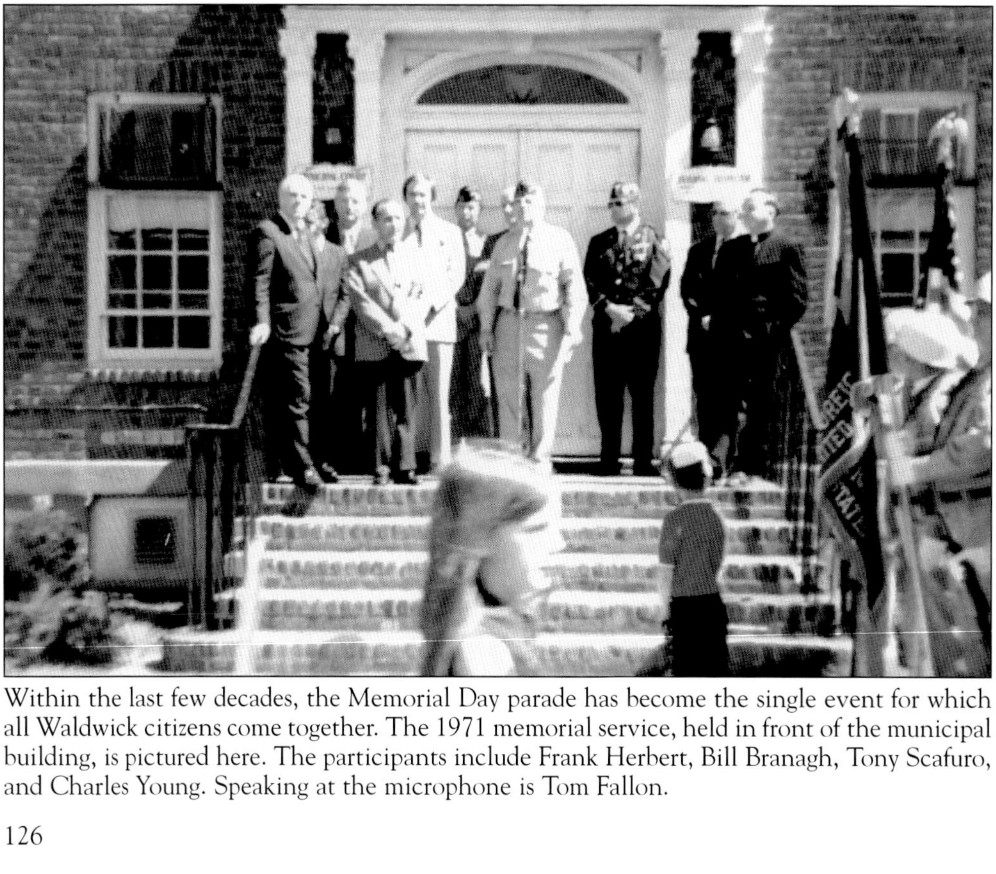

Within the last few decades, the Memorial Day parade has become the single event for which all Waldwick citizens come together. The 1971 memorial service, held in front of the municipal building, is pictured here. The participants include Frank Herbert, Bill Branagh, Tony Scafuro, and Charles Young. Speaking at the microphone is Tom Fallon.

"Main Line" through Waldwick

The trains keep rolling through—Back and forth,
Keeping to their scheduled times, as they have for more than a century.
The center of activity—
Bringing people, commerce, even life to the town.

They've watched Waldwick grow and change.
From yesteryear's stream trains and trolley,
From a quiet, sleepy community—Small town America,
To the technology and rushing, fast pace of today.

Trees are cut down. Streets are widened.
Old houses are razed. Cars are more modern and more plentiful.
Some of the people have moved out, some have died, others have changed.

Dreams and creations of yesterday have been torn down.
Some are rusting away. Others are covered over by weeds—Forgotten.
A way of life is lost, except to one's memory.

The N.J.R.T. trolley line is torn up.
The "old Waldwick School" is razed—Its cement cannon lost forever.
The Bamper Hotel burns down.
Marconi Hall closes its doors—The Italian "Feast" but a memory.
Jackson's Pond is filled in.
The Middle School is sold.
Borrelli's Barber Shop closes its doors.
Cracas' candy store—Which sold newspapers and Sen-Sen to Erie commuters,
And brought sweet delight to children—Is no more.
The signal tower and train depot remain,
And sit quietly amidst present-day transience, competition, and impatience.

The railroad and trolley like umbilical cords,
Connected Waldwick with Paterson, Hoboken, and New York City.
And, through those connections, a town was given birth, nurtured, and grew—
Till it was out of sight of the rail lines—Independent of them.

People independent of each other—
Trying to stay connected to each other through terminals in their homes.
Forgetting, perhaps not caring, how we've evolved to what we are today.
Yesterday's community dependence has yield to today's independence.

But, still the train keeps rolling through—Back and forth.
Keeping to their scheduled times, as they have for more than a century.
Consistent and grounded in their basic effort—
Bringing people, commerce, even life, to the old town.

Their whistles keep sounding. Reminding us—
Of what is still the center of activity and life,
Of what is still important,
Of what brought us to where we are now.

—Thomas J. Ursetti
August 1996, May 2003

BIBLIOGRAPHY

Amster, Ruth, ed. *Bergen Herald* (1948–1972).
Cannon, Beatrice. "Waldwick," 2 vols. Ridgewood Historical Society.
———. "Home of Beatrice Cannon," Ridgewood Historical Society.
———. "Waldwick Methodist Church," Ridgewood Historical Society.
Clayton, W. Woodward. *History of Bergen and Passaic Counties*. March 1882.
Hudson, Susan. *Background of Ho-Ho-Kus History*. Women's Club of Ho-Ho-Kus, 1953.
Kinsey and Larue. "Day Book" (1823–1830), Ridgewood Historical Society.
Lambert, Virginia, ed. *Waldwick: Then and Now*. Waldwick History Committee, 1994.
Lucas, Walter. *From the Hills to the Hudson: Railroadians of America*. New York, 1944.
Nelson, William. *History of the City of Paterson and the County of Passaic New Jersey*. Paterson: The Press Printing and Publishing Company, 1901.
Orvil Township–Waldwick borough clerk journals, 1895–1930.
Quimby, E.J. *Interurban Interlude: A History of the North Jersey Rapid Transit Company*. Ramsey: Model Craftsman Publishing Company, 1968.
Schlivek, Louis B., *Man in Metropolis*. New York: Doubleday, 1965.
Smith, Alfred P., ed. *Landscape* (1882–1901), Saddle River.
Traphagen, Julia A. *Our Neighborhood: A History of Waldwick*, 1953.
VanBenschoten, Sandra G. *The History of Saddle River*, 1996.
Van Valen. *History of Bergen County*. New Jersey Publishing and Engraving Company, 1900.
Waldwick Coal and Lumber Company account books (1909–1923), Waldwick Historical Society.
Westervelt, Frances. *History of Bergen County*. New York: Lewis Historical Publishing Company, 1923.

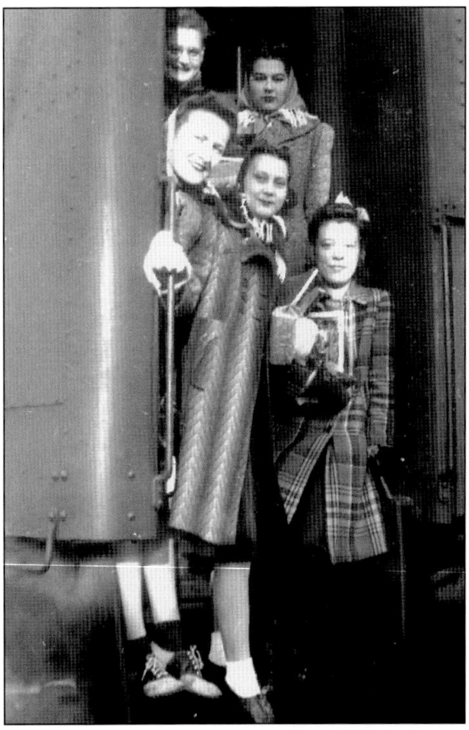

In this c. mid-1940s photograph, students say good-bye as they head by train to Ramsey High School. From left to right are the following: (front row) Jean Lion, Nellie Heddy, and Doris Wagner; (back row) Jean Van Dyke and Anne Heidelburger. Ramsey High School, then Midland Park High School, educated Waldwick students until Waldwick High School was erected in 1963.